A Data Scientist's Guide to Acquiring,
Cleaning, and Managing Data in R

A Data Scientist's Guide to Acquiring, Cleaning, and Managing Data in R

Samuel E. Buttrey and Lyn R. Whitaker
Naval Postgraduate School, California, United States

Registered Offices
John Wiley & Sons, Inc., 111 River Street, Hoboken, NJ 07030, USA
John Wiley & Sons Ltd, The Atrium, Southern Gate, Chichester, West Sussex, PO19 8SQ, UK

Editorial Office
9600 Garsington Road, Oxford, OX4 2DQ, UK

For details of our global editorial offices, customer services, and more information about Wiley products visit us at www.wiley.com.

Wiley also publishes its books in a variety of electronic formats and by print-on-demand. Some content that appears in standard print versions of this book may not be available in other formats.

Library of Congress Cataloging-in-Publication Data applied for

Hardback ISBN: 9781119080022

Cover Design: Wiley
Cover Image: © Nongkran_ch/Gettyimages

Set in 10/12pt WarnockPro by SPi Global, Chennai, India

To Elinda and Mike

Contents

About the Authors

Samuel E. Buttrey received a bachelor's degree in statistics from Princeton University in 1983. After 8 years as a Wall Street computer systems analyst, he returned to graduate school and received MA and PhD degrees in statistics from the University of California at Berkeley, the latter in 1996. In that year, he joined the faculty of the Department of Operations Research at the Naval Postgraduate School in Monterey, California. He has published papers on nearest-neighbor and other classification methods and on applied problems ranging from numismatics and oceanography to human vision. He has also published papers describing his implementations of algorithms in software. His interests include classification, computationally intensive methods, and statistical graphics, and most recently, inter-point distance measures for mixed categorical and numeric data. He lives in Pacific Grove, California, with wife Elinda, son John, and some cats.

Lyn R. Whitaker received a bachelor's degree in genetics in 1978 and a PhD in statistics from the University of California, Davis, in 1985. She was an Assistant Professor in the Department of Statistics and Applied Probability at the University of California at Santa Barbara from 1985 to 1988, and joined the faculty of the Department of Operations Research at the Naval Postgraduate School in 1988. Her interests are applied statistics relevant to defense issues. These include unsupervised methods for large and messy data, the statistical aspects of reliability and survival analysis, and most recently, jointly with Buttrey, development and use of inter-point distances for mixed data types. She resides in Monterey, California, with husband Mike, father Fred, and, occasionally, children Alex, Lee, and Mary.

Preface

Statisticians use data to build models, and they use models to describe the world and to make predictions about what will happen next. There has been a large number of very good books that describe statistical modeling, but these modeling efforts usually start with a set of "clean," well-behaved data in which nothing is missing or anomalous.

In real life, data is messy. There will be missing values, impossible values, and typographical errors. Data is gathered from multiple sources, leading to both duplication and inconsistency. Data that should be categorical is coded as numeric; data that should be numeric can appear categorical; data can be hidden inside free-form text; and data can be in the form of dates in a wide number of possible formats. We estimate that 80% of the time taken in any data analysis problem is taken up just in reading and preparing the data. So, any analyst needs to know how to acquire data and how to prepare it for modeling, and the steps taken should be automatic, as far as possible, and reproducible.

This book describes how to handle data using the R software. R is the most widely used software in statistics, and it has the advantage of being free, open-source, and available on every major computing platform. Whatever software you use, you will find yourself facing the issues of acquiring, cleaning, and merging data, and documenting the steps you took. We hope this book will help you do these things efficiently.

Monterey, California, USA   Sam Buttrey and Lyn Whitaker
November 30, 2016

Acknowledgments

Our book is about how to use R to process data. We use R because it is powerful, versatile, and extensible. We thank the developers of R for their service to the statistical community for producing a high-quality open-source piece of software. We also thank the long list of colleagues and students who have helped frame our thinking about questions of statistics and data.

About the Companion Website

Don't forget to visit the companion website for this book:

www.wiley.com/go/buttrey/datascientistsguide

There you will find valuable material designed to enhance your learning, including:

- A complete listing of all the R code in the Book
- Example datasets used in the Exercises

1

R

1.1 Introduction

This book focuses on one problem that is common to almost every statistical problem – indeed, to almost any problem involving any sort of analysis. That problem is acquiring and preparing the data. Across our many years of data analysis, we have learned that seemingly 80% of our time – maybe more – goes into the data preparation steps (a belief echoed by others such as Dasu and Johnson, 2003). Collectively, we call these actions *data cleaning*, although, as we will discuss later, we sometimes use that term for something a little more specific. Regardless of the name, almost any analysis requires that you (i) acquire that data, that is, read it into the computer program; (ii) clean the data, that is, identify entries that are duplicated or clearly erroneous or anomalous, and take other preparation steps (e.g., combining entries such as "Female," "female," and "F"); (iii) merge data from different sources; and (iv) prepare the data for modeling, which might involve dividing a set of numeric values into subsets, combining states into regions, and so on. This book discusses some approaches for accomplishing these four steps in the R language (R Core Team, 2013). A fifth problem, which receives less emphasis, is the problem of long-term curation of the data. Which parts of the data must be saved and in what way? We address that question by reference to the idea of *reproducible research*, which we discuss later in this chapter, and later in the book as well.

1.1.1 What Is R?

R is a computer program that lets you analyze data. By "analyze" we mean, first, read the data into the program and then operate on it – drawing graphs and charts, manipulating values, fitting statistical models, and so on. (Notice that we prefer to call data "it" rather than "them." We discuss this choice briefly toward the end of the chapter.) R is both a statistical "environment" and also

A Data Scientist's Guide to Acquiring, Cleaning, and Managing Data in R, First Edition.
Samuel E. Buttrey and Lyn R. Whitaker.
© 2018 John Wiley & Sons Ltd. Published 2018 by John Wiley & Sons Ltd.
Companion website: www.wiley.com/go/buttrey/datascientistsguide

a programming language, and it is very widely used both in commercial and academic settings. R is free and open-source and runs on Windows, Apple, and Linux operating systems. It is maintained by a group of volunteers who release bug fixes and new features regularly.

1.1.2 Who Uses R and Why?

R started as a tool for statisticians, evolving from a language called S that was created in the 1970s. Today, R remains the primary language of academic statisticians, and it also has a prominent place among analysts in business and government as well. It is used not only for building statistical models but also for handling and cleaning data, as in this book, and for developing new statistical methods, building simulations, for visualization, and generally for all the data-handling tools the statistician and the data scientist require. Because of the ease with which users can develop and distribute new methods, R has also become the tool of choice in certain fast-growing fields such as biostatistics and genetics. Articles on "surveys of the top tools used by data scientists" inevitably name R as one of the important tools with which data scientists, as well as statisticians, should be familiar. Moreover, R's popularity is such that there are extensions to R (see "packages" in Section 1.4.4) that allow you to connect to other programs such as the Python and Java languages, the H2O machine-learning system, the ArcGIS geographical information system, and many more.

1.1.3 Acquiring and Installing R

The primary way to acquire R is to download it from the Internet. The main R website for R is www.r-project.org, and the www.cran.r-project.org page ("CRAN" standing for "Comprehensive R Archive Network") is where you can download R itself. There are in fact dozens of "mirror" sites for CRAN – that is, websites that are essentially copies of the CRAN site – so as to reduce the load on the CRAN site. You can probably find a mirror near you on the "mirrors" page. After you download R, install it in the way you would normally install a program on your operating system.

At any one time, users around the world will be running slightly different versions of R, since new ones are released fairly frequently. For example, at this writing the current version of R was called 3.3.2, but many users are still using 3.2 or earlier versions. This will almost never cause problems, but it is a good idea to update your version of R from time to time.

There are also several slightly different versions of R distributed other than at CRAN. Microsoft R Open is a particular version of R that uses a different set of math libraries intended to make certain computations faster. Like "regular" R, Microsoft R Open is free, although it does not run on OS X. Other versions of R are intended to communicate with relational databases or with other big-data platforms. For this book, we will assume you are running "regular" R – but in any case for our purposes all versions of R should behave exactly the same way.

1.1.4   Starting and Quitting R

The way you start R depends on your operating system. Normally double-clicking on an R icon will be enough to get R started. In the command-line interface of many Linux systems, or using the OS X terminal window, it may be enough just to type the upper-case letter R (or, for Windows command lines, Rgui). When R has started, you will see the command prompt >. This is the R *console*, the place where commands are entered. At this point, you can start typing commands to R. When it comes time to quit R, you can either "kill" the window in the usual way (for OS X, the red dot, the lightswitch in the top right, or via the File dialog; for Windows, the red X or File dialog) or you can type the q() command. In either case, R will then ask you if you want to "Save workspace image." If you answer "yes" to this question, R will save to the disk any changes you made during the current session, whereas if you answer "no," R will return its workspace to the condition it was in when R was last started. We almost always want to answer "yes" to this question!

1.2   Data

Data is information about the elements of whatever problem we are investigating. Data comes in many forms, but for our purposes it will always be presented in a set of computer-ready values. For example, a database concerning birds might include text about the habits of the birds, numbers giving lengths and weights of the individuals, maps showing migration patterns, images showing the birds themselves, sound recordings of the birds' calls, and so on. Although they look very different, all of these different pieces of information can be represented in the computer in digital form in one way or another. In this example, one of our primary tasks might be to ensure that each bird's description is correctly matched with the correct map, image, and song file. Our data analysis projects rarely include data quite so disparate, but in almost every case we need to acquire data, clean it (a process we start to describe in what follows and continue throughout the book), and prepare it for modeling, and in almost every case we expect our data to consist of both numeric and textual values.

1.2.1   Acquiring Data

The first step in a data analysis project, of course, is to get the data into R where it can be manipulated. We are old enough to remember the days when this involved typing all the data from the back of a book or journal paper into a statistics package by hand, but happily this is not necessary today. On the other hand, data now comes in a variety of formats, few of which were created with the convenience of the data scientist in mind. In Chapter 6, we describe some of these common formats and how to use R to read data effectively.

1.2.2 Cleaning Data

We "clean" data when we detect (and, in many cases, remove) anomalies. Anomalies will very often be missing values, but they might also be absurd ones, as when people's ages are reported as 999 or −1. Sometimes, as in our earlier example, we might have genders reported as "Female," "female," and "F" and we want to combine these three values. In the cleaning process we might learn, for example, that one data source produced no data at all in August 2016; this sort of fact will need to be brought to the attention of the data provider. The data cleaning process also involves merging data from different sources, extracting subsets or reshaping the data in some way. All in all, data cleaning is the process of turning raw data, received from one or more providers, into a data set that can be used in visualization, modeling, and decision-making.

In practice these steps are iterative. Our cleaning process not only informs the modeling, but it sometimes leads us to re-acquire the data in a different, more usable form. Similarly, insights from modeling will often lead us to prepare the data in a new and more revealing way – because it is when we model that we often discover anomalies or other interesting attributes of the data.

1.2.3 The Goal of Data Cleaning

What a "clean" data set should look like depends on what your goals are. One useful perspective is given by Wickham (2014), who describes what he calls "tidy" data. A tidy data set is rectangular (or tabular); each row describes one unit of analysis (an observation), and each column gives one measurement (a variable). For example, in a data set giving measurements about people, each row would concern itself with a person, and the columns might give height, weight, age, blood type, and so on.

In some problems, it is not immediately clear what the unit of analysis is. For example, imagine data that describes the locations of boats over the course of a month, as recorded by GPS. For some purposes, a "tidy" data set would have one row per GPS ping, each row giving a ship identifier, a location, and a time. For other purposes, we might prefer a data set with one row per boat, each row giving the southernmost point that ship reaches, or perhaps giving a binary indicator of whether the ship did, or did not, spend time in international waters. Some data – images and sound, for example – do not lend themselves to this "tidy" approach.

The exact layout of your final data will depend on what you plan to do with it – and in some cases this won't be known until after you have operated on the data.

1.2.4 Making Your Work Reproducible

It is vital that other people be able to reproduce the actions you took on your data. Ideally, you or another analyst should be able to start with your raw data, run all the steps you applied to it, and emerge with exactly the same clean, prepared data sets. This will be useful to you when you encounter a situation similar to the one in the previous paragraph, where the form of the new data needs to be designed. But it is even more important for another analyst, since if you or another analyst can reproduce your results there will be no disagreement about the data. The act of making research reproducible has, in recent years, been rightfully recognized as a cornerstone of scientific progress. Record and document every step you take so that others can repeat them.

1.3   The Very Basics of R

This book is about handling data in R. It cannot teach you the very basics of R in detail – although, happily, there are many good books and online resources that can. (We give a few examples at the end of this chapter.) In this section, we list a few of the most basic facts about R, but, again, this book is not intended to teach you R. Rather, we focus on the details of R and of the way data is represented in R, in order to help you understand some of the ways to acquire, clean, and handle data inside R.

1.3.1   Top Ten Quick Facts You Need to Know about R

In this section, we give a few of the most important facts about R a beginner needs to know. There will be more detail on these facts later in the chapter and throughout the book.

1) The **prompt** is (by default) >. If you leave a command incomplete, maybe because there is an unclosed parenthesis or quotation mark, R gives you the continuation prompt, which is +. The Esc key (Windows) or control-C (other systems) produces the **break** command, which will take you back to the regular prompt. In this example, we show what a completed command looks like – in this case, R is computing the value of 3 divided by 2.

```
> 3 / 2
[1] 1.5
```

Here, R produced the prompt (>), and we typed 3 / 2 and pressed the Enter (or "Return") key. R then produced the output. We will talk about the [1] part in Chapter 2, but the computed value of 1.5 is shown. In the following example, we show what happens when we press Enter after typing the slash character:

```
> 3/
+ 2
[1] 1.5
```

Here, since the expression on the first line was incomplete, R produced the continuation prompt, +. When we typed 2 and hit Enter, the expression was complete and the result was shown. In case of confusion, press break until the original > prompt is showing.

In examples in this book where we want to show the R output, we also show the > prompt in front of our code. Remember, that > is produced by R; you don't need to type that yourself. (At the end of the chapter, we tell you where you can get all the code from the book in electronic form.)

2) R is **case-sensitive**, which means that upper- and lower-case letters are different in R. For example, the built-in R object LETTERS gives all 26 upper-case letters. A different item called letters contains the lower-case versions of the alphabet. There is no built-in object called Letters.

3) **Show** an object by typing its name. For example, if you type ls by itself, you see the contents of the function whose name is ls, the one that lists all the objects in your workspace (which we define later). To actually run the function and see the objects, you need to type the function's name together with parentheses. In this case, list your objects by typing ls().

4) Get **help** for a function or object named thing with the command help(thing) or ?thing. For example, to see the help for the ls() function, type help(ls). If you don't know the name, try help.search() with a relevant word in quotation marks; for example, try help.search ("matrices") to see functions that handle matrices.

5) **Assign** a value or object to a name with the left-arrow (less-than plus hyphen): for example, the command a <- 1 creates a new object named a with value 1. (You can also assign with a command such as a = 1, but we don't recommend it.) The assignment will over-write any existing object named a you might have had. Once you create an object, it is in your "workspace," and your workspace can be saved when you quit. So unless your computer crashes, when you create an object it will persist until you delete it. **Display** the set of objects in your workspace with objects() or ls(); remove an object with remove() or rm(). Not every character is permitted in the name of an R object. Start a name

with a letter or a dot, and then stick to numbers, letters, underscores, and dots. Names cannot contain spaces. In this example, we show some assignments that succeed and some that do not.

```
> a <- 1
> a.1 <- 1
> 2a <- 1
Error: unexpected symbol in "2a"
> a 2 <- 1
Error: unexpected numeric constant in "a 2"
```

The first two of these assignments succeed, because a and a.1 are valid names. The last two fail because they refer to invalid names.

6) The **comment character** is #. A comment ends at the end of the line. If you want a comment to span multiple lines, you need to start each comment line with #.

7) **Recall** earlier commands with the up-arrow. You can edit an earlier command and then press the Enter key to run the new version. The history() command shows a list of your recent commands; put a number in (as in history(500)) to see more.

8) When referring to file names, R itself uses the **forward slash** in the console. The Windows file system uses the backward slash, so Windows users may use that, too, but in that case you have to type \\ (we talk more about this later on). For example, a Windows user who wants to access a file named c:\temp\mycode.R in an R command will need to type either c:/temp/mycode.R or c:\\temp\\mycode.R. You'll need to use a regular, single backslash if you are interacting with the Windows operating system and not R – if, for example, you are presented with a graphical "select file" window. The file systems for OS X and Linux users use the forward slash at all times.

9) Just about any function you want is built into R, so R makes an excellent **calculator**. For example,

```
> sin (log (34))
[1] -0.375344
```

This says that the sine (using radians) of the logarithm (base e) of 34 is −0.375344. Most functions allow you to specify "arguments," values you pass to the function to modify its behavior. Some must be specified; others have default values. For example, log (34, 10) produces the base 10 logarithm instead of the natural logarithm. If a function accepts multiple arguments, you will need to specify them in the proper order – or by name. In this example, the arguments to log are named x and base (see the help at ?log), so we could have entered log(base = 10, x = 34) too.

10) R's **operators** include the comparison operators ! = for "not equal," == for "is equal to," < = and > = for "less than or equal to" and "greater than or equal to," and the arithmetic operators * for "multiplied by" and ^ for "raised to the power of."

1.3.2 Vocabulary

As we get started, it will be worthwhile for us to repeat some of the vocabulary of R, and of data, that you should be familiar with. In this section, we define some of the terms that are commonly used in discussion of R, both in this book and elsewhere.

vector A *vector* is the simplest piece of data in R. It consists of one or more entries (also called "items" or "elements") that are all either text or all numbers or all "logical" (i.e., TRUE or FALSE). (Technically, a vector might have length 0, and there are some other types, but that last sentence covers 99% of what you will do with R.) For example, the value of the famous constant π is built into R as the object pi, and the R object pi is a numeric vector with length 1. We talk about vectors in Chapter 2.

matrix A *matrix* is just a two-dimensional vector in rectangular shape. While matrices are important in statistics, they are less important in the data cleaning process. Still, it is useful to know about matrices in preparation for using data frames (below). We discuss matrices at the start of Chapter 3.

list A *list* is an R object that can hold other R objects. Lists are everywhere in R and you will need to know how to create them and access their elements. We discuss lists starting in Section 3.3.

data frame A *data frame* is a cross between a matrix and a list. Like a matrix, it is rectangular, but like a list it can contain items of different sorts – numeric, text, and so on – as its columns. You can think of a data frame as a list of vectors all of which are the same length. Most of the data we encounter will be in the form of data frames, and, if it isn't, we will usually try to put it into a data frame. We talk about data frames starting in Section 3.4.

object An *object* is a general word for anything in R. Usually, we will use this to refer to data objects such as vectors, matrices, lists, or data frames, but we might use "object" to refer to a function, a file handle, or anything else with a name in R.

rows and columns A data frame and a matrix are two-dimensional rectangular objects, consisting of *rows* and *columns*. Our goal, in a data cleaning problem, is almost always to produce one or more data frames whose rows correspond to the things being measured, and whose columns give the different measurements. For example, in a military manpower problem each row might represent a soldier, and the columns would give measurements such as age, sex, rank, and years in service. Statisticians sometimes call rows and columns "observations" and "variables" (although that second word has another meaning in R, see the following discussion). Confusingly, other terms exist too: authors in machine learning talk of "instances" (or "entities") and "attributes" ("features"). We will use "rows" and "columns" when the emphasis is on the representation of the data in a data frame, and "observations" and "variables" when the emphasis is on the role being played by the data.

variable A *variable* is also a generic term for an R object, especially one of the objects in our workspace. The name is slightly misleading because the object's value doesn't have to change. We would call `pi` a "variable," at least in casual conversation.

operator An *operator* describes an action on one or two objects – often vectors – and produces a result. For example, the * operator, placed between two numbers, produces their product. Most operators act on two things – we say they are "binary." The + and - operators can also be "unary," meaning they act on one number. So in the expression -3, the - is a unary operator. Operations are often "vectorized," meaning they act separately on each item of a vector.

function A *function* is a kind of R object that can take an action. Functions often accept arguments to control the computations they make, and produce "return values," the results of the computation. For example, the cos () function takes as its one argument the size of an angle, in radians, and produces, as its return value, the cosine of that angle. So typing cos (1) invokes a function and produces a value of about 0.54. Operators are functions, too, although they don't look like it. For example, you can multiply two numbers by calling the * function explicitly with two arguments, though you'll need quotation marks; "*"(3, 4) operates * on 3 and 4 and produces 12. Functions are covered in detail in Chapter 5.

expression An *expression* is a legal R "phrase" that would produce an action if you entered it into R. For example, a <- 3 is an expression that, if evaluated, would cause an item a to be created and given the value 3. That expression is called an *assignment*. pi > 3 is an expression that would produce TRUE, since the number pi is greater than 3. This is an example of a *comparison*. Just typing 2 is also an expression; the system interprets this as being the same as print (2), and prints out the value 2. Most expressions involve the use of functions or operators, as well as R variables.

command We often use the word "command" as a casual shortcut to mean "function," "operator," or "expression." For example, we might say "use the help command" instead of "run the help function."

script A *script* is a text file that can list R commands. We use script files in all of our projects and we recommend that you do, too. We discuss scripts in Chapter 5.

workspace The *workspace* is the set of objects (data and functions) in our current environment. These are objects we have created.

working directory The *working directory* is the folder on your computer where your R data is stored. By default, R will look in this directory for any external files you might ask for. We talk more about the working directory in the following section.

With this vocabulary in mind it is easier to discuss some of the ways that R operates. As an example, it's not always obvious what the different operators in R will do in weird cases. We know that 3 < 10 is TRUE. What is the value of 3 < "10"? The answer is FALSE. R cannot compare a number to a character, so converts both values into characters. Then the comparison is made alphabetically. So just as "Apple" < "Banana" is TRUE because "Apple" comes first in alphabetical order, so too does "10" come before "3" – since, as always, we compare the initial characters first, and the 1 character precedes the 3 character in our computer's sorting system. We talk much more about the different types of data in R, and converting between them, in Chapter 2.

Another example of unexpected behavior has to do with the way R reads commands typed in at the command line. We saw that the command a <- 3 assigns the value 3 to an object a. However, what happens when you type a < - 3, with a space between < and -? The answer is that R attaches the hyphen to the value 3, and then compares the value of a to the number -3. In general, spaces will not affect your R commands – but in this case the space "broke" the assignment operator <-.

R objects have names and names have to conform to a small set of rules. If data is brought in from outside R, perhaps from a spreadsheet, names will be changed if they need to be made valid (details can be seen in the help for the make.names() function). Technically it is possible to force R to use invalid names, but don't do that. A few names in R are *reserved*, meaning they cannot be used as the name of an R variable. For example, you cannot name an object TRUE; that name is reserved. (You may name an object T, because that name isn't reserved, but we don't recommend it.) It is also wise to try to avoid giving an object the name of an existing R function (although there are lots of R functions and some are obscure). If you name a vector sum, and then use the sum() function to add things up, R will be smart enough to differentiate your vector from the system's function. But if you create a function called sum() in your workspace, R will use that one (since your function will appear first on the search path; see "search path" in Section 1.4.1). This is almost never what you want. The R functions c() and t() provide good examples of names to avoid.

Finally, R can operate in an "object-oriented" way. A number of R functions are "generic," meaning that have specific methods to handle specific data types. For example, the summary() function applied to a numeric vector gives some information about the values in the vector, but the same function applied to the output of a modeling function will often give summary statistics about the model. The exact action that the generic function takes depends on the "class" (i.e., the type) of the object passed to it. We run across a few of these generic functions in the following few chapters and discuss object-oriented programming briefly in Section 5.6.3

1.3.3 Calculating and Printing in R

R performs calculations and prints results. In this section, we talk about some of the differences between what R computes and what it prints, as well as how text data is represented.

Floating-Point Error

This is a good place to discuss an issue that arises in a lot of data cleaning problems and has caught us and our students off-guard more than once. For almost all computations, R uses "double-precision floating-point" arithmetic, as most other systems do. What this means is that R can represent numbers up to about $\pm 1.79 \times 10^{\pm 308}$ with at least some accuracy. However, double precision is not exact. Consider this example, in which we multiply together the numbers (1/49) and 49.

```
> 1/49 * 49
[1] 1                          # as expected
> 1 - (1/49 * 49)
[1] 1.110223e-16
> (49 * 1/49) == (1/49 * 49) # should be TRUE
[1] FALSE
```

The first computation shows the "expected" product of (1/49) and 49 – the value 1. In fact, though, the second computation shows that this product is not exactly 1; it differs from 1 by a tiny amount that we might call "floating-point error." That amount was so small that it wasn't displayed in the first computation, according to R's default display conditions. (The command print(1/49 * 49, digits = 16) will reveal that this product is computed as a number very slightly less than 1.) This is not a bug in R; it's a statement about the way double-precision floating-point arithmetic works, analogous to the way that in ordinary arithmetic, the number 0.333333 ... is not quite 1/3. The final computation shows the practical effect of this: if you compare two floating-point values directly, they might be recorded as being different just because of floating-point error. You will need to be aware of this when you compare the results of doing the same computation in two different ways.

Significant Digits

In the above-mentioned example, we saw how R printed 1 even though the number in question was slightly different. While R's computations use double-precision floating point, its display will generally print a smaller number of digits than are available. Moreover, R formats outputs in a neat way, so that typing 2.00 produces 2, but typing 2.01 prints out as 2.01. These formatting choices are most noticeable when many values are being shown. The display that R chooses does not affect the precision with which it does calculations. Of course you can force R to round off the results of its calculation; we discuss formatting, rounding, and scientific notation in Chapter 4.

Character Strings

We will spend a lot of time in this book handling text or character data, data in the form of letters such as "Oakland" or "Missing". Sometimes, as is common, we will call a set of characters a *string*. In R, strings are enclosed by quotation marks, and either the double-quotation mark " or the single one ' can be used. A string delineated by single-quotation marks is converted into the other kind. The two kinds of quotation marks make it possible to insert a quote into a string, such as this: "She said 'No.' " (If you typed "She said "No." ", you would see R produce an error.) If you type 'She said "No." ', the outside quotes are converted to double quotes. Then, since there are double quotes on the inside, too, those interior quotation marks are "protected" by preceding them with the backslash character. The result is converted into "She said \"No.\" "

This idea of "protecting" certain special characters goes beyond quotation marks. The character that marks the end of a line of text is called "new-line" and is written as \n, backslash followed by n. Typing this character requires two keystrokes, but it counts as only one character. In general, special characters are "protected" by the backslash characters. Besides the quotation mark and the new-line, the important special characters are \t, the tab, and \\, the backslash itself. The backslash also serves to introduce strings in special formats, such as hexadecimal (e.g., "\xb1" produces the character with hexadecimal value b1, which displays as the plus-minus sign, ±) or Unicode (e.g., "\U20ac" uses Unicode to display the Euro currency symbol). We talk much more about text in general and Unicode in particular in Chapter 4.

1.4 Running an R Session

Once you start using R you may find yourself using it for lots of different projects. Although this is partly a matter of taste, we find it useful to keep separate sets of data for separate projects. In this section, we describe where R keeps your data, and some other aspects of R with which you will need to be familiar.

1.4.1 Where Your Data Is Stored

When you start R, you start it in a *working directory*, and this directory forms the starting point for where R looks for, and stores, data. For example, typing `list.files()` will list all of the files in your working directory. When you quit R and save the workspace, a file with all of your R objects will be created in that same directory. This file is named `.RData`. The leading dot in the name is important, because some terminal programs, such as the "bash" command interpreter, do not by default list files whose names start with a dot. We don't recommend changing the name of the `.RData` file.

This provides a natural mechanism for project management. To prepare for a new project on a system with a command-line interface, just create a new directory and start R from there (see "starting R" above). On systems with desktop icons, copy an existing R icon, edit the properties to point to the new directory, and add the project name to the icon. The details of this operation will depend on your operating system. In this way, you can keep the different `.RData` files for your different projects separate.

When you start R, it will use an existing `.RData` file if there is one in the working directory, or create a new, empty one if there is not. Often we have a certain number of objects from earlier projects that we want in the new project. There are two mechanisms for acquiring those existing R objects. In one case, we literally copy all the objects from another `.RData` in a different project's directory into the existing workspace, using the `load()` function. This can be dangerous because objects being copied will over-write existing ones with the same names. A second mechanism uses `attach()`, which puts the other `.RData` on the "search path." The search path is a list of places where R looks for objects when you mention them. You can examine your current search path with the `search()` command. The first entry on the search path is the current `.RData` file (although it carries the confusing name `.GlobalEnv`); most of the other entries on the search path are put there by R itself. When you use a name such as `pi`, R looks for that object in your workspace, and then in each of the packages or directories named in the search path until it finds one by that name. You can attach other `.RData` files anywhere in the search path, except in the first position; usually we put them into position two so that they are searched right after the local workspace. We talk more about getting data into and out of R in Chapter 6.

1.4.2 Options

R maintains a list of what it calls "options," which describe aspects of your interaction with it. For example, one option sets the text editor that R calls when you edit a function, one describes how much memory is set aside for R, one lets you change the prompt character from its default, and so on. Generally, we find the default values reasonable, but the help for the `options()` function describes the possible values and running `options()` shows you the current ones. Changes to the options last only for this R session. Section 3.3.2 shows an example of setting one of the options.

1.4.3   Scripts

Most of the work we do with R is interactive – that is, we issue commands and wait for R's response. This use of R is best when we are exploring data and developing approaches to handling and modeling it. As we develop sets of commands for a particular project, we can combine these into "scripts," which are simply files full of commands. Having a set of commands together allows us to execute them in exactly the same way every time, and it allows us to add comments and other notes that will be useful to us and to other users whom we share the code with. This approach, while still interactive, is best when we have developed an approach and want to use it repeatedly. Scripts also provide a natural mechanism for project management: often we start with an empty workspace and use scripts to populate the workspace by reading and preparing data, loading from other sources, or attaching other directories, before starting on the modeling steps.

R can also be run in batch mode – that is, it can start, run a single set of commands, and then stop. This approach can be used when the same task needs to be performed repeatedly, perhaps on different data – say, every day to process data gathered overnight. We talk about scripts and batch use of R in Chapter 5.

1.4.4   R Packages

A *package* is a set of functions (and maybe data and other stuff too) that provides an extension to R. R comes with a set of packages, some of which are automatically placed onto the search path, and others of which are not. If a package is present on your computer but not in your search path, you can access (or "load") it with the `library()` or `require()` command (these two differ only in how they react if a package cannot be found). A package only needs to be loaded once per R session, but when you re-start R you will need to re-load packages. There are also thousands of additional packages that have been contributed by R users that can be found on the Internet, primarily at the main repository at `cran.r-project.org` and its mirror sites. If your computer is connected to the Internet, you can install a package (if you know its name) with the `install.packages()` command. If that works, the package will still need to be loaded with the `library()` command. If your computer is not connected to the Internet, you can still install packages from a disk file if one is available. Most of the code in this book requires no additional packages, although in some cases we will point out cases where additional packages make particular tasks easier, more efficient, or, in rare cases, possible.

It is possible to force certain packages to be loaded whenever you start R. When we anticipate needing a package, our preference is to include a call to `library()` or `require()` inside our scripts.

1.4.5   RStudio and Other GUIs

The "look" of R depends on your operating system. At its most basic – and we often see this when we are connecting to remote servers – R consists only of a command line. On the most popular platforms – Windows and OS X – running R produces a graphical user interface, or GUI. This is a set of windows containing a number of menu items giving selections, or buttons that help you perform common tasks. Most of the GUI, though, consists of the console. A few enhanced GUIs are available. Perhaps the most widely used among these is RStudio (RStudio Team, 2015), a development environment that includes a console window, a set of script window tabs, and better handling of multiple graphics windows. RStudio comes in free and paid versions for all operating systems and is available from its maker at `rstudio.com`. We have found that many of our students prefer the more interactive, perhaps more modern feel of RStudio to the standard R interface – but underneath, the R language is exactly the same.

1.4.6   Locales and Character Sets

R is essentially the same program whether you run it on Windows, OS X, or Linux. (There are minor differences in the way you access external files and in some low-level technical functions that will not be relevant in data cleaning.) In particular, R is an English-language program, so a "for" loop is always indicated by `for()`. Speakers of many languages can arrange to have error messages delivered in their language, if this ability is configured at the time R is installed – see the help for the `Sys.setenv()` function and for "environment variables."

Even though R is in English, it is possible to set the "locale" of R. This allows you to change the way that R does things such as format currency values. English speakers use the dot as the decimal separator and the comma to set off thousands from hundreds, but many Europeans use those two characters in reverse. Other locale settings affect the abbreviations in use for days of the week and months of the year. We discuss some of these in Chapter 3, but one important one to note here is the "collation" setting. This describes how R sorts alphabetical items. Under the usual choices on Windows and OS X, lower- and upper-case letters are sorted together, so that "a" precedes "A" in alphabetical order, but both precede "b." To continue an earlier example, this ensures that `"apple"` < `"banana"` and `"apple"` < `"Banana"` are both TRUE. However, on some Linux systems the so-called "C" collation sequence is used. In that scheme, all the upper-case letters come before any of the lower-case ones – so that `"apple"` < `"banana"` is TRUE, but `"apple"` < `"Banana"` is FALSE. Moreover, as the help for `Comparison` points out, "in Estonian, S comes between S and T." You have to be aware of your both locale and the relevant language whenever you compare strings.

Another aspect of character handling is the use of different character sets. Text in non-Roman languages such as Hebrew or Korean requires some special considerations. We discuss these at some length in Chapter 4.

1.5 Getting Help

R has a number of ways of getting help to you. "Help" can mean information about the specific syntax of individual R commands, about putting the pieces of R together in programs, or about the details of the various statistical models and tools that R provides. In this section, we describe some of the resources available to help you learn about R.

1.5.1 At the Command Line

The most basic help is provided at the command line, through the commands `help()`, `?` and `help.search()`. The first two commands act identically and will be most useful when you need information on a particular R function or operator whose name you know. In most cases, the argument doesn't need to be in quotation marks, though it may be – so `help(matrix)` or `?"matrix"` both bring up a page about some matrix functions. Quotation marks will be required when looking for help on some elements of the R language – so `?"for"` gives the help page for the `for` looping term and `help("==")` produces the page on comparison operators. The `help.search()` command is useful when the subject, rather than the name, is known; this command opens a window (depending on your operating system) that gives links to associated R objects. A related command is the `apropos()` function, which takes a character argument (as in `apropos("matrix")`) and returns a vector of names of objects containing that string (in this example, every object with `matrix` in its name). A final piece of command-line help is provided by the `args()` function, which takes a function and displays the set of arguments expected by, and default values provided by that function.

1.5.2 The Online Manuals

When you install R, you are given the opportunity to install the online manuals with it. These manuals are generally correct and complete, but they are intended as references, and are not always useful as tutorials.

1.5.3   On the Internet

The main page for the R project is `r-project.org`. This is the central repository for R and its documentation. If you are interested in participating in a community of R users, you might consider joining one of the mailing lists, which you can find under `mail.html` at that page.

R is very popular and there are lots and lots of blogs, pages, and other web documents that address R and solve specific problems. Your favorite Internet search engine will be able to find dozens of these.

1.5.4   Further Reading

A lot of documentation comes with R when you install in the usual way. You can find a list of these manuals under Help | Manuals in Windows, or Help | R Help on OS X, or with `help.start()`. The "Introduction to R" manual is a good place to start.

The book "The Art of R Programming" (Matloff, 2011) is a nice tour of many R features ranging from beginning to advanced. As its name suggests, the emphasis is on writing powerful and efficient R programs. Many other books introduce the use of R, or describe its application in specific fields such as economics or genomics. The `r-project` website has a list of over 150 books using R. As we mentioned earlier, that site also maintains mailing lists for interested users, and a quick web search will reveal scores of blogs and web pages devoted to R and to answering R questions.

The recent book by Wickham and Grolemond (2016) describes those authors' approach to not only data cleaning but a set of additional tasks, including visualization and modeling, which we think of as beyond the scope of data acquisition and cleaning. That approach requires an entire set of tools from packages outside R – although they come conveniently bundled together – as well as a new vocabulary. This ecosystem has its adherents, but we prefer to use base R where possible.

1.6   How to Use This Book

1.6.1   Syntax and Conventions in This Book

We reproduce a lot of R code in this book. R code is indicated in a fixed-width font `like this`. Since R is case-sensitive, our text will exactly match what is typed into R – except that in the prose we capitalize letters of R objects if they appear at the beginning of sentences. Inside a paragraph, or when we want to show a sequence of commands, we reproduce exactly what we type, like this:

`sqrt (pi)`. When we also want to show what R returns, the code will be shown with the prompt and the literal R output, like this:

```
> sqrt (pi)
[1] 1.772454
```

Unlike the example in the "top ten quick fact" #1, we suppress the continuation prompt +, so that it is not confused with the ordinary plus sign.

There are several different schemes for formatting code that you can find described on the Internet, and they do not always agree. To us the most important rule is to make your code easy to read. This means, first, use spacing and indenting in a helpful and consistent way, and second, add plenty of comments to help the reader. There is always a temptation to write code as quickly as possible, with an eye toward worrying about neatness later. Resist that temptation! Code is for sharing and for re-use.

On a lighter note, we know that the word "data" originated as the plural of the singular "datum," but it has long been permitted to construe "data" in the singular, and we do that in this book. You will find us saying "the data is..." rather than "are." This is intentional.

1.6.2 The Chapters

In order to use R wisely, you have to understand what data looks like to R. The following three chapters describe the sorts of data that R recognizes, and how to manipulate R's objects. We start by describing vectors, the simplest form of data in R, in Chapter 2. This chapter describes the common types of vectors, the different ways to extract subsets from them, and how to change values in vectors. It also describes how R stores missing values, an integral part of almost every data cleaning problem. The chapter concludes with a look at the important `table ()` function and some of the basic operations on vectors – sorting, identifying duplicates, computing unions and intersections of sets, and so on.

Chapter 3 describes more complicated data structures: matrices, lists, and finally data frames. Understanding how data frames work is critical to using R intelligently. We defer until this chapter discussion of how R handles times and dates, because part of that discussion requires an understanding of lists.

The final data chapter, Chapter 4, discusses the last important data type – text or character data. Text data is stored in vectors and data frames such as other kinds, but there are a number of operations specific to text. This chapter describes how to manipulate text in R – changing case, extracting and assembling pieces of strings, formatting numbers into strings, and so on. One important topic is *regular expressions*, a set of tools for finding strings that contain a pattern of characters. This chapter also discusses the UTF-8 system of encoding non-Roman alphabets such as Greek or Chinese and R's concept of *factors*, which are important in modeling but often cause problems during the data cleaning process.

Chapter 5 discusses two types of tool used to automate computations in R: functions and scripts. These different, but related, tools, will be part of every analysis you ever do, so you should understand how to construct them intelligently. We also look briefly at "shell scripts," which are a special sort of script that let you run R in batch, rather than interactive mode, and discuss some of the tools available in R for debugging.

This is a book about cleaning data, but the data to be cleaned needs to come from somewhere. Chapter 6 describes the different ways to bring data into R: from other R sessions, from spreadsheet-like text files, from relational databases, and so on. We describe two of the formats in which data is commonly found in modern applications: XML and JSON. We also describe how to acquire data programmatically from web pages.

Chapter 7 takes a bigger view of the data cleaning process. While the earlier chapters focus on the nuts and bolts of R as they relate to data cleaning, this chapter describes the sort of challenges in a real-life data cleaning project. We talk about how to combine data from different sources and give examples of the sort of anomalies that you have to expect in dealing with real data. In almost every case you will have to rely on judgment, rather than just on a cookbook of techniques. We spend some time discussing the role of judgment on data cleaning.

The Exercise

The culmination of the book is the data cleaning exercise presented in Chapter 8. This chapter presents a complicated data acquisition and cleaning problem that, while artificial, reflects many of the problems and challenges we have seen over our years of real-life data handling experience. If you can find your way through to the end of the exercise, we expect that you will be well prepared to handle the data the real world sends your way.

Critical Data Handling Tools

In every chapter, we have set aside the final section to recap commands and tools we think are particularly important when it comes to data handling and manipulation. If you can master the use of these tools, and apply them wisely, you can reduce the risk of missing important information in your data.

The Code

All of the code reproduced in this book appears in scripts in the `cleaning Book` package you can download from the CRAN website. You can open these scripts in R and run the code from there – although since most examples are very short, we suggest that you consider typing them in yourself, to get a feel for the R language.

2

R Data, Part 1: Vectors

The basic unit of computation in R is the *vector*. A vector is a set of one or more basic objects *of the same kind*. (Actually, it is even possible to have a vector with no objects in it, as we will see, and this happens sometimes.) Each of the entries in a vector is called an *element*. In this chapter, we talk about the different sorts of vectors that you can have in R. Then, we describe the very important topic of *subsetting*, which is our word for extracting pieces of vectors – all of the elements that are greater than 10, for example. That topic goes together with *assigning*, or replacing, certain elements of a vector. We describe the way missing values are handled in R; this topic arises in almost every data cleaning problem. The rest of the chapter gives some tools that are useful when handling vectors.

2.1 Vectors

By a "basic" object, we mean an object of one of R's so-called "atomic" classes. These classes, which you can find in help(vector), are logical (values TRUE or FALSE, although T and F are provided as synonyms); integer; numeric (also called double); character, which refers to text; raw, which can hold binary data; and complex. Some of these, such as complex, probably won't arise in data cleaning.

2.1.1 Creating Vectors

We are mostly concerned with vectors that have been given to us as data. However, there are a number of situations when you will need to construct your own vectors. Of course, since a scalar is a vector of length 1, you can construct one directly, by typing its value:

```
> 5
[1] 5
```

A Data Scientist's Guide to Acquiring, Cleaning, and Managing Data in R, First Edition.
Samuel E. Buttrey and Lyn R. Whitaker.
© 2018 John Wiley & Sons Ltd. Published 2018 by John Wiley & Sons Ltd.
Companion website: www.wiley.com/go/buttrey/datascientistsguide

R displays the [1] before the answer to show you that the 5 is the first element of the resulting vector. Here, of course, the resulting vector only had one entry, but R displays the [1] nonetheless. There is no such thing as a "scalar" in R; even *π*, represented in R by the built-in value pi, is a vector of length 1. To combine several items into a vector, use the c() function, which combines as many items as you need.

```
> c(1, 17)
[1] 1 17
> c(-1, pi, 17)
[1] -1.000000  3.141593 17.000000
> c(-1, pi, 1700000)
[1] -1.000000e+00  3.141593e+00  1.700000e+06
```

R has formatted the numbers in the vectors in a consistent way. In the second example, the number of digits of pi is what determines the formatting; see Section 1.3.3. In example three, the same number of digits is used, but the large number has caused R to use scientific notation. We discuss that in Section 4.2.2. Analogous formatting rules are applied to non-numeric vectors as well; this makes output much more readable. The c() function can also be used to combine vectors, as long as all the vectors are of the same sort.

Another vector-creation function is rep(), which repeats a value as many times as you need. For example, rep(3, 4) produces a vector of four 3s. In this example, we show some more of the abilities of rep().

```
> rep (c(2, 4), 3)                # repeat a vector
[1] 2 4 2 4 2 4
> rep (c("Yes", "No"), c(3, 1)) # repeat elements of vector
[1] "Yes" "Yes" "Yes" "No"
> rep (c("Yes", "No"), each = 8)
 [1] "Yes" "Yes" "Yes" "Yes" "Yes" "Yes" "Yes" "Yes" "No"
[10] "No"  "No"  "No"  "No"  "No"  "No"  "No"
```

The last two examples show rep() operating on a character vector. The final one shows how R displays longer vectors – by giving the number of the first element on each line. Here, for example, the [10] indicates that the first "No" on the second line is the 10th element of the vector.

2.1.2 Sequences

We also very often create vectors of sets of consecutive integers. For example, we might want the first 10 integers, so that we can get hold of the first 10 rows in a table. For that task we can use the colon operator, : . Actually, the colon operator doesn't have to be confined to integers; you can also use it to produce a sequence of non-integers that are one unit apart, as in the following example, but we haven't found that to be very useful.

```
> 1:5
[1] 1 2 3 4 5
> 6:-2
[1]  6  5  4  3  2  1  0 -1 -2  # Can go in reverse, by 1
> 2.3:5.9
[1] 2.3 3.3 4.3 5.3            # Permitted (but unusual)
> 3 + 2:7                      # Watch out here! This is 3 +
[1]  5  6  7  8  9 10          # (vector produced by 2:7)
> (3 + 2):7
[1] 5 6 7                      # This is 5:7
```

In that last pair of examples, we see that R evaluates the 2 : 7 operation before adding the 3. This is because : has a higher precedence in the order of operations than addition. The list of operators and their precedences can be found at ?Syntax, and precedence can always be over-ridden with parentheses, as in the example – but this is the only example of operator precedence that is likely to trip you up. Also notice that adding 3 to a vector adds 3 to each element of that vector; we talk more about vector operations in Section 2.1.4.

Finally, we sometimes need to create vectors whose entries differ by a number other than one. For that, we use seq(), a function that allows much finer control of starting points, ending points, lengths, and step sizes.

2.1.3 Logical Vectors

We can create logical vectors using the c() function, but most often they are constructed by R in response to an operation on other vectors. We saw examples of operators back in Section 1.3.2; the R operators that perform comparisons are <, <=, >, >=, == (for "is equal to") and != (for "not equal to"). In this example, we do some simple comparisons on a short vector.

```
> 101:105 >= 102              # Which elements are >= 102?
[1] FALSE  TRUE  TRUE  TRUE  TRUE
> 101:105 == 104              # Which equal (==) 104?
[1] FALSE FALSE FALSE  TRUE FALSE
```

Of course, when you compare two floating-point numbers for equality, you can get unexpected results. In this example, we compute 1 - 1/46 * 46, which is zero; 1 - 1/47 * 47, and so on up through 50. We have seen this example before!

```
> 1 - 1/46:50 * 46:50 == 0
[1]  TRUE  TRUE  TRUE FALSE  TRUE
```

We noted earlier that R provides T and F as synonyms for TRUE and FALSE. We sometimes use these synonyms in the book. However, it is best to beware of using these shortened forms in code. It is possible to create objects named

T or F, which might interfere with their usage as logical values. In contrast, the full names TRUE and FALSE are reserved words in R. This means that you cannot directly assign one of these names to an object and, therefore, that they are never ambiguous in code.

The Number and Proportion of Elements That Meet a Criterion

One task that comes up a lot in data cleaning is to count the number (or proportion) of events that meet some criterion. We might want to know how many missing values there are in a vector, for example, or the proportion of elements that are less than 0.5. For these tasks, computing the sum() or mean() of a logical vector is an excellent approach. In our earlier example, we might have been interested in the number of elements that are ≥ 102, or the proportion that are exactly 104.

```
> 101:105 >= 102
[1] FALSE   TRUE   TRUE   TRUE   TRUE
> sum (101:105 >= 102)
[1] 4                              # Four elements are >= 102
> 101:105 == 104
[1] FALSE FALSE FALSE   TRUE FALSE
> mean (101:105 == 104)
[1] 0.2                            # 20% are == 104
```

It may be worth pondering this last example for a moment. We start with the logical vector that is the result of the comparison operator. In order to apply a mathematical function to that vector, R needs to convert the logical elements to numeric ones. FALSE values get turned into zeros and TRUE values into ones (we discuss conversion further in Section 2.2.3). Then, sum() adds up those 0s and 1s, producing the total number of 1s in the converted vector – that is, the number of TRUE values in the logical vector or the number of elements of the original vector that meet the criterion by being $\geq$ 102. The mean() function computes the sum of the number of 1s and then divides that sum by the total number of elements, and that operation produces the proportion of TRUE values in the logical vector, that is, the proportion of elements in the original vector that meet the criterion.

2.1.4 Vector Operations

Understanding how vectors work is crucial to using R properly and efficiently. Arithmetic operations on vectors produce vectors, which means you very often do not have to write an explicit loop to perform an operation on a vector. Suppose we have a vector of six integers, and we want to perform some operations on them. We can do this:

```
> 5:10
[1]   5   6   7   8   9 10
> (5:10) + 4
```

```
[1]    9 10 11 12 13 14
> (5:10)^2                          # Square each element;
[1]    25   36   49   64   81 100   # parentheses necessary
```

Just to repeat, arithmetic and most other mathematical operations operate on vectors and return vectors. So if you want the natural logarithm of every item in a vector named x, for example, you just enter `log(x)`. If you want the square of the cosine of the logarithm of every element of x, you would use `cos(log(x))^2`, and so on. There are functions, such as `length()`, `sum()`, `mean()`, `sd()`, `min()`, and `max()`, that operate on a vector and produce a single number (which, to be sure, is also a vector in R). There are also functions such as `range()`, which returns a vector containing the smallest and largest values, and `summary()`, which returns a vector of summary statistics, but one of the sources of R's power is the ability to perform computations on every element of a vector at once.

In the last two examples above, we operated on a vector and a single number simultaneously. R handles this in the natural way: by repeating the 4 (in the first example) or the 2 (in the second) as many times as needed. R calls this *recycling*. In the following example, we see what R does in the case of operating on two vectors of the same length. The answer is, it performs the operation between the first elements of each vector, then the second elements, and so on. In the opening command, we have the usual assignment, using < -, and also an additional set of parentheses outside that command. These additional parentheses cause the result of the assignment to be printed. Without them, we would have created thing1, but its value would not have been displayed.

```
> (thing1 <- c(20, 15, 10, 5, 0)^2)
[1] 400 225 100   25    0
> (thing2 <- 105:101)
[1] 105 104 103 102 101
> thing2 + thing1
[1] 505 329 203 127 101
> thing2 / thing1
[1] 0.2625000 0.4622222 1.0300000 4.0800000        Inf
```

In the last lines, R computes the ratios element by element. The final ratio, 101/0, yields the result Inf, referring to an infinite value. We discuss Inf more in Section 2.4.4. The following example compares a function that returns a single, summary value to one that operates element by element.

```
> max (thing2, thing1)
[1] 400
> pmax (thing2, thing1)
[1] 400 225 103 102 101
```

The max() function produces the largest value anywhere in any of its arguments – in this case, the 400 from the first element of thing1. The pmax () ("parallel maximum") function finds the larger of the first element of the two vectors, and the larger of the second element of the two vectors, and so on.

Two logical vectors can also be combined element by element, using the | logical operator for "or" (i.e., returning TRUE if either element is TRUE) and the & operator for "and" (i.e., returning TRUE only if both elements are TRUE). These operators differ in a subtle way from their doubled versions || and &&. The single versions evaluate the condition for every pair of elements from both vectors, whereas the doubled versions evaluate multiple TRUE/FALSE conditions from left to right, stopping as soon as possible. These doubled versions are most useful in, for example, if () statements.

Recycling

There can be a complication, though: what if two vectors being operated on are not of the same length?

```
> 5:10 + c(0, 10, 100, 1000, 10000, 100000)   # Two 6-vectors
[1]     5   16    107   1008   10009 100010 # Add by element
> 5:10 + c(1, 10, 100)              # A 6-vector and a 3-vector
[1]     6   16    107 9   19 110    # The 3-vector is replicated
> 5:10 + 3:7                        # A 6-vector and a 5-vector
[1]   8 10 12 14 16 13              # 5+3, 6+4, ..., 9+7, 10+3
Warning message:
In 5:10 + 3:7 :
  longer object length is not a multiple of shorter length
```

It is important to understand these last two examples because the problem of mismatched vector lengths arises often. In the first of the two examples, the 3-vector (1, 10, 100) was added to the first three elements of the 6-vector, and then added again to the second three elements. Once again R is recycling. No warning was issued because 3 is a factor of 6, so the shorter vector was recycled an exact number of times. In the final example, the 5-vector was added to the first five elements of the 6-vector. In order to finish the addition, R recycled the first element of the 5-vector, the value 3. That value was added to the last entry of the 6-vector, 10, to produce the final element of the result, 13. The recycling only used part of the 5-vector; since 5 is not a factor of 6, a warning was issued.

Recycling a vector of length 1, as we did when we computed (5:10) + 4, is very common. Recycling vectors of other lengths is rarer, and we suggest you avoid it unless you are certain you know what you are doing. When you see the longer object length... warning as we did in the last example, we recommend you treat that as an error and get to the root of that problem.

Tools for Handling Character Vectors

Almost every data cleaning problem requires some handling of characters. Either the data contains characters to start with – maybe names and addresses, or dates, or fields that indicate sex, for example – or we will need to construct some (perhaps turning sexes labeled 1 or 2 into M and F). We also often need to search through character strings to find ones that match a particular pattern; remove commas or currency signs that have been put into formatted numbers (such as "$2500.00"); or discretize a numeric variable into a smaller number of groups (such as turning an Age field into levels Child, Teen, Adult, Senior). Character data is so important, and so common, that we have devoted an entire chapter (Chapter 4) to special techniques for handling it.

2.1.5 Names

A vector may have *names*, a vector of character strings that act to identify the individual entries. It is possible to add names to a vector, and in this section we give examples of that. More commonly, though, R adds names to a table when you tabulate a vector using the table() function. We will have more to say about table(), and the names it produces, in Section 2.5. In the meantime, here is a simple example of a vector with names. Notice that the third name has an embedded space. This name is not "syntactically valid" according to R's rules. A syntactically valid name has only letters, numbers, dots, and underscores and starts either with a letter or a dot and then a non-numeric character. It is usually a bad practice to have a vector's names be invalid, but, as we show in the following example, it is possible. See Section 3.4.2 for information on how to ensure that your names are valid.

```
> vec <- c(101, 102, 103)
> names(vec)
NULL
> names(vec) <- c("a", "b", "Long name")
> names(vec)
[1] "a"          "b"          "Long name"
```

After the second line, R returned the special value NULL to indicate that the vector had no names. (We talk more about NULL in Section 2.4.5.) The names() function then assigned names to the elements of the vector. We can also assign names directly in the c() function, as in this example.

```
> c(a = 101, b = 102, Long.name = 103)
        a         b Long.name
      101       102       103
```

In this case, we used a syntactically valid name; an invalid one would have had to be enclosed in quotation marks.

2.2 Data Types

The three data types we have mentioned so far – numeric, logical, and character – are the ones we most often use. R does support several other data types. In this section, we mention these data types briefly, and then discuss the important topic of converting data from one type to another. Sometimes this is an operation we do explicitly and intentionally; other times R performs the conversion automatically.

2.2.1 Some Less-Common Data Types

Integers

R can represent as integer values between $-(2^{31} - 1)$ and $2^{31} - 1$. (This number is 2,147,483,647.) Values outside this range may be displayed as if they were integers, but they will be stored as doubles. When doing calculations, R automatically converts values that are too big to be integers into doubles, so the only time integer storage will matter is if you explicitly convert a really large value into an integer (see Section 2.2.3). If you need R to regard an item as an integer for some reason, you can append L on its end. So, for example, 123 is numeric but 123L is regarded as an integer value. Of course, it only makes sense to add L to a thing that really is an integer.

Raw

"Raw" refers to data kept in binary (hexadecimal) form. This is the format that data from images, sound, or video will take in R. We rarely need to handle that kind of file in a data cleaning problem. However, we do sometimes resort to using raw data when a file has unexpected characters in it, or at the beginning of an analysis when we do not know what sort of data a file might have. In that case, the data will be read into R and held as a vector of class raw. A raw vector is a string of bytes represented in hexadecimal form. It can be converted into character data (when that makes sense) with the rawToChar() function. We talk more about reading raw data, particularly to handle the case of unexpected characters, in Section 6.2.5.

Complex Numbers

R has the ability to manipulate complex numbers (numbers such as $1.3 - 2.4i$, where i is $\sqrt{-1}$). Since complex numbers almost never arise in data cleaning, we will not discuss them in this book.

2.2.2 What Type of Vector Is This?

You can usually tell what sort of vector you have by looking at a few of its entries. Character data has entries surrounded by quotes; numeric entries have no quotes; and logical entries are either TRUE or FALSE. So, for example, the value "TRUE", with quotation marks, can only belong to a character vector. There are also several functions in R that tell you explicitly what sort of thing you have. Two of these functions, mode() and typeof(), tell you the basic type of vector. They are essentially identical for our purposes, except that typeof() differentiates between integer and double, whereas mode()

calls them both `numeric`. The `str()` function (for "structure") not only tells you the type of vector but also shows you the first few entries. A related function, `class()`, is a more general operator for complex types.

A second group of functions gives a `TRUE/FALSE` answer as to whether a specific vector has a specific mode. These functions are named `is.logical()`, `is.integer()`, `is.numeric()`, and `is.character()`, and each returns a single `logical` value describing the type of the vector. A more general version, `is()`, lets you specify the class as an argument: so `is.numeric(pi)` is identical to `is(pi, "numeric")`. This more general form is particularly useful when testing for more complicated, possibly user-defined classes.

2.2.3 Converting from One Type to Another

It is important to remember that a vector can contain elements of only one type. When types are mixed – for example, if you inadvertently insert a character element into a numeric vector – R modifies the entire vector to be of the more complicated type. Here is an example:

```
> c(1, 4, 7, 2, 5)        # Create numeric vector
[1] 1 4 7 2 5
> c(1, 4, 7, 2, 5, "3")   # What if one element is character?
[1] "1" "4" "7" "2" "5" "3"
```

In this example, the entire vector got converted to `character`. The rule is that R will convert every element of a vector to the "most complicated" type of any of the elements. `Logical` is the least complicated type, followed by `raw`, `numeric`, `complex`, and then `character`. (Raw vectors behave a little differently from the others. See Section 6.2.5.)

It is important to know what values the less complicated types get when they are converted to more complicated ones. `Logical` elements that are converted into `numeric` become 0 where they have the value `FALSE` and 1 where they are `TRUE`. A logical converted into a character, however, gets values `"FALSE"` and `"TRUE"`. A number gets converted into a high-accuracy text representation of itself, as we see in these examples.

```
> 1/7
[1] 0.1428571             # by default, 7 digits are displayed
> c(1/7, "a")
[1] "0.142857142857143" "a"
```

One instance where R frequently performs conversions automatically is from integer to numeric types.

Conversion Functions
R will convert less complicated types into more complicated ones where required. Sometimes you need to force the elements of a vector back into a

less complicated representation. Just as there are functions whose names start with `is.` for testing the type of an object, there is a set of `as.` functions for converting from one type to another. The rules are these: a character will be successfully converted to a numeric if it has the syntax of a number. It may have leading or trailing spaces (or new-lines or tabs), but no embedded ones; it may have leading zeros; it may have a decimal point (but only one); it may not have embedded commas; it may have a leading minus or plus sign, and, if it is in scientific notation, the exponent character E may be in upper- or lower-case and may also be followed by a minus or plus sign. In this example, we show some character strings that do and do not get converted to numbers. Notice that the elements of the vector that do not get converted turn into missing values (NA). We discuss missing values in Section 2.4.

```
> as.numeric (c(" 123.5   ", "-123e-2", "4,355", "45. 6",
                "$23", "75%"))
[1] 123.50  -1.23      NA      NA      NA      NA
Warning message:
NAs introduced by coercion
```

In this case, the first two elements were successfully converted. The third has a comma, the fourth has an embedded space, and the last two have non-numeric characters. In order to convert strings such as those into numbers, you would have to remove the offending characters. We describe how to manipulate text in Chapter 4.

The warning message you see here is a very common one. Unlike most warning messages, this one will often arise naturally in the course of data cleaning – but make sure you understand exactly where it's coming from.

The only `character` values that can be successfully converted into `logical` are "T", "TRUE", "True", and "true" and "F", "FALSE", "False", and "false". In this case, no extraneous spaces are permitted. All other character values are converted into NAs.

The rule is simple for converting `numeric` values into `logical` ones. Numeric values that are zero become FALSE; all other numbers become TRUE. The only issue is that sometimes numbers you expect to be zero aren't quite because of floating-point error. In this example, we convert some numbers and expressions to `logical`.

```
> as.logical (c(123, 5 - 5, 1e-300, 1e-400, 1 - 1/49 * 49))
[1]  TRUE FALSE  TRUE FALSE  TRUE
```

The first element here is clearly non-zero, so it gets converted to TRUE. The second evaluates to exactly zero and produces FALSE. The third is non-zero, but the fourth counts as zero since it is outside the range of double precision (see Section 1.3.3). The last element is our running example of an expression that "should" be zero but is not (again, see Section 1.3.3). Since it is not zero, it gets converted to TRUE. Numeric, non-missing values never produce NA when converted to logical.

2.3 Subsets of Vectors

We very often need to pull out just a piece of a vector. This is called *subsetting* or *extracting*. In most cases, where we extract a subset, we can use a similar expression to replace (or *assign*) new values to a subset of the elements in a vector. Knowing how to do this is crucial to data cleaning in R; you cannot work efficiently in R without understanding this material.

2.3.1 Extracting

We constantly perform this operation in one form or another when cleaning data: we look at subsets of rows or columns, we examine a vector for anomalous entries, we extract all the elements of one vector for which another has a specific value, and so on. There are three methods by which we can extract a subset of a vector. First, we can use a numeric vector to specify which elements to extract. This numeric vector is an example of a "subscript" and its entries are called "indices." Second, we can use a logical subscript; and, third, we can extract elements using their names.

Numeric Subscripts
The most basic way to extract a piece of a vector is to use a numeric subscript inside square brackets. For example, if you have a vector named a, the command a[1] will extract the first element of a. The result of that command is a vector of length 1, of the same mode as the original a. The command a[2:5] will produce a vector of length 4, with the second through fifth elements of a. If you ask for elements that aren't there – if, for example, a only had three elements – then R will fill up the missing spots with missing (NA) values. We discuss those further in Section 2.4. In this example, we have a vector a containing the numbers from 101 to 105.

```
> (a <- 101:105)
[1] 101 102 103 104 105
> a[3]
[1] 103
```

It's possible to pull out elements in any order, just by preparing the subscript properly. You can even use a numeric expression to compute your subscript, but *only do this if you're sure your expression is an integer.* If the result of your expression isn't an integer, even if it misses by just a tiny bit, you will get something you might not expect.

```
> a[c(4, 2)]
[1] 104 102
> a[1+1]                    # A simple expression; this works
[1] 102
> a[2.999999999999999]      # This is truncated to 2, but...
[1] 102
> a[2.9999999999999999]     # exactly 3 in double-precision.
[1] 103
> a[49 * (1/49)]            # This index gets truncated to zero;
integer (0)                 # R produces a vector of length zero
```

There are two kinds of special values in numeric subscripts: negative values and zeros. Negative values tell R to omit those values, instead of extracting them – so a[-1], for example, returns everything *except* the first element of a. You can have more than one negative number in your subscript, but you cannot mix positive and negative numbers, and that makes sense. (For example, in the expression a[c(-1, 3)], should the second element be returned or not?)

Zeros are another special value in a subscript. They are simply ignored by R. Zeros appear primarily as a result of the match() function; you will rarely use them intentionally yourself. Knowing that zeros are permitted helps make sense of the error message in the following example, though.

```
> a[-2]                  # Omit element 2
[1] 101 103 104 105
> a[c(-1, 3)]            # Illegal
Error in a[c(-1, 3)] : only 0's may be mixed
    with negative subscripts
> a[-1:2]    # Illegal, because -1:2 evaluates to -1, 0, 1, 2
Error in a[-1:2] : only 0's may be mixed
    with negative subscripts
> a[-(1:2)] # -(1:2) is (-1, -2): omit elements 1 and 2.
[1] 103 104 105
```

Logical Subscripts

Logical subscripts are also very powerful. A logical subscript is a logical vector of the same length as the thing being extracted from. Values in the original vector that line up with TRUE elements of the subscript are returned; those that line up with FALSE are not.

We almost never construct the logical subscript directly, using c(). Instead it is almost always the result of a comparison operation. In this example, we start with a vector of people's ages, and extract just the ones that are > 60.

```
> age <- c(53, 26, 81, 18, 63, 34)
> age > 60
[1] FALSE FALSE  TRUE FALSE  TRUE FALSE
> age[age > 60]
[1] 81 63
```

The age > 60 vector has one entry for each element of age, so it is easy to use that to extract the numeric values of age, which are > 60. But the power of logical subscripting goes well beyond that. Imagine that we also knew the names of each of the people. Here we show how to extract the names just for the people whose ages are >60.

```
> people <- c("Ahmed", "Mary", "Lee", "Alex", "John", "Viv")
> age > 60              # Just as a reminder
[1] FALSE FALSE  TRUE FALSE  TRUE FALSE
> people[age > 60]      # Return name where (age > 60) is TRUE
[1] "Lee"  "John"
```

This particular manipulation – extracting a subset of one vector based on values in another – is something we do in every data cleaning problem. It is important to be sure that you know exactly how it works.

One case where results might be unexpected is when you inadvertently cause a logical subscript to be converted to a numeric one. In the example above, suppose we had saved the logical vector as a new R object called age.gt.60. In the following example, we show what happens if R is allowed to convert that logical vector into a numeric one.

```
> age.gt.60  <- age > 60
> people[age.gt.60]
[1] "Lee"  "John" # as expected
> people[0 + age.gt.60]
[1] "Ahmed" "Ahmed"
> people[-age.gt.60]
[1] "Mary"    "Lee"     "Alex"    "John"    "Viv"
```

In the 0 + age.gt.60 example, R has to convert the logical subscript to numeric in order to perform the addition. After the addition, then, the subscript has the values 0 0 1 0 1 0, and the extraction produces the first element of the vector two times, ignoring the zeros. In the following example, the negative sign once again causes R to convert the logical subscript to numeric; after the application of the sign operator the subscript has the values 0 0 -1 0 -1 0. The extraction drops the first element (because of the -1 value) and the rest are returned. This is a mistake we sometimes make with a logical subscript – in this example, we probably intended to enter people[!age.gt.60], with the ! operator, in order to return people whose ages are not greater than 60.

When using a logical subscript, it is possible for the two vectors – the data and the subscript – to be of different lengths. In that case R recycles the shorter one, as described in Section 2.1.4. This might be useful if, say, you wanted to keep every third element of your original vector, but in general we recommend that your logical subscript be the same length as the original vector.

The which() function can be used to convert a logical vector into a numeric one. It returns the indices (i.e., the position numbers) of the elements that are

TRUE. So this is particularly useful when trying to find one or two anomalous entries in a long vector of logical values. To find the locations of the minimum value in a vector y, you can use which(y == min(y)), but the act of finding the index specifically of the minimum or maximum value is so common that there are dedicated functions, called which.min() and which.max(), for this task. There is one difference, though: these two functions break ties by selecting the first index for which y is at its maximum or minimum, whereas which() returns all the matching indices.

Using Names

The third kind of subscripting is to use a vector's names. Since names are characters, a name subscript will need to be a character as well. Here is a named vector, together with an example of subscripting by name.

```
> (vec <- c(a = 12, b = 34, c = -1))
 a  b  c
12 34 -1
> vec["b"]
 b
34
> vec[names(vec) != "a"]
 b  c
34 -1
```

To show all the values except the one named a, it is tempting to try something like vec[-"a"]. However, R tries to compute the value of "negative a," fails, and produces an error. The final example above shows one way to exclude the element with a particular name from being extracted.

Named vectors are not uncommon, but they do not come up very often in data cleaning. The real use of names will become clearer in Chapter 3, where we will encounter rectangular structures that have row names, column names, or, very often, both.

2.3.2 Vectors of Length 0

Any of these extraction methods can produce a vector of length 0, if no element meets the criterion. This happens particularly often when all of the elements of a logical subscript are FALSE. A vector of length 0 is displayed as integer(0), numeric(0), character(0), or logical(0). In this example, we show how such a vector might arise.

```
> (b <- c(101, 102, 103, 104))
[1] 101 102 103 104
> a <- b[b < 99] # Reasonable, but no elements of b are < 99
> a
numeric(0)        # a has length 0
```

A zero-length vector cannot be used intelligently in arithmetic, and watch out: the sum() of a numeric or logical vector of length 0 is itself zero. If a zero-length vector is used as the condition in an if() statement, an error results. This is an error that arises in data cleaning, as in this example:

```
> sum (a)
[1] 0                    # Possibly unexpected
> sum (a + 12345)
[1] 0                    # Definitely unexpected
> if (a < 2) cat ("yes\n")
Error in if (a < 2) cat("yes\n") : argument is length zero
```

In the last example, we made use of the cat() function, which writes its arguments out to the screen, or, as R calls it, the console. The \n represents the new-line, to return the cursor to the left of the screen. When writing functions to do data cleaning (Chapter 5), we will need to check that the conditions being tested are not vectors of length 0.

2.3.3 Assigning or Replacing Elements of a Vector

Every operation that extracts some values can also be used to replace those values, simply using the extraction operation on the left side of an assignment. Of course, R will require that the resulting vector have all its entries of the same type. So, for example, a[2] <- 3 will replace the second entry of a with the value 3. If a is logical, this operation will force it to be numeric; if a is character, the second entry of a will be assigned the character value "3". Just as we can extract using logical subscripts or names, we can use those subscripting techniques for assignment as well. These examples show replacement with numeric and logical subscripts.

```
> (a <- c(101, 102, -99, 104, -99, 9106)) # last item should
[1]   101   102   -99  104   -99 9106          # have been 106
> a[6] <- 106                    # numeric subscript
> a
[1] 101 102 -99 104 -99 106
> a[a < 0] <- 9999               # logical subscript
> a
[1]   101   102 9999   104 9999   106
```

As we mentioned, a logical subscript will almost always have the same length as the data vector on which it is operating. In the preceding example, the logical subscript a < 0 has the same length as a itself.

These examples show how names can be used to assign new values to the elements of a vector.

```
> b <- c("A", "missing", "C", "D")
> names (b) <- c("Red", "White", "Blue", "Green")
```

```
> b
      Red      White      Blue      Green
      "A" "missing"       "C"        "D"
> b["White"] <- "B"           # name subscript
> b
  Red White  Blue Green
  "A"   "B"   "C"   "D"
```

It is also possible to assign to elements of a vector out past its end. This is one way to combine two vectors. Elements that are not assigned will be given the special NA value (see the following section). Another way to combine two vectors is with the c() command, but either way, if two vectors of different types are combined, R will need to convert them to the same type. In this example, we combine two vectors.

```
> a <- 101:103
> b <- c(7, 2, 1, 15)
> c(a, b)                     # Combine two vectors
[1] 101 102 103   7   2   1   15
> a                           # Unchanged; no assignment made
[1] 101 102 103
> a[4:7] <- b                 # index non-existent values
> a
[1] 101 102 103   7   2   1   15
> b
[1]   7   2   1 15
> b[6] <- 22                  # index non-existent value
> b
[1]   7   2   1 15 NA 22      # b[5] filled in with NA
```

In the last example, b[6] was assigned, but no instruction was given about what to do with the newly created fifth element of b. R filled it in with the special missing value code, NA. The following section describes how NA values operate in R.

2.4 Missing Data (NA) and Other Special Values

In R, missing values are identified by NA (or, under some circumstances, by <NA>; see Sections 2.5 and 4.6). This is a special code; it is not the two capital letters N and A put together. Missing values are inevitable in real data, so it is important to know the effect they have on computations, and to have tools to identify them and replace them where necessary. In this section, we discuss NA values in vectors; subsequent chapters expand the discussion to describe the effect of NA values in other sorts of R objects.

Missing values arise in several ways. First, sometimes data is just missing – it would make sense for an observation to be present, but in fact it was lost or never recorded. Second, some observations are inherently missing. For example, a field named `MortPayRat` might contain the ratio of a customer's monthly home mortgage payment to her monthly income. Customers with no mortgage at all would presumably have no value for this field. An `NA` value would make more sense than a zero, which would suggest a mortgage payment of zero. Third, as we saw in the last section, missing values appear when we try to extract an item that was never present in a vector. For example, the built-in item `letters` is a vector containing the 26 lower-case letters of the English alphabet. The expression `letters[27]` will return an `NA`. Finally, we sometimes see other special values `Inf` or `-Inf` or `NaN` in response to certain computations, like trying to divide by zero. Those special values can often be treated as if they were `NA` values. We discuss these and a final special value, `NULL`, in this section.

Since all the elements of a vector must be of the same kind, there are actually several different kinds of `NA`. An `NA` in a logical vector is a little different from an `NA` in a numeric or character one. (There are actually objects named `NA_real_`, `NA_integer_`, and `NA_character_`, which make this explicit.) Normally, the difference will not matter, but there is one case where knowing about the types of `NA` can explain some behavior that both arises fairly often and also seems mysterious. We mention this in Section 2.4.3.

2.4.1 The Effect of NAs in Expressions

A general, if imprecise, rule about `NA` values is that any computation with an `NA` itself becomes an `NA`. If you add several numbers, one of which is an `NA`, the sum becomes `NA`. If you try to compute the range of a numeric with missing values, both the minimum and maximum are computed as `NA`. This makes sense when you think of an `NA` as an unknown that could take on any value. Basic mathematical computations for numeric vectors all allow you to specify the `na.rm = TRUE` argument, to compute the result after omitting missing values.

2.4.2 Identifying and Removing or Replacing NAs

In every data cleaning problem we need to determine whether there are `NA` values. What you *cannot* do to identify missing values is to compare them directly to the value `NA`. Just as adding an `NA` to something produces an `NA`, comparing an `NA` to something produces `NA`. So if a variable `thing` has value 3, the expression `thing == NA` produces `NA`, and if `thing` has value `NA`, the expression `thing == NA` also produces `NA`. To determine whether any of your values are missing, use the `anyNA()` function. This operates on a vector and returns a logical, which is `TRUE` if any value in the vector is `NA`. More useful, perhaps, is the `is.na()` function: if we have a vector named `vec`, a call to `is.na(vec)` returns a vector of logicals, one for each element in `vec`, giving TRUE for the elements that are NA and FALSE for those that are not. We can also use which(is.na(vec)) to find the numeric indices of the missing elements. Here, we show an example of a vector with NA values and some example of what operations can, and cannot, be performed on them.

```
> (nax <- c(101, 102, NA, 104))
[1] 101 102  NA 104
> nax * 2                     # Arithmetic on NAs gives NAs...
[1] 202 204  NA 208
> nax >= 102                  # ...as do comparisons
[1] FALSE  TRUE   NA  TRUE
> mean (nax)                  # One NA affects the computation
[1] NA
> mean (nax, na.rm = TRUE) # na.rm = TRUE excludes NAs
[1] 102.3333
> is.na (nax)                 # Locate NAs with logical vector
[1] FALSE FALSE  TRUE FALSE
> which (is.na (nax))         # Numeric indices of NAs
[1] 3
```

When your data has NA or other special values, you are faced with a decision about how to handle them. Generally they can be left alone, replaced, or removed. Removing missing values from a single vector is easy enough; the command vec[!is.na(vec)] will return the set of non-missing entries in vec. A more sophisticated alternative is the na.omit() function, which not only deletes the missing values but also keeps track of where in the vector they used to be. This information is stored in the vector's "attributes," which are extra pieces of information attached to some R objects.

```
> nax[!is.na (nax)]         # Return the non-missing values
[1] 101 102 104
> (nay <- na.omit (nax)) # This keeps track of deleted ones
[1] 101 102 104
attr(,"na.action")
[1] 3
attr(,"class")
[1] "omit"
```

Data cleaners will very often want to record information about the original location of discarded entries. In this example, these can be extracted with a command like attr(nay, "na.action").

Things get more complicated when the vector is one of many that need to be treated in parallel, perhaps because the vector is part of a more complicated structure like a matrix or data frame. Often if an entry is to be deleted, it needs to be deleted from all of these parallel items simultaneously. We talk more about these structures, and how to handle missing values in them, in Chapter 3. (We also note that most modeling functions in R have an argument called na.action that describes how that function should handle any NA values it encounters. This is outside our focus on data cleaning.)

2.4.3   Indexing with NAs

When an NA appears in an index, NA is produced, but the actual effect that R produces can be surprising. This arises often in data cleaning, since it is common to have a vector (usually fairly long and as part of a larger data set) with many NAs that you may not be aware of. Suppose we have a vector of data b and another vector of indices a, and we want to extract the set of elements of b for which a has the value 1, like this: b[a == 1]. The comparison a == 1 will return NA wherever a is missing, and b[NA] produces NA values. So the result is a vector with both the entries of b for which a == 1 and also one NA for every missing value in a. This is almost never what we want. If we want to extract the values of b for which a is both not missing and also equal to 1, we have to use the slightly clunky expression b[!is.na(a) & a == 1]. This example shows what this might look like in practice.

```
> (b <- c(101, 102, 103, 104))
[1] 101 102 103 104
> (a <- c(1, 2, NA, 4))
[1]  1  2 NA  4
> b[!is.na (a) & a == 2] # We probably want this...
[1] 102
> b[a == 2]              # ...and not this.
[1] 102  NA
```

In the following example, we show how two commands that look alike are treated slightly differently by R.

```
> b[a[2]]              # a[2] = 2; extract element 2 of b
[1] 102                # ... which is 102
> b[a[3]]              # a[3] is NA
[1] NA
> (a <- as.logical (a))  # Now convert a to logical
[1] TRUE TRUE   NA TRUE
> b[a[3]]              # a[3] is NA
[1] NA NA NA NA
```

In the first example of b[a[3]], the value in a[3] was a numeric NA, so R treated the subscripting operation as a numeric one. It returned only one value. In the second example, a[3] was a logical NA, and when R subscripts with a logical – even when that logical value is NA – it recycles the subscript to have the same length as the index (we saw this in Section 2.1.4).

The lesson here is that when you have an NA in a subscript, R may return something other than what you expect.

2.4.4 NaN and Inf Values

A different kind of special value can arise when a computation is so big that it overflows the ability of the computer to express the result. Such a value is expressed in R as Inf or -Inf. On 64-bit machines Inf is a bit bigger than 1.79×10^{308}; it most often appears when a positive number is accidentally divided by zero. Inf values are not missing, and is.na(Inf) produces FALSE. Another special value is NaN, "not a number," which is the result of certain specific computations such as 0/0 or Inf + -Inf or computing the mean of a vector of length 0. Unlike Inf, an NaN value is considered to be missing. As with NA values, Inf and NaN values take over every computation in which they are evaluated. There are rules for when more than one is present – for example, Inf + NA gives NA, but NaN + NA gives NaN. From a data cleaning perspective, all of these values cause trouble and you will generally want to identify any of these values early on. The function is.finite() is useful here; this produces TRUE for numbers that are neither NA nor NaN nor Inf or -Inf. So in that sense it serves as a check on valid values. To see whether every element of a numeric vector vec consists of values that are not any of these special ones, use the command all(is.finite(vec)).

2.4.5 NULL Values

A final sort of special value is the R value NULL. A NULL is an object with zero length, no contents and no class. (A vector of length 0 has no contents, but since it has a class – numeric, logical, or something else – it is not NULL.) In data cleaning, NULLs most often arise when attempting to access an element of a list, or a column of a data frame, which does not exist. We discuss this in Section 3.4.3. For the moment, the important point is that we can test for NULL values with the is.null() function, and that if you index using a NULL value the result will be a vector of length 0.

2.5 The table() Function

The table() function is so important in data cleaning that it merits its own section. This command, as its name suggests, produces a table giving, for each of the unique values in its argument, the number of times that value appears. In this example, we will create a vector with some color names in it, and we will add in an NA as well.

```
> vec <- rep (c("red", "blue", NA, "green"), c(3, 2, 1, 4))
> vec
 [1] "red"    "red"    "red"    "blue"  "blue"  NA
 [7] "green" "green" "green" "green"
> table (vec)
```

```
vec
 blue green   red
    2     4     3
```

There are a couple of things to notice here. First, the ordering of the results in the table is alphabetical, rather than being determined by the order the entries appear in the vector vec. Second, the resulting object is not quite a named vector, as you can see by the word vec that appears above the word blue. (We omit this line in many future displays to save space.) In fact, this object has class table, but it can be treated like a named vector – so, for example, table(vec)["green"] produces 4. Third, *by default* table *omits* NA as well as NaN values. In data cleaning this is almost never what we want. There are two different arguments to the table() function that serve to declare how you want missing values to be treated. The first of these is named useNA. This argument takes the character values "no" (meaning exclude NA values, which was the default as seen earlier), "ifany" (meaning to show an entry for NAs if there are any, but not if there aren't) and "always", meaning to show an entry for NAs whether there are any NA values or not. In our current example, where there is one NA, the table() command with useNA set to "ifany" or "always" will produce output like this:

```
> table (vec, useNA = "always")
 blue green   red  <NA>
    2     4     3     1
```

Notice that R displays the entry for NA values as <NA>, with angle brackets. This makes it easier to use the characters "NA" as a regular character string, perhaps for "North America" or possibly "sodium." (This angle bracket usage will appear again later.) R will not be confused if you have both NA values and also actual character strings with the angle brackets, such as "<NA>", but it is definitely a bad practice. To see what happens when there are no NAs, let us look at the same vector without its missing entry, which is number 6.

```
> table (vec[-6], useNA="ifany")
 blue green   red
    2     4     3
> table (vec[-6], useNA="always")
 blue green   red  <NA>
    2     4     3     0
```

For data cleaning purposes, we almost always want to know about missing values, so we will almost always want useNA to be "ifany" or "always". The second missing-value argument, exclude, allows you to exclude specific values from the table. By default, exclude has the value c(NA, NaN), which is why those values do not appear in tables. Most commonly we set this value to NULL to signify that no entries should be excluded, although sometimes we exclude certain very common values. Here we might want to exclude the common value green while tabulating all other values, including NAs. The following example shows how we can do that. It also shows the use of exclude = NULL.

```
> table (vec, exclude="green")
blue   red <NA>
   2     3    1
> table (vec, exclude=NULL)
 blue green    red   <NA>
    2     4      3      1
```

It is possible to supply both useNA and exclude at the same time, but the results may not be what you expect. We recommend using either useNA or exclude to display missing values in every table.

2.5.1 Two- and Higher-Way Tables

If we give two vectors of the same length to the table () function, the result is a two-way table, also called a cross-tabulation. For example, suppose we had a vector called years, one for each transaction in our data set, with values 2015, 2016, and 2017; and suppose we also had a vector called months, of the same length, with values such as "Jan", "Feb", and so on. Then table (years, months) would produce a 3 × 12 table of counts, with each cell in the table telling how many entries in the two vectors had the values for the cell. That is, the top-left cell would give the number of entries from January 2015; the one to the right of that would give the number of entries for February 2015; and so on. (If there are fewer than 12 months represented in the data, of course, there will be fewer than 12 columns in the table.) This is an important data cleaning task – to determine whether two variables are related in ways we expect. If, for example, we saw no transactions at all in March 2016, we would want to know why.

In R, a two-way table is treated the same as a *matrix*; we discuss matrices in detail in the following chapter. For very large vectors, the data.table () function in the data.table package (Dowle *et al.*, 2015) may prove more efficient than table (). Three- and higher-way tables are produced when the arguments to table () are three or more equal-length vectors. These tables are treated in R as *arrays*; we give an example in Section 3.2.7. The xtabs () function is also useful for creating more complex tables.

2.5.2 Operating on Elements of a Table

The table () command counts the number of observations that fall into a particular category. In the example above, the table (years, months) command produces a two-way table of counts. Often we want to know more than just how many observations fall into a cell. R has several special-purpose functions that operate on tables. The prop.table () function takes, as its first argument, the output from a call to table (), and depending on its second argument produces proportions of the total counts in the table by cell, or by row, or by column. In this example we set up three vectors, each of length 15. Then we show the effect of calling table (), and of calling prob.table () on the result. By default, prop.table () computes the proportions of observations in each cell of the table. In the final example, we use the second argument of 2 to compute the proportions within each column; supplying 1 would have produced the proportions within each row.

```
> yr <- rep (2015:2017, each=5)
> market <- c("a", "a", "b", "a", "b", "b", "b", "a", "b",
              "b", "a", "b", "a", "b", "a")
> cost <- c(64, 87, 71, 79, 79, 91, 86, 92, NA,
            55, 37, 41, 60, 66, 82)
> (tab <- table (market, yr))
      yr
market 2015 2016 2017
     a    3    1    3
     b    2    4    2
> prop.table (tab)     # These proportions sum to 1
      yr
market       2015       2016       2017
     a 0.20000000 0.06666667 0.20000000
     b 0.13333333 0.26666667 0.13333333
> prop.table (tab, 2) # Each column's proportions sum to 1
      yr
market 2015 2016 2017
     a  0.6  0.2  0.6
     b  0.4  0.8  0.4
```

The margin.table () command produces the marginal totals from a table – that is, row or column totals (controlled by the second argument) for a two-way table, and corresponding sums for a higher-way one. The addmargins () function incorporates those totals into the table, producing a new row or column named Sum (or both). This is often a summary statistic we want, but watch out – the convention regarding the second argument of addmargins () is not the same as that of prop.table () and margin.table (). This example shows addmargins () in action.

```
> addmargins (tab)              # append row and column sums
      yr
market 2015 2016 2017 Sum
     a    3    1    3   7
     b    2    4    2   8
   Sum    5    5    5  15
> addmargins (tab, 2)           # append column sums
```

```
       yr
market 2015 2016 2017 Sum
     a    3    1    3   7
     b    2    4    2   8
```

We might also want to know the average, standard deviation, or maximum of entries in a numeric variable, broken down by which cell they fall into. In our example, we might want the maximum `cost` among the three observations from 2015 with market a, and for the two from 2015 and market b, and so on. For this purpose we use the `tapply()` function, whose name reminds us that it applies a function to a table. This function's arguments are the vector on which to do the computation (in our example, `cost`), an argument named `INDEX` describing the grouping (here, we might use the vector `yr`), and then the function to be applied. The following example shows `tapply()` at work. In the first line, we use the `min()` function to produce the minimum value for each year – but an `NA` is produced for 2016 since one `cost` for that year is `NA`. We can pass the `na.rm = TRUE` argument into `tapply()`, which then passes it into `min()` as in the following example, if we want to compute the minimum value among non-missing entries.

```
> tapply (cost, yr, min)        # find minimum within each yr
2015 2016 2017
  64   NA   37
> tapply (cost, yr, min, na.rm = TRUE)
2015 2016 2017
  64   55   37
```

It is possible to extend this example to the two-way case of minimum cost, or another statistic, by both market and year. Here the tabularization part, represented by the argument `INDEX`, needs to be a list. We discuss lists starting in Section 3.3; for the moment, just know that a list is required when grouping with more than one vector. In the first example as follows, we compute the mean of the `cost` values for each combination of market and year (using `na.rm = TRUE` as above, and the `list()` function to construct the list). In the second example, we show how we can supply our own function "in line," which makes it more transparent than if we had written a separate function. The details of writing functions are covered in Chapter 5, but here our function takes one argument, named `x`, and returns the value given by the sum of the squares of the entries of `x`. (In this example, we pass the `na.rm = TRUE` argument directly to sum to keep our function simpler.) The `tapply()` function is in charge of calling our function six times, once for each cell of the table.

```
> tapply (cost, list (market, yr), mean, na.rm = TRUE)
      2015     2016     2017
a 76.66667 92.00000 59.66667
b 75.00000 77.33333 53.50000
```

```
> tapply (cost, list (market, yr),
                function (x) sum (x^2, na.rm = TRUE))
    2015   2016   2017
a 17906   8464  11693
b 11282  18702   6037
```

2.6   Other Actions on Vectors

In this section, we describe additional actions on vectors that we find particularly important for data cleaning. This includes rounding numeric values, sorting, set operations, and the important topics of identifying duplicates and matching.

2.6.1   Rounding

R operates on numeric vectors using double-precision arithmetic, which means that often there are more significant digits available than are useful. Results will often need to be displayed with, say, two or three significant digits. The natural way to prepare displays like this is through formatting the numbers – that is, changing the way they display, but not their actual values. We discuss formatting in Section 4.2. But sometimes we want to change the numbers themselves, perhaps to force them to be integers or to have only a few significant digits. The round() function and its relatives do this. Round() lets the user specify the number of digits to the right of the decimal place to be saved; the signif() function lets him or her specify the total number of significant digits retained. So round(123.4567, 3) produces 123.457, while signif(123.4567, 3) produces 123. A negative second argument produces rounding the nearest power of 10, so round(123.4567, -1) rounds to the nearest 10 and produces 120, while round(123.4567, -2) rounds to the nearest 100 and produces 100. The trunc() function discards the part the decimal and produces an integer; floor() and ceiling() round to the next lower and next higher integer, respectively, so floor(-3.4) is -4 while trunc(-3.4) is -3. Rounding of problematic entries (like those that end in a 5) can be affected by floating-point error (see Section 1.3.3).

2.6.2   Sorting and Ordering

It is common to have to sort the elements of a vector, and the sort() function performs that task in R. By default, the sort is from smallest to largest, but the decreasing = TRUE argument will reverse the order. There are two minor complications. First, sort() will drop NA and NaN values by default, giving a vector shorter than the original when these values are present. This behavior is controlled by the na.last argument, which itself defaults to NA. If set to TRUE, this argument will have the sort() function place NA and NaN values at the end, and, if FALSE, at the beginning of the sorted output.

A second complication is in sorting character vectors. Sorting in this case is alphabetical, of course, so if the characters are text representations of numbers such as "1", "2", "5", "10", and "18", the resulting output, sorted alphabetically, will be "1", "10", "18", "2", and "5". Moreover, the sorting order depends on the character set and locality being used. We mentioned this in Section 1.4.6 and address it further in Section 4.5.

The related order() function returns a set of indices that you can use to sort a vector. This is useful when you want to re-arrange one vector's values in the order specified by a second vector. (If that sounds as if it wouldn't be a common task, wait until Section 3.5.4.) In this example, we have a vector of names, and a vector of scores, and we want the names in ascending order of score.

```
> nm <- c("Freehan", "Cash", "Horton",
    "Stanley", "Northrop", "Kaline")
> scores <- c(263, 263, 285, 259, 264, 287) # 2 tied at 263
> nm[order(scores)]                # ascending order of score
[1] "Stanley"  "Freehan"   "Cash"
[4] "Northrop" "Horton"    "Kaline"
> nm[order(scores, nm)]                     # tie broken by nm
[1] "Stanley"  "Cash"      "Freehan"   # (alphabetically)
[4] "Northrop" "Horton"    "Kaline"
> nm[order (scores, decreasing = TRUE)] # descending
[1] "Kaline"   "Horton"    "Northrop"
[4] "Freehan"  "Cash"      "Stanley"
```

As in the example, the order() function can be given more than one vector. In this case, the second vector is used to break ties in the first; if a third vector were supplied, it would be used to break any remaining ties, and so on. It is very common to re-order a set of data that has time indicators (month and year, maybe) from oldest to newest. The order() function has the same na.last argument that sort() has, although its default value is TRUE.

2.6.3 Vectors as Sets

Often we need to find the extent to which two vectors have values that overlap. For example, we might have customer data from two sources and we want to determine the extent to which the customer IDs agree; or we might want to find the set of states in which none of our customers reside. These call for techniques that treat vectors as sets and that will normally be most useful when the data is a small number of integers, character data, or factors, about which we say more in Section 4.6. They can be used with non-integer data as well, but as always we cannot rely on two floating-point numbers that we expect to be equal actually being equal.

The essential set membership operation is performed by the %in% function. R has a few functions with names like this, surrounded by percentage signs.

This allows us to use a command like a `%in%` b, rather than the equivalent, but perhaps less transparent, `is.element(a, b)`. The return value is a vector the same length as a, with a logical indicating whether each element of a is found anywhere in b. In data cleaning we very often tabulate the result of this function call; so a command like `table(a %in% b)` produces a table of `FALSE` and `TRUE`, giving the number of items in a that were not found in b, and the number that were. For this purpose, an `NA` value in a matches only an `NA` in b, and similarly an `NaN` value in a matches only an `NaN` value in b. In this example, we compare some alphanumeric characters to the built-in data set `letters` containing the 26 lower-case letters of the alphabet.

```
> c("g", "5", "b", "J", "!") %in% letters
[1]  TRUE FALSE  TRUE FALSE FALSE
> table (c("g", "5", "b", "J", "!") %in% letters)
FALSE  TRUE
    3     2
```

The `union()`, `intersect()`, and `setdiff()` functions produce the union, intersection, and difference between two sets. This example shows those functions in action.

```
> union (c("g", "5", "b", "J", "!"),
                 letters)      # elements in either vector
 [1] "g" "5" "b" "J" "!" "a" "c" "d" "e" "f" "h" "i" "j"
[14] "k" "l" "m" "n" "o" "p" "q" "r" "s" "t" "u" "v" "w"
[27] "x" "y" "z"
> intersect (c("g", "5", "b", "J", "!"),
                 letters)      # elements in both vectors
[1] "g" "b"
> setdiff (c("g", "5", "b", "J", "!"),
                 letters)      # elements of a not in b
[1] "5" "J" "!"
```

2.6.4 Identifying Duplicates and Matching

Another data cleaning task is to find duplicates in vectors. The `anyDuplicated()` function tells you whether any of the elements of a vector are duplicates. The `unique()` function extracts only the set of distinct values (including, by default, `NA` and `NaN`). The distinct values appear in the output in the order in which they appear in the input; for data cleaning purposes we will often sort those unique values.

Often it will be important to know which elements are duplicates. The `duplicated()` function returns a logical vector with the value `TRUE` for the second and subsequent entries in a set of duplicates. However, the first entry in a set of duplicates is not indicated. For example, `duplicated (c(1, 2, 1, 1))` returns `FALSE FALSE TRUE TRUE`; the first 1 is not considered duplicated under this definition. (Alternatively, the fromLast = TRUE argument reads from the end of the vector back to the beginning, but again the "first" member of a set of duplicates is not indicated.) Combining a call with fromLast = FALSE and one with fromLast = TRUE, using the union() function, identifies all duplicates.

A common task is to find all the entries that are duplicated anywhere in the data set (or that are never duplicated). One way to do this is via table(). Any value that appears more than once is, of course, duplicated (but remember that floating-point numbers might not match exactly). In this example, we construct a vector from the lower-case letters, but add a few duplicates.

```
> let <- c(letters, c("j", "j", "x"))
> (tab <- table (let))
let
 a b c d e f g h i j k l m n o p q r s t u v w x y z
 1 1 1 1 1 1 1 1 1 3 1 1 1 1 1 1 1 1 1 1 1 1 1 2 1 1
> which (tab != 1) # table locations where duplicates appear
  j  x
 10 24               # 10th & 24th table entries aren't ones
> names (tab)[tab != 1]
[1] "j" "x"
```

It is often useful to use table() twice in a row. This example counts the number of entries that appear once, twice, and so on in the original data. Consider this example:

```
> table (table (let))

 1  2  3
24  1  1               # 24 entries are 1, one is 2, one is 3
```

The last line shows that there are 24 entries in let that appear once; one entry, x, that appears twice; and one entry, j, that appears three times. We use this in almost every data cleaning problem to find entries that appear more often than we expect. In a real application, we might have tens of thousands of elements and only a few duplicates. The which(tab != 1) command shows us the elements that are duplicated, but not how many times each one appears; the table(table(let)) command shows us how many duplicates there are, but not which letter goes with which count.

Another important task is *matching*, which is where we identify where, in a vector, we can find the values in another vector. We will find this particularly useful when merging data frames in Section 3.7.2. There are two ways to handle elements that do not match; they can be returned as NA, preserving the length of the original argument in the length of the return value, or, with the nomatch = 0 argument, they can be returned as 0, which allows the return value to be used as an index. In this example, we match two sets of names.

```
> nm <- c("Jensen", "Chang", "Johnson",
    "Lopez", "McNamara", "Reese")
> nm2 <- c("Lopez", "Ruth", "Nakagawa", "Jensen", "Mays")
> match (nm, nm2)
[1]   4 NA NA   1 NA NA
> nm2[match (nm, nm2)]
[1] "Jensen" NA          NA          "Lopez"  NA          NA
```

The third command tells us that the first element of nm, which is Jensen, appears in position 4 of nm2; the second element of nm, Chang, does not appear in nm2, and so on. We can extract the elements that matched from the nm2 vector as in the last line – but the NA entries in the output of match() produce NAs in the vector of names. An easier approach is to supply the nomatch = 0 argument, as in this example.

```
> match (nm, nm2, nomatch = 0)
[1] 4 0 0 1 0 0
> nm2[match (nm, nm2, nomatch = 0)]
[1] "Jensen" "Lopez"
```

We use match() (or its equivalent) in any data cleaning problem that requires combining two data sets. Understanding how match() works makes data cleaning easier. Match() is, in fact, a more powerful version of %in%.

2.6.5   Finding Runs of Duplicate Values

During a data cleaning problem, it often happens that a particular identifier – a name or account number, perhaps – appears many times in an input data set. As an example we might be given a list of payments, with each payment identified by a customer number and each customer contributing dozens of payments. It will be useful to count the number of times each repeated item appears. We also use this on logical vectors to find, for example, the locations and lengths of sets of payments that are equal to 0. The rle() function (the name stands for "run length encoding") does exactly this: given a vector, it returns the number of "runs" – that is, repetitions – and each run's length. In this example, we show what the output of the rle() function looks like.

```
> rle (c("a", "b", "b", "a", "c", "c", "c"))
Run Length Encoding
  lengths: int [1:4] 1 2 1 3
  values : chr [1:4] "a" "b" "a" "c"
```

This output shows that the vector starts with a run of length 1 (the first element in the lengths vector) with value a (the values vector); then a run of length 2 with value b; and so on. The output is actually returned in the form of a list with two parts named lengths and values; in Section 3.3, we discuss how to access the pieces of a list individually.

2.7 Long Vectors and Big Data

Starting in version 3.0.0, R introduced something called a *long vector*, a special mechanism that allows vectors to be much longer than before. Since there are only $2^{31} - 1$ values of an integer, entries in a long vector beyond that point will have to be indexed by `double` indices. Other than that, this extension should, in principle, be invisible to users. One exception is that the `match()` function, and its descendants, `is.element()` and `%in%`, do not work on long vectors. On long vectors, `table()` can be very slow and the `data.table` package provides some faster alternatives. R's documentation suggests avoiding the use of long vectors that are characters.

2.8 Chapter Summary and Critical Data Handling Tools

This chapter introduces R vectors, which come in several forms, primarily logical, numeric, and character. The `mode()`, `typeof()`, and `class()` functions give you information about the class of a vector. The set of `is.` functions like `is.numeric()` returns a TRUE/FALSE result when an object is of the specified model, and the set of `as.` functions performs the conversion. Remember that logicals are simpler than numerics, and numerics simpler than character, and that converting from a simpler to a more complicated mode is straightforward. Converting from a more complicated to a simpler mode follows these rules:

- Converting character to numeric produces NA for things that aren't numbers, like the character strings `"TRUE"` or `"$199.99"`.
- Converting character to logical produces NA for any string that isn't `"TRUE"`, `"True"`, `"true"`, `"T"`, `"FALSE"`, `"False"`, `"false"` or `"F"`.
- Converting numeric to logical produces FALSE for a zero and TRUE for any non-zero entry (and watch out for floating-point error here).

Extracting and assigning subsets of vectors are critical parts of any data cleaning project. We can use any of the modes as an index or "subscript" with which to extract or assign. A logical subscript returns the values that match up with its TRUE entries. Logical subscripts are extended by recycling where necessary (but most often when we do this it is by mistake). A numeric subscript returns the values specified in the subscript – and, unsurprisingly, numeric subscripts are not recycled. The `which()` command identifies TRUE values in a logical vector, so you can use that to convert a logical subscript to a numeric one. Finally, a character subscript will extract, from a named vector, elements whose names are present in the subscript (and, again, this kind of subscript is not recycled).

Any kind of vector can have missing values, indicated by NA, and there are a few other special values as well. Missing values influence computations they are involved in, so we often want to supply an argument like na.rm = TRUE to a function computing a sum, mean or other summary statistic on numeric data. You should expect to encounter missing values in any data set from any source and be prepared to accommodate them.

The table() function is critical to data cleaning. It tabulates a vector, returning the number of times each unique value appears, with names corresponding to the original values in the data set. Passing two or more vectors to table() produces a two- or higher-way cross-tabulation. We recommend adding the useNA = "ifany", useNA = "always", or exclude = NULL arguments to ensure that table() counts and displays the number of NA values, unless you're certain no values are missing. Using table() on the output of table() – as in table(table(x)) – tells us how many items in a vector x appear once, twice, and so on. This is useful for detecting entries that appear more often than expected.

Using names() on the output of table() will produce the unique entries in a vector, but we also use the unique() function to find these. We spend a lot of energy in identifying duplicates, and the duplicated() function is useful here – although, remember, it does not return TRUE for the first item in a set of duplicates. The is.element() and %in% functions help determine the extent to which two sets of values overlap; both of these are simpler versions of the match() function, which is critical to combining data from different sources.

3

R Data, Part 2: More Complicated Structures

3.1 Introduction

R data is made up of vectors, but, as you already know, there are more complicated structures that consist of a group of vectors put together. In this chapter, we talk about the three major structures in R that data handlers need to know about. The most important of these is the *data frame*, in which, eventually, almost all of our data will be held. But in order to build up to the data frame, we first need to describe matrices and lists. A data frame is part matrix, part list, and in order to use data frames most efficiently, you need to be able to think of it in both ways. Furthermore, we do encounter matrices in the data cleaning world, since the `table()` command can produce something that is basically a matrix.

3.2 Matrices

A *matrix* (plural *matrices*) is essentially a vector, arrayed in a (two-dimensional) rectangle. As with a vector, every element of a matrix needs to be of the same type – logical, numeric, or character. Most of the matrices we will see will be numeric, but it is also possible to have a logical matrix, typically for subscripting, as we shall see. We start using the vector of 15 numbers, 101, 102, ..., 115, to produce a 5 × 3 (i.e., five rows by three columns) numeric matrix.

```
> (a <- matrix (101:115, nrow = 5, ncol = 3))
     [,1] [,2] [,3]
[1,]  101  106  111
[2,]  102  107  112
[3,]  103  108  113
[4,]  104  109  114
[5,]  105  110  115
```

A Data Scientist's Guide to Acquiring, Cleaning, and Managing Data in R, First Edition.
Samuel E. Buttrey and Lyn R. Whitaker.
© 2018 John Wiley & Sons Ltd. Published 2018 by John Wiley & Sons Ltd.
Companion website: www.wiley.com/go/buttrey/datascientistsguide

There are a couple of points to mention here. First, the matrix is filled column by column, with the first column being filled before the second one starts. We often intuitively expect the matrix to be filled row by row, because our data comes in rows, and we read English left-to-right, but this is not how R works. If you need to load your data into your matrix by rows, use the `byrow` = `TRUE` argument. This arises when you copy a matrix off of a web page, for example; we expect the entries to be read along the top line, but R stores them down the first column. (We come back to this example in Section 6.5.3.)

Second, notice the row and column indicators such as `[4,]` and `[,2]`. In the following section, we will see how to use those numbers to extract elements from the matrix, or to assign new ones.

Third, the `length()` operator can be used on a matrix, but it returns the total number of elements in the matrix. More often we want to know the number of rows and columns; that information is returned by the `nrow()` and `ncol()` functions, or jointly by the `dim()` function, which gives the numbers of rows and columns in that order:

```
> length (a)
[1]  15
> dim (a)
[1]  5 3
```

Fourth, in our example, we used the `matrix()` function to create the matrix from one long vector. An alternative is to create a matrix from a set of equal-length vectors. The `cbind()` function ("c" for column) combines a set of vectors into a matrix column by column, while `rbind()` performs the operation row by row. If the vectors are of unequal length, R will use the usual recycling rules (Section 2.1.4). Again, all of the elements of a matrix need to be of the same sort, so if any vector is of type character, the entire matrix will be character.

As with vectors, arithmetic operations on matrices are performed element by element, so `A^2` squares each element of A and A `*` B multiplies two matrices element by element. There are special symbols for matrix-specific operations: for example, A `%*%` B performs the usual kind of matrix multiplication, `t(A)` transposes a matrix, and `solve()` inverts a matrix. These operations do not tend to come up much in data cleaning, but often, we want to perform an operation on a matrix row by row or column by column. We come back to these row and column operations in Section 3.2.3.

3.2.1 Extracting and Assigning

Since a matrix is just a vector, it is possible to use a subscript just like the one we used in Section 2.3.1 to pull out or replace an element. In the example above, a `[6]` would produce 106 (remember that we count by columns first), and a `[6]` `<-` `999` would replace that element with 999. However, it is much more common to identify elements of a matrix by two subscripts, one for the row and one for the column. These two subscripts are separated by a comma. In our example, a[1,2] would produce 106, and a[1,2] <- 999 would replace that value.

Of course, it is possible to ask for more than one entry at a time. In this example, we ask for a 3 × 2 sub-matrix from our original matrix a:

```
> a[c(4, 2), c(3, 1)]
      [,1] [,2]
[1,]   114  104
[2,]   112  102
```

The two rows we asked for, numbers 4 and 2, in that order, are returned, with the corresponding entries from columns 3 and 1, in that order. Just as when we use subscripts on a vector, we may use duplicate subscripts; a vector of negative numbers indicates that the corresponding entries should be removed.

If you leave one of the two subscripts empty, you are asking for an entire row or column. This command says "give me all the rows except for number 2, and all the columns."

```
> a[-2,]
      [,1] [,2] [,3]
[1,]   101  106  111
[2,]   103  108  113
[3,]   104  109  114
[4,]   105  110  115
```

Notice here that some rows have been renumbered. The row that had been number 5 in the original a is now the fourth row. This is not surprising, but it raises the question as to whether we might be able to keep track of rows that have been deleted, since that would help us audit changes we have made to the data. We will describe one way to do that using row names in Section 3.2.2.

In addition to using a numeric subscript, we can use a logical one. Logical subscripts for rows or columns act exactly as logical subscripts for vectors (see Section 2.3.1). Whether you use numeric or logical subscripts, subscripting a matrix with row and column indices will return a rectangular object. To extract values from, or assign new values to, a non-rectangular set of entries, you can use a matrix subscript, which we describe in Section 3.2.5.

Demoting a Matrix to a Vector

In order to turn a matrix into a vector, use the c() function on it. Just as c() creates vectors from individual elements (see, e.g., Section 2.1.1), it also creates vectors from matrices. In our example, c(a) will produce a vector of 15 numbers. The entries in that vector come from the first column, followed by the second column, and so on. In order to extract data row by row, transpose the matrix first, using the t() function in a command like c(t(a)).

Sometimes, though, R produces a vector from a matrix when we did not expect it. In this example, see what happens when we ask for, say, the second column of a. Remember that a has five rows and three columns.

```
> a[,2]
[1]  106 107 108 109 110
```

The result of this operation is not a matrix with five rows and one column; it is a vector of length 5. This reduction – or "demotion" – from a matrix to a vector follows a general rule in R under which dimensions of length 1 are usually removed ("dropped") by default. This can cause trouble when you have a function that is expecting a matrix, perhaps because it plans to use dim() to find the number of rows. If you pass a single column of a matrix, that is, a vector, such a function would call dim() on a vector, which returns the value NULL. The way around this is to specify that this dropping should not take place, using the drop = FALSE argument, like this:

```
> a[,2,drop = FALSE]
      [,1]
[1,]   106
[2,]   107
[3,]   108
[4,]   109
[5,]   110
```

The result of that operation is a matrix with five rows and one column. When building functions that take subsets of matrices, it is often a good idea to use drop = FALSE to ensure that the resulting subset is itself a matrix and not a vector value.

3.2.2   Row and Column Names

It is very convenient to have a matrix whose rows and columns have names. We can assign (and extract) row and column names with the dimnames() function, described in Section 3.3.2, and there are also functions named rownames() and colnames() to do the same job. (There is also an equivalent row.names() function, spelled with a dot, but, interestingly, there is no col.names() function.) Rows and columns are named automatically by the table() function (technically, a two-way table has class table, not matrix, but that distinction will not matter here). We start this extended example by constructing a table.

```
> yr <- rep (2015:2017, each = 5)
> market <- c(2, 2, 3, 2, 3, 3, 3, 2, 3, 3, 2, 3, 2, 3, 2)
> (tbl <- table (market, yr))
```

```
        yr
market 2015 2016 2017
     2    3    1    3
     3    2    4    2
```

Notice that the row-name entries ("2" and "3" under market) are not a column of the table; they are merely identifiers. This table has three columns, not four. Now we show the column names and demonstrate how they can be changed using the colnames() function.

```
> colnames (tbl)
[1] "2015" "2016" "2017"
> colnames (tbl) <- c("FY15", "FY16", "FY17")
> tbl
        yr
market FY15 FY16 FY17
     2    3    1    3
     3    2    4    2
```

Once row or column names have been assigned, we can refer to them by name as well as by number. This makes it possible to refer to a row or column in a consistent way, without having to know its location. Notice, though, that dimension names are characters, even if they look numeric. So, for example, tbl [2,] will produce the second row of the matrix tbl, while tbl ["2",] will produce the row whose name is "2", regardless of what number that row has – and even if earlier rows have been removed.

```
> tbl [2,]
FY15 FY16 FY17
   2    4    2
> tbl ["2",]
FY15 FY16 FY17
   3    1    3
```

3.2.3   Applying a Function to Rows or Columns

There are lots and lots of operations on matrices supported by R, but many of them are mathematical and not useful in data cleaning. One operation that does come up, though, is running a function separately on each row or column of a matrix. A few of these are so common that they are built in. Specifically, there are functions named colSums() and rowSums(), which compute all of the column sums or row sums, and corresponding functions for the means, colMeans() and rowMeans(). Very often, though, you want to apply some custom function, such as the one that tells how many entries are NA or missing. The facility for doing this is the apply() function, to which you supply the matrix, the direction of travel (1 for across rows, 2 for down columns), and then the function that is to be applied to each row or column. This last can be a function built into R, a function you have written yourself, or even a function defined on the fly.

```
> a <- matrix (101:115, 5, 3)
# These four commands produce identical results
> rowSums (a)
> apply (a, 1, sum)
# Pass argument na.rm into the sum() function
> apply (a, 1, sum, na.rm = T)
> apply (a, 1, function (x) sum (x))
[1] 318 321 324 327 330
# User-written command selects the second-smallest entry
# in each column
> apply (a, 2, function (x) sort(x)[2])
[1] 102 107 112
```

If each call to the function returns a vector of the same length, apply() creates a matrix. In this example, we use the range() function to produce two values for each column of a.

```
> apply (a, 2, range)
      [,1] [,2] [,3]
[1,]   101  106  111
[2,]   105  110  115
```

When apply() is used with a vector-valued function, such as range() in the last example, the output is arranged in columns, regardless of whether the operation was performed on the rows or the columns of the original matrix. This does not always match our intuition, particularly when the operation was performed on rows. In this example, we show the row-by-row ranges of the a matrix and then transpose using the t () function.

```
> apply(a, 1, range)
      [,1] [,2] [,3] [,4] [,5]
[1,]   101  102  103  104  105
[2,]   111  112  113  114  115
# Use t() to transpose that matrix
> t(apply(a, 1, range))
      [,1] [,2]
[1,]   101  111
[2,]   102  112
[3,]   103  113
[4,]   104  114
[5,]   105  115
```

A difficulty arises when different calls to the function produce vectors of different lengths. In that case, R cannot construct a matrix and has to return the results in the form of a list (we discuss lists in Section 3.3). This might arise, say, when looking for the locations of unusual values by column. In this example, we look for the locations in each column of values greater than 109 in the matrix a.

```
> apply (a, 2, function (x) which (x > 109))
[[1]]
integer(0)

[[2]]
[1] 5

[[3]]
[1] 1 2 3 4 5
```

This result tells us that the first column has no entries >109, the second column's fifth entry is >109, and all five entries in the third column are >109. In general, you have to be aware that apply () might return a list if the function being applied can return vectors of different lengths.

3.2.4 Missing Values in Matrices

One very common use of apply () is to count the number of missing values in each row or column, since missing values always affect how we do data cleaning. This code shows how to count the number of NA value in each column. To show off some more of R's capabilities, we use the semicolon, which allows multiple commands on one line, and the multiple assignment operation, which lets us assign several things at once.

```
> a <- matrix (101:115, 5, 3); a[5, 3] <- a[3, 1] <- NA; a
     [,1] [,2] [,3]
[1,]  101  106  111
[2,]   NA  107  112
[3,]  103  108  113
[4,]  104  109  114
[5,]  105  110   NA
> apply (a, 2, function (x) sum (is.na (x)))
[1] 1 0 1
```

From the last command, we see there is one missing value in each of columns 1 and 3.

We saw how to use which () to identify missing values in a vector back in Section 2.4, and the same command can also identify missing values in a matrix. By default, which (is.na (vec)) will return the indices of vec with missing values as if vec had been stretched out into a long vector (column by column, as always). However, the arr.ind = TRUE argument will supply the row and column indices of the items selected by which (). This is extremely useful in tracking down a small number of missing values. In this example, we use which () to identify the missing entries in a.

```
> which (is.na (a))
[1]   3 15
> which (is.na (a), arr.ind = TRUE)
      row col
[1,]   2   1
[2,]   5   3
```

Here, which() returns a matrix with two named columns and two unnamed rows. Of course, this approach is not limited to finding NAs. It can also be used to find negative values, or anything else that is unexpected and needs to be cleaned.

3.2.5 Using a Matrix Subscript

In the last example, we saw how which() with arr.ind = TRUE returns a matrix giving a vector of rows and a vector of columns that, together, identify the cells that had NA values. One underused feature of R is that we can use a matrix subscript, such as the one returned by which() with arr.ind = TRUE to extract from, or assign to, another matrix. We can also use the vector returned by the ordinary use of which(), but the matrix approach sometimes makes it much easier to extract the necessary rows or columns. In this example, we construct a matrix with five columns of data and a sixth column named "Use". This final column tells us which of the data columns should be extracted for each of the rows.

```
> b <- matrix (1:20, nrow = 4, byrow = TRUE)
> b <- cbind (b, c(3, 2, 0, 5))
> colnames (b) <- c("P1", "P2", "P3", "P4", "P5", "Use")
> rownames (b) <- c("Spring", "Summer", "Fall", "Winter")
> b
      P1 P2 P3 P4 P5 Use
[1,]   1  2  3  4  5   3
[2,]   6  7  8  9 10   2
[3,]  11 12 13 14 15   0
[4,]  16 17 18 19 20   5
```

Since the first row's value of Use is 3, we want to extract the third element of that row; since the second row's value of Use is 2, we want the second element of that row; and so on. Without the ability to use a matrix subscript, we might be forced to loop through the rows of b, but in R we can extract all these items in one call. Our matrix subscript has two columns, one giving the rows from which we are extracting (in this case, all the rows of b in order) and another giving the column from which to extract (in this case, the values in the Use column of b). Here we show we can construct this matrix subscript and use it to extract the relevant entries of b.

```
> (subby <- cbind (1:nrow(b), b[,"Use"]))
     [,1] [,2]
[1,]    1    3
[2,]    2    2
[3,]    3    0
[4,]    4    5
> b[subby]
[1]   3   7 20
```

Notice that in this example the value of Use in the third row was zero – and therefore no value was produced for that row of the matrix subscript (see "zero subscripts" in Section 2.3.1). Negative values cannot be used in a matrix subscript.

As a real-life example of where this might occur, we were recently given a matrix of customer payments. The first 96 columns contained monthly payment amounts. The last column gave the number of the month with the last payment in it. Our task was to extract the payment amount whose month appeared in that final column. So if, in the first row, that column had the value 15, we would have extracted the amount from the 15th column of the payment matrix; and so on for the second and subsequent rows.

Two points here: notice that we extracted in our example earlier using b[subby] using no additional commas. The matrix subscript defines both rows and columns. Second, remember to use cbind() to construct the subscript argument (our subby above). Make sure that the matrix subscript really is a matrix, and not two separate vectors, or you will extract rows and columns separately. Matrix subscripting works with names, too. If our matrix b had had both row and column names, we could have used a character matrix in exactly the same way as the numeric subby. In that case, b would need both row and column names so that both columns of the subscript argument could be character. We cannot have one vector be numeric and the other character, because we need to combine them into a matrix, and all the entries in a matrix have to be of the same type. It is also possible to have a logical matrix act as a subscript – but the results are surprising and we do not recommend it.

3.2.6   Sparse Matrices

A *sparse* matrix is one whose entries are largely zero. For example, in a language processing application we might form a matrix with words in the rows and documents in the columns. Then a particular cell, say, the ijth one, would have a zero if word i did not appear in document j, and since, in many examples, most words do not appear in most documents that matrix might have a high proportion of zeros. There are a number of schemes for representing sparse matrices. The recommended Matrix package (Bates and Maechler, 2016) implements many of these. We encounter sparse matrices in our work, but rarely in the context of data cleaning, so we will not discuss them in this book.

3.2.7   Three- and Higher-Way Arrays

Three-way (and higher-way) matrices are called *arrays* in R. An array looks like a matrix in that all of its elements need to be of the same type, but a three-way array requires three subscripts, a four-way array requires four subscripts, and so on. The only time we seem to have encountered such a thing in data cleaning is when constructing a three- or higher-way table(). In this example, we show a three-way table made from three vectors each of length 8, and then we extract the value 3 from the second row of the first column of the first "panel."

```
> who <- rep (c("George", "Sally"), c(2, 6))
> when <- rep (c("AM", "PM"), 4)
> worked <- c(T, T, F, T, F, T, F, T)
> (sched <- table (who, when, worked))
, , worked = FALSE

          when
who        AM PM
  George   0   0
  Sally    3   0

, , worked = TRUE

          when
who        AM PM
  George   1   1
  Sally    0   3
> sched[2,1,1]
[1] 3
```

Many commands that work on matrices, like, apply() and prop.table(), operate on arrays as well. You can also use c() on an array to produce a vector – in this case, the first column of the first panel is followed by the second column of the first panel, and so on. The aperm() function plays the role of t() for higher-way arrays.

3.3   Lists

A *list* is the most general type of R object. A list is a collection of things that might be of different types or sizes; a list might include a numeric matrix, a character vector, a function, another list, or any other R object. Almost every modeling function in R returns a list, so it is important to understand lists when using R for modeling, but we also need to describe lists because one special sort of list is the data frame, which we describe in the following section.

Normally, we will encounter lists as return values from functions, but we can create a list with the list() function, like this:

```
> (mylist <- list (alpha = 1:3, b = "yes", funk = log, 45))
$alpha
[1] 1 2 3

$b
[1] "yes"

$funk
function (x, base = exp(1))  .Primitive("log")

[[4]]
[1] 45
```

Lists also appear as the output from the split() function, which divides a vector into (possibly unequal-length) pieces according to the value of another vector. We use this frequently in data cleaning. For example, we might divide a vector of people's ages according to their gender. In this simple example, we show how split() produces a list; later, in Section 3.5.1, we show how that list can be put to use.

```
> ages <- c(26, 45, 33, 61, 22, 71, 43)
> gender <- c("F", "M", "F", "M", "M", "F", "F")
> split (ages, gender)
$F
[1] 26 33 71 43

$M
[1] 45 61 22
> split (ages, ages > 60)
$`FALSE`
[1] 26 45 33 22 43

$`TRUE`
[1] 61 71
```

It is worth noting that if the second argument – gender in this case – has missing values, those values will be dropped from the output of split(). Notice also that in the second example the names of the list elements have been surrounded by backward quotes. This is for display, because FALSE and TRUE are not valid names here, but the character strings "FALSE" and "TRUE" are.

The length of a list, as found using length(), is the number of elements, regardless of how big each individual element is. The lengths() function returns a vector of lengths, one for each element on the list. In our example, `length(mylist)` returns the value 4, whereas `lengths(mylist)` returns a vector with four lengths in it (including the length of 1 that is returned for the function `funk()`). The `str()` command we described in Section 2.2.2 works on lists as well. The resulting value printed to the screen gives a description of every element on the list – one line for atomic elements and multiple lines for lists within lists. This is one way to help understand the structure of your data quickly.

3.3.1 Extracting and Assigning

In the first example in this section, the first three elements were given names and the fourth was not. That output hints at how to extract items from a list. You can use double square brackets – so `mylist[[4]]` will return 45 – or, if an element has a name, you can use the dollar sign and the name – so `mylist$b` will return `"yes"`, and `split(ages, ages > 60)$"TRUE"` will return the vector of ages >60. Single square brackets can be used, with a numeric, logical, or name subscript, but there's a catch – single square brackets return a list, not the contents of the list. This is useful if you want only a couple of pieces of a list. For example, `mylist[1:2]` will return a list with the first two elements of `mylist`, and `mylist[1]` will return a list with the first element of `mylist` – not as a vector but as a list. A logical subscript will also work here: `mylist[c(T, T, F, F)]` will return the same list as `mylist[c(1,2)]` or `mylist[c("alpha", "b")]`. Most of the lists we run into will have names, and we usually extract elements one at a time with the dollar sign, but the distinction between single and double brackets is still important. Single brackets create lists; double brackets extract contents. And what happens in our example if you ask for `mylist[[2:3]]` or `mylist[[c(F, T, T, F)]]`? Unsurprisingly, these commands generate errors.

When you request a list item using single brackets and a name that is not present on the list, R returns a list with one NULL element; with double brackets or the dollar sign, it returns the NULL itself. This is consistent with the rule that says single brackets produce lists, while double brackets and dollar signs extract contents. Using double brackets with a numeric subscript greater than the number of elements in the list, such as `mylist[[11]]` in our example, produces an error rather than a NULL.

Of course, to extract elements of a list by name, we need to know the names. We can determine the names a list has using the `names()` function. If the list has no names at all, this function will return NULL; if some elements have names, the `names()` function will return an empty string for those elements with no names. This example shows the names of the `mylist` list.

```
> names(mylist)
[1] "alpha" "b"       "funk"    ""
```

We can also use the names () function on the left-hand side of an assignment to change the names of the elements on a list. For example, the commands names (mylist) [4] <- "RPM" would change the name of the fourth element of mylist to "RPM".

Unlike when you use single or double square brackets, when using the dollar sign to extract an item, you don't need its full name. (Technically, you can pass the exact argument into double square brackets to control this behavior, but we don't.) You only need enough to identify the item unambiguously. In this example, mylist$a would be enough to produce the same numeric vector returned by mylist$alpha, but if there were two items on the list, say alpha and algorithm, typing mylist$a would produce NULL. You would need to specify at least mylist$alp in order to be unambiguous. It's often convenient to use these abbreviated names, but that approach is best suited for quick work at the command line. We recommend using full names in functions and scripts, to avoid confusion or even an error if new items get added to the list later.

To replace an item on a list, just re-assign it. If you want to add a new item to a list, just assign the new item to a new name. Here, naturally, you need to use the item's full name. If your mylist has an item called alpha and you use the command mylist$alp <- 3, you will create a new item named alp and leave the old one, alpha, unchanged. To delete an item from a list, you can use subscripting as we did for a vector. For example, either mylist <- mylist[c(1, 2, 4)] or mylist <- mylist[-3] will drop the third entry. But another, possibly easier, way is to assign NULL to the name or number. In this example, mylist$funk <- NULL or mylist[[3]] <- NULL would remove the item named funk from mylist. This behavior means that it is difficult to intentionally store a NULL value in a list, but this does not seem to be much of a limitation.

Another useful function for operating on lists is unlist(), which, as its names suggests, tries to turn your entire list into a vector. When the list contains unusual objects, such as the function element of the mylist list in our example, the results of unlist() can be difficult to predict. This example shows the effect of unlist() operating on a list of regular vectors, which we create by excluding the function element of mylist().

```
> unlist (mylist[-3])
alpha1 alpha2 alpha3        b
   "1"    "2"    "3"  "yes"     "45"
```

Here we can see that R has produced names for each of the elements from the vector mylist$a, and in a well-behaved list these names can be useful.

3.3.2 Lists in Practice

Generally, we do not need lists much when data cleaning. As we have noted, lists arise as the output of many R functions – a function in R cannot return more than one result, so if a function computes two things of different sizes, it will need to return a list. For example, the rle() function we described in Chapter 2 returns the lengths of runs and, separately, the value associated with each run. It is then your job to extract the pieces from the list. The pieces will almost always be named, so they will be able to be extracted using the $ operator. (In the case of rle(), the pieces are called lengths and values.) Lists also arise as the output from the split() command. Normally, after calling split() we would then call an apply()-type function on each element of the resulting list. We describe this in Section 3.5.1. And, of course, the apply functions can themselves produce lists, as we saw in Section 3.2.3.

Another common context in which lists arise concerns the dimension names of a matrix. The dimnames() function returns NULL when applied to a matrix without row or column names. Otherwise, it returns a list with two elements: the vector of row names and the vector of column names. In general, this return has to be a list, rather than a matrix, because the number of rows and number of columns will be different. Either of the two entries may be NULL, because a matrix may have row names without column names, or vice versa. The dimnames() function may be used to assign, as well as extract, dimension names. These examples continue the earlier ones using the two-way table tbl and the three-way table sched from Sections 3.2.2 and 3.2.7, respectively, and show dimnames() at work. Notice that dimnames() produces a list with three vectors of names from the three-way table.

```
> dimnames(tbl)
$market
[1] "2" "3"

$yr
[1] "FY15" "FY16" "FY17"

> dimnames (sched)
$who
[1] "George" "Sally"

$when
[1] "AM" "PM"

$worked
[1] "FALSE" "TRUE"
```

As we have seen before, dimension names are always characters. So in the three-way array example, the names for the worked dimension are the character strings "FALSE" and "TRUE", not the logical values. In the following example, we show how we can modify an element of the dimnames() list.

```
> dimnames(tbl)[[2]][1] <- "Archive"
> tbl
      yr
market Archive FY16 FY17
     2       3    1    3
     3       2    4    2
```

In the dimnames() assignment we change the first column name. Here, dimnames(tbl) produces a list, the [[2]] part extracts the vector of column names, and the [1] part accesses the element we want to change. Of course, we could have achieved the same result with dimnames (tbl)$yr[1] <- "Archive".

Another list that arises from R itself is the list of session options, returned from a call to the options() function. This list includes dozens of elements describing things such as the number of digits to be displayed, the current choice of editor, the choices going into scientific notation, and many more. Calling names(options()) will produce a vector of the names of the current options. You can examine a particular option, once you know its name, with a command like options()$digits. To set an option, pass its name and value into the options() function, with a command like options(digits = 9).

3.4 Data Frames

Now that we understand how matrices and lists work, we can focus on the most important object of all, the *data frame*. A data frame (written with a dot in R, as data.frame) is a list of vectors, all of which are the same length, so that they can be arrayed in a matrix-like rectangle. (Technically, the elements of a data frame can also be matrices, as long as they are of the right size, but let us avoid that complication. For our purposes, the elements of a data frame will be ordinary vectors.) The vectors in the list serve as the columns in the rectangle. A data frame looks like a matrix, with the critical difference that the different columns can be of different types. One column can be numeric, another character, a third factor, a fourth logical, and so on. Each vector has elements of one type, as usual, but the data frame allows us to store the sort of data we get in real life. So a data frame about people might contain their names (which would probably be character), their ages (often numeric, but possibly factor), their gender (possibly character, possibly factor), their eligibility for a particular program (which might be logical), and so on. In this example, we use the data.frame() function to construct a data frame. In data cleaning, our data frames are very often produced by functions that read in data from the disk, a database, or some other source. We describe methods of acquiring data in Chapter 6, but for the moment we will use this simple example.

```
> (mydf <- data.frame (
        Who = letters[1:5], Cost = c(3, 2, 11, 4, 0),
        Paid = c(F, T, T, T, F), stringsAsFactors = FALSE))
    Who Cost  Paid
1     a    3 FALSE
2     b    2  TRUE
3     c   11  TRUE
4     d    4  TRUE
5     e    0 FALSE
```

There are a few points worth noting here. First, R has provided row names (visible as 1 through 5 on the left) to the data frame automatically. A matrix need not have row names or column names, and a list need not have names, but a data frame must always have both row names and column names. R will create them if they are not explicitly assigned, as it did here. The data.frame() function ensures (unless you specify otherwise) that column names are valid and not duplicated. You may specify row names explicitly, using the row.names argument, in which case they must be not duplicated and not missing. Column names can be examined and set using the names() command, as with a list, or with the colnames() or dimnames() commands, as with a matrix. Generally, you will probably find the names() or colnames() approaches to be easier, since they involve vectors and not a list. For row names, the rownames() and row.names() functions allow the row names of a data frame to be examined or assigned. Section 3.2.2 describes how row names can be useful when handling matrices, and those points are true for data frames as well.

A second point is that, by default, the data.frame() function turns character vectors into factors. Factors are discussed in Section 4.6, and, as we mention there, they are useful, even required, in some modeling contexts. They are rarely what we want in data cleaning, however. The best way to keep factors out of data frames is to not allow them in the first place; we accomplished this in the example above by passing the stringsAsFactors = FALSE argument to the data.frame() function. Without that argument, the Who column of mydf would have been a factor variable with five levels. Another way to prevent factors from being created is to set the stringsAsFactors global option to be FALSE, using the options(stringsAsFactors = FALSE) command. However, we cannot rely on all of the users of our code having that setting in place, so we always try to remember to turn this option off explicitly when we call data.frame(). This issue will arise again when we talk about combining data frames later in this section, and about reading data in from outside sources in Chapter 6.

There are several functions that help you examine your data frame. Of course, in many cases, it will be too big to simply print out and examine. The `head()` and `tail()` functions display only the first or last six rows of a data frame, by default, but this can be changed by the second argument, named n. So `head(mydf, n = 10)` will show the first 10 rows, `tail(mydf, 12)` will show the last 12, and, using a negative argument, `head(mydf, -120)` will show all but the last 120. The `str()` function prints a compact representation of a data frame that includes the type of each column, as well as the first few entries. Other useful functions include `dim()`, to report the numbers of rows and columns, and `summary()`, which gives a brief description of each column.

3.4.1 Missing Values in Data Frames

Because the columns of a data frame can be of different classes, missing values can be of different classes, too. A missing value in a numeric column will be a numeric missing value, while in a character column, the missing value will be of the character type. We discussed missing values at some length in Section 2.4. It is always good to know where missing values come from and why they exist – often investigating the causes of "missingness" will lead to discoveries about the data. The `is.na()` function operates on a data frame and returns a logical-valued matrix showing which elements (if any) are missing; the `anyNA()` function operates on data frames as well. One approach to handling missing data is to simply omit any observations (rows) of the data frame in which one or more elements is missing. R's `na.omit()` function does exactly that. (For this purpose, `NaN` is missing but `Inf` and `-Inf` are not.) This is the default behavior for a number of R's modeling functions, but in general we do not recommend deleting records with missing values until the reason for the values being missing is understood.

3.4.2 Extracting and Assigning in Data Frames

Since a data frame is matrix-like and also list-like, we can use both matrix-style and list-style subsetting operations on a data frame. One difference appears when we select a single row. With a matrix, selecting a single row returns a vector, unless you specify `drop = FALSE` (see Section 3.2.1). However, with a data frame, even a single row is returned as a data frame with one row because in general even one row of a data frame will contain entries of different types.

With that one difference, we extract rows from a data frame just as we extract rows from a matrix – by number, including negatives; using a logical vector; or by names (as we mentioned, the rows of a data frame, and the columns, always have names). We can extract columns using either list-style access or matrix-style access. List-style access uses single brackets to produce sub-lists, which in this case means that using single brackets will produce a data frame. Double bracket subscripts, or the dollar sign, will produce a vector. The difference is that double brackets require an exact name, unless exact = FALSE is set, whereas the dollar sign only requires enough of the name to be unambiguous. If there are two columns with similar names, and your request is not sufficient to determine a unique answer, nothing at all (i.e., NULL) is returned. Therefore, it makes sense, particularly when writing functions for other people, to use full names for columns.

Matrix-style access uses column names or numbers; just as with a matrix, selecting only one column will produce a vector unless you explicitly set drop = FALSE. This example shows a number of ways of extracting columns from data frames. We start by showing list-style access using single brackets.

```
> mydf[2]              # Numeric subscript
  Cost
1    3
2    2
3   11
4    4
5    0
> mydf["Cost"]         # Subscript by name
  Cost
1    3
2    2
3   11
4    4
5    0
> mydf[c(F, T, F)]     # Logical subscript
  Cost
1    3
2    2
3   11
4    4
5    0
```

Each of those operations produced a data frame with five rows and one column (which is, of course, a list). In the following examples, we use double brackets together with a numeric or character subscript and produce a vector. As with a list, a logical subscript with more than one TRUE inside a pair of double brackets will produce an error. (You might have expected the same result with a numeric subscript; in fact, a numeric subscript of length 2 can be used; it acts as a one-row matrix subscript.) When using a character index inside double brackets, you can specify exact = FALSE to permit the same sort of matching that we get with the dollar sign.

```
> mydf[[2]]
[1]  3  2 11  4  0
> mydf[["Cost"]]
[1]  3  2 11  4  0
> mydf[["C"]]
NULL
> mydf[["C", exact = FALSE]]
[1]  3  2 11  4  0
```

Notice that the result in each of these cases is a vector. In the following examples, we show the use of the dollar sign to extract a column. In this case, as we mentioned, we need to specify only enough of the name to be unambiguous.

```
> mydf$W                        # Extracts the "Who" column
[1] "a" "b" "c" "d" "e"
```

The dollar sign can only refer to one column at a time. To extract more than one column, we can use single brackets as above, or matrix-style access in which we explicitly specify rows and columns. As with a matrix, leaving one of those two indices blank will select all of them, and R will produce vectors from single columns unless the drop = FALSE argument is specified. This example shows extraction using matrix-style syntax.

```
> mydf[1:2, c("Cost", "Paid")]
  Cost  Paid
1    3 FALSE
2    2  TRUE
> mydf[,"Who", drop = FALSE] # Example of drop = FALSE
  Who
1   a
2   b
3   c
4   d
5   e
```

Removing a column from a data frame is exactly like removing an element from a list and is accomplished in the same way – by assigning NULL to the column reference. Running the command mydf$Paid <- NULL will remove the column Paid from the data frame using list-style notation, and mydf[,"Paid"] <- NULL performs the same task using matrix-style notation.

To replace subsets of elements you can once again use the matrix-style or list-style syntax. So, for example, mydf[c(1,3), "b"] <- "A" and mydf$b[c(1,3)] <- "A" both replace the first and third entries of the b column of mydf with "A". (Of course, if that column had been numeric or logical before, this operation will force R to convert it to character.)

3.4.3   Extracting Things That Aren't There

The critical difference between a matrix and a data frame is that the columns of a data frame can be vectors of different types. Another difference manifests itself when you try to access an element that isn't there, maybe because you asked for a row or column number that was too big or a row or column name that didn't exist. In a vector, attempts to extract an item beyond the end of the vector will produce NAs. But if you ask a matrix for a row or column that doesn't exist, R will produce an error. This example shows the difference:

```
> (mat <- matrix (1001:1006, 2, 3)) # Matrix with six items
# Ask for a non-existent entry, using vector-like indexing
> mat[8]
[1] NA
> mat[,4] # Ask for a non-existent column
Error in mat[, 4] : subscript out of bounds
```

In general, we prefer the error. A function that sees an NA will often try to carry on, whereas an error will force you to stop and figure out what has happened.

The situation with data frames (and lists) is different. Supplying subscripts for which there are no rows produces one row with all NAs for every unusable subscript. The entries in these rows will have the same classes (numeric, character, etc.) that the data frame had. This arises when some rows have been deleted, and then you, or a program, try to access one of the deleted rows by name. In this example, we show how asking for rows that don't exist can cause trouble.

```
> mydf2 <- data.frame (alpha = 1:5, b = c(T, T, F, T, F),
  NX = c("NA", "NB", "NC", "ND", "NE"),
  stringsAsFactors = FALSE,
  row.names = c("Red", "Blue", "White", "Reddish", "Black"))
> mydf2
         alpha       b NX
Red          1    TRUE NA
Blue         2    TRUE NB
White        3   FALSE NC
Reddish      4    TRUE ND
Black        5   FALSE NE
# Let's ask for rows that don't exist.
> mydf2[c(9, 4, 7, 1),]
         alpha      b   NX
NA          NA     NA <NA>
Reddish      4   TRUE   ND
NA.1        NA     NA <NA>
Red          1   TRUE   NA
```

In this example, we see that the resulting data frame has four rows, two of which contain only NA values. The character column's NAs are represented with angle brackets, as <NA>, to make it easy to distinguish a missing value from the legitimate character string NA in row 1. The first two columns' NAs are numeric and logical. As elsewhere (e.g., Section 2.4.3), logical subscripts will recycle – which is rarely what you want – and usually produce unwanted results when they contain NAs.

In the following example, we show one more operation that can produce rows with NAs in them. Since our data frame has rows named both "Red" and "Reddish", asking for a row named "Re" is ambiguous and produces a row of NAs. (In contrast, the row names of a matrix may not be abbreviated; supplying a name that is not an exact row name produces an error.)

```
> mydf2["Re",]              # Not enough to be unambiguous
    alpha  b    c
NA     NA NA <NA>
```

A much more frequent problem happens when accessing columns. If you access a non-existent column in the matrix or list styles, using an abbreviation, R produces an error. In our example, mydf2[, "gamma"] (referring to a non-existent column), mydf2[, "N"] (referring to an abbreviated name, with a comma), and mydf2["N"] (without the comma) all produce errors. In contrast, when using the double-bracket notation, NULL is returned when a name is abbreviated or non-existent. (As we mentioned with lists, there is in fact an exact argument to the double brackets that we do not use.) Just like the NA returned when accessing a non-existent element of a vector, this NULL has the potential to be more trouble than an error would have been. The use of the dollar sign, as we mentioned, permits the use of unambiguously abbreviated names but produces a NULL when used with a non-existent name. In this example, we show how asking for a non-existent name can produce an unexpected result.

```
# Ask for the first column by abbreviated name.
> mydf2$alph
[1] 1 2 3 4 5                # No problem
# Create another column with a similar name
> mydf2$alpha.plus.1 <- mydf2$alpha + 1
> mydf2$alph
NULL
> mydf2$alph + 1             # No error, but..
numeric(0)                   # probably unexpected
```

The second-to-last operation produced NULL because alph was not sufficient to differentiate between the columns alpha and alpha.plus.1. If a row or column name matches exactly, R will extract it properly (so if you have alpha and alpha.plus.1 and ask for alpha, there is no ambiguity). It is a good practice to use complete names, unless there is a strong reason not to.

3.5   Operating on Lists and Data Frames

Very often we will want to operate on each of the elements of a list or each
of the rows or columns of a data frame. For example, we might want to know
how many missing values are in each column. In Section 3.2.3, we saw a matrix
using apply(), but apply() does not work on a list (since a list doesn't have
dimensions). The apply() function does work on data frames, but it first converts the data frame into a matrix. This conversion will only be sensible when all
the columns are of the same type, as with the all-numeric data frame described
in Section 3.5.2. In other cases, the results can be quite unexpected. In this
example, we operate on the rows of a data frame, using apply(), to show how
this can go wrong.

```
> (dd <- data.frame (a = c(TRUE, FALSE), b = c(1, 123),
      cc = c("a", "b"), stringsAsFactors = FALSE))
      a    b c
1   TRUE   1 a
2 FALSE  123 b
> apply (dd, 1, function (x) x)
    [,1]     [,2]
a   " TRUE"  "FALSE"
b   "  1"    "123"
cc  "a"      "b"
```

Here the function passed to apply() does nothing but return whatever it
passed to it. Since data frame dd has a character column, apply() converted
the whole data frame into a character matrix. It does this in part by calling
the format() function column by column, producing the results seen here:
a value " TRUE" with a leading space in row 1 (formatted to be the same
length as the string "FALSE"), and " 1" with two leading spaces in row 2
(formatted to be the same length as the string "123"). Analogous conversions
happen whenever a data frame with at least one column that is neither logical
nor numeric is passed to apply(), used in other matrix functions such as t()
(transpose), or accessed with a matrix subscript.

   A general approach to this sort of operation (element by element for a list, column by column for a data frame) is supplied by sapply() and lapply().
The lapply() function always returns a list, whereas sapply() runs
lapply() and then tries to make the output into a vector (if the function
always returns a vector of length 1) or a matrix (if the function returns a
vector of constant length). Be careful, though, because if the different function
calls return items of different lengths, sapply() will need to return a list,
just as the ordinary apply() function did back in Section 3.2.3. Moreover,
if the function returns elements of different types (perhaps as a row of a
data frame), sapply() will try to convert these to a common type. In these

cases, use `lapply()`. The following example shows one very common use of `sapply()`, which is to return the classes of each column in a data frame.

```
> sapply (mydf2, class)
      alpha           b          NX alpha.plus.1
  "integer"   "logical"   "character"   "numeric"
```

In this example, the regular `apply()` function will convert the whole data frame to character first, before computing the classes, which it would report as all character.

It is easy to operate on the columns of a data frame (or the elements of a list) with `lapply()` and `sapply()` functions. As we have seen, it is more difficult to operate on the rows. These two functions provide a solution to this problem. They can be used with an ordinary numeric vector as their first argument, in which case they act like a `for()` loop, applying their function to each element of the vector. The `for()`-like behavior of `lapply()` and `sapply()` is most useful when using a complicated function on each row of a data frame. The command `sapply (1:nrow(ourdf), function (i) fancy (ourdf[i,]))` runs a user-written function called `fancy()` on each row of a data frame. supplied by `sapply()` and `lapply()`. The argument to `fancy()` really is a data frame, and not one that has been converted into a matrix. In this example, we show how we might identify rows that contain the number 1. Note that the naïve use of `apply()` does not find the number 1 in the first row.

```
> apply (dd, 1, function (x) any (x == 1))
[1] FALSE FALSE
> sapply (1:2, function (i) any (dd[i,] == 1))
[1]  TRUE FALSE
```

3.5.1 Split, Apply, Combine

The family of `apply()` functions all operate as part of strategy that Wickham (2011) calls "split-apply-combine." The data is split (possibly by row, possibly by column), a function is applied to each piece, and the results recombined. We have already met the `tapply()` function (Section 2.5.2), which performs exactly this set of operations on vectors. We can also do this explicitly via `split()` and `sapply()` or `lapply()`. We start the following example by constructing a data frame with some people's ages, genders, and ages of spouses, and computing the average value of Age by Gender. In this example, we do not specify `stringsAsFactors = FALSE`.

```
> age <- data.frame (Age = c(35, 37, 56, 24, 72, 65),
  Spouse = c(34, 33, 49, 28, 70, 66),
  Gender = c("F", "M", "F", "M", "F", "F"))
```

```
> split (age$Age, age$Gender)
$F
[1] 35 56 72 65

$M
[1] 37 24
> sapply (split (age$Age, age$Gender), mean)
   F    M
57.0 30.5
```

Here the split() function returns a list with the elements of Age divided by value of Gender. Then sapply() operates the mean() function on each element of the list and returns a vector (i.e., it performs both the "apply" and "combine" operations). In this example, we could have used tapply(age$Ages, age$Gender, mean) to produce an identical result.

However, unlike tapply(), split() can operate on a data frame, producing a list of data frames. We can then write a function to operate on each data frame. In this example, we split our data frame by Gender and then use summary() on each of the resulting data frames to return some information about every column. Summary() applied to the factor column Gender is more informative than when applied to a character column; this is why we did not specify stringsAsFactors = FALSE earlier. The result of the calls to summary() appears as a specially formatted table.

```
> split (age, age$Gender)
$F
  Age Spouse Gender
1  35    34      F
3  56    49      F
5  72    70      F
6  65    66      F

$M
  Age Spouse Gender
2  37    33      M
4  24    28      M
> lapply (split (age, age$Gender), summary)
$F
      Age              Spouse           Gender
 Min.   :35.00    Min.   :34.00     F:4
 1st Qu.:50.75    1st Qu.:45.25     M:0
 Median :60.50    Median :57.50
 Mean   :57.00    Mean   :54.75
 3rd Qu.:66.75    3rd Qu.:67.00
 Max.   :72.00    Max.   :70.00
```

```
$M
        Age             Spouse         Gender
Min.    :24.00   Min.    :28.00   F:0
1st Qu.:27.25    1st Qu.:29.25    M:2
Median :30.50    Median :30.50
Mean   :30.50    Mean   :30.50
3rd Qu.:33.75    3rd Qu.:31.75
Max.   :37.00    Max.   :33.00
```

Using `sapply()` in this case produces an unexpected result (try it!). That function tries hard to construct a vector or matrix whenever it can. A single command that produces essentially the same final result, without letting you save the list, is the `by()` function. In this example, `by(age, age$Gender, summary)` performs the `summary()` operation on each column, broken down by gender.

Under some circumstances, the three tasks of split, apply, and combine might require separate functions, each of which may have its own arguments and conventions. The `dplyr` package Wickham and Francois (2015) presents a set of tools that aim to make this sort of processing more consistent. Although this package is intended for data frames, the earlier `plyr` Wickham (2011) package handles lists and arrays as well. Both are intended to be fast and efficient and to permit parallel computation, which we address in Section 5.5. We have been accustomed to performing these tasks in regular R, and we recommend that users know how to perform these tasks there, since lots of existing code and users take that approach.

3.5.2 All-Numeric Data Frames

We noted above that it is difficult to apply a function to the rows of a data frame because the entries of a row may have different classes. All-numeric data frames, though – those whose columns are all logical or numeric – behave specially in these situations. When one of these data frames is converted to a matrix the numeric nature of the columns is preserved (with logicals being converted to numeric). These data frames can also be transposed, or accessed with a matrix subscript, without losing their numeric nature. All-numeric data frames provide a useful way of storing numbers in a matrix-like way while being able to use data-frame-like syntax – but, again, as soon as one character column (perhaps an ID) is added, the nature of the data frame changes.

Just as there are functions `as.numeric()` and so on to convert vectors from one class to another (see Section 2.2.3), R provides `as.matrix()` and `as.data.frame()` functions to convert data frames to matrices and vice versa. This is mostly useful for all-numeric data frames or for older functions that require numeric matrices.

3.5.3   Convenience Functions

We encourage users to use long names for their data objects and for their column names, for increased readability. However, this often leads to a situation where to use a simple expression we need a long line like the one in this example:

```
CustPayment2016$JanDebt +   CustPayment2016$FebPurch -
                            CustPayment2016$FebPmt
```

The `with()` and `within()` functions provide an easier way to perform operations such as these, and they are particularly useful when the same operation needs to be done multiple times on multiple data objects, usually data frames. For each of these functions, we pass the data frame's name and then the expression to be performed, like this:

```
with (CustPayment2016, JanDebt + FebPurch - FebPmt)
```

One issue that if the expression includes an assignment, the assignment is ignored. In order to create a new column in `CustPayment2016` we would need code like this:

```
CustPayment2016$FebDebt <- with (CustPayment2016,
                    JanDebt + FebPurch - FebPmt)
```

As an alternative, the `within()` function can perform assignments; it returns a copy of the data with the expression evaluated. In this case, we could add a new column called `FebDebt` to the data frame with a command like this:

```
CustPayment2016 <- within (CustPayment2016,
                    FebDebt <- JanDebt + FebPurch - FebPmt)
```

Notice that in this example `within()` returns a copy, which then needs to be saved.

Two more convenience functions are the `subset()` and `transform()` functions. Much beloved of beginners, they make the subsetting and transformation process easier to follow by helping do away with square brackets. For example, we might extract all the rows of data frame d for which column `Price` is positive with a command like `d[ d$Price > 0,]`; `subset()` allows us to use the alternative `subset(d, Price > 0)`. It is also possible to extract a subset of columns at the same time. The `transform()` function allows the user to specify transformations to existing columns in a data frame and returns the updated version. The help pages for both of these functions are accompanied by warnings that recommend using them interactively only, not for programming, and we generally avoid them.

A final convenience function is the ability to "pipe" provided by the `%>%` function in the `magrittr` package (Bache and Wickham, 2014). This is intended to make code more readable by allowing one function's output to serve as another's input directly at the command line, rather than requiring nested calls. For example, consider this evaluation of a mathematical expression:

```
> cos (log (sqrt (8 - 3)))
[1] 0.6933138
```

In R, we have to read this from the inside out: we compute $8 - 3$; take the square root of the result; take the logarithm of that result; and finally compute the cosine of the result from the `log()` function. Using the pipe notation, we can pass the results of one computation to the next in the order in which they are performed. This example shows the same computation performed using the pipe notation.

```
> (8 - 3) %>% sqrt %>% log %>% cos
[1] 0.6933138
```

The pipe notation is particularly useful for nested functions and can be brought to bear on data frames. However, be aware that not every function is suitable for piping, and notice that the order of precedence required that we surround the $8 - 3$ with parentheses.

3.5.4 Re-Ordering, De-Duplicating, and Sampling from Data Frames

Data frames can be re-ordered (i.e., sorted) using a command that extracts all the rows in a new order. This ordering will usually be a vector of row indices constructed with the `order()` function (see Section 2.6.2). So if a data frame named `cust` has columns `ID` and `Date`, then `ord <- order (cust$ID, cust$Date)` (or the slightly more convenient alternative, `ord <- with(cust, order (ID, Date))`) will produce a vector `ord` that shows the ordering of the data frame's rows by increasing `ID`, and then by increasing `Date` within `ID`. Therefore, the command `cust <- cust[ord,]` will replace the old `cust` with the newly ordered one.

In Section 2.6.4, we saw that the `unique()` function returns the unique entries in a vector, while its counterpart `duplicated()` returns a logical vector that is `TRUE` for any entry that appears earlier in the vector. These two functions operate directly on matrices and data frames as well. So the command `unique(mydf)` takes a data frame named `mydf` and returns the set of non-duplicated rows. As always, floating-point error can be a problem when detecting whether two things are identical.

One more operation that comes up is random sampling from a data frame. This is a good plan when the original data set is so big that it cannot be easily used for testing, for example, or plotting. As with re-ordering, the idea is to construct a sample of row indices and then to subset the data frame with that sample. The `sample()` command is useful here. In its most basic form, we pass an integer named x giving the number of rows in the data frame and an argument named `size` giving the desired sample size. The result is a random set of integers selected without replacement with each value from 1 to x being equally likely. To sample 200 rows from a data frame named mydf, we could use the command sam <- sample (nrow (mydf), 200) to get a vector of 200 row numbers, and then mydf [sam,] to do the sampling. (This presumes that there are 200 or more rows in mydf. If not, R produces an error.) Of course, the new data frame's rows will maintain the numbers they had in the original mydf, so the row names of the new version will be out of order. If that bothers you, a quick sam <- sort (sam) prior to subsetting will fix that. The sample () function also has a number of more sophisticated features, including sampling with replacement and the ability to specify different probabilities for different choices.

3.6   Date and Time Objects

Most data cleaning problems will include dates (and sometimes times). The most important tasks we face with dates in data cleaning are doing arithmetic (e.g., adding a number of days to a date or finding the number of days between two dates) and extracting each date's day, day of the week, month, calendar quarter, or year. Objects representing dates and times come in several forms in R, but since one of them takes the form of a list, we have postponed discussion of those objects until here.

3.6.1   Formatting Dates

There are lots of ways to display a date in text, and during data cleaning it will feel like you meet all of them. Americans might write July 4, 2017 as "7/4/17," but to most of the rest of the world, this indicates April 7th. Furthermore, this representation leaves unclear precisely where in the string the day starts; it starts in the third character for an American's "7/4/17" but in the first for an internationally formatted date like "26/05/17." The two unambiguous formats "2017-07-04" and "2017/07/04" are good starting points for storing dates, especially in text files outside of R. (The value "2017-7-4" is permitted, but this format leads to date strings of different lengths; 20170704 is easy to mistake for an integer.)

The simplest date class in R is called Date, and an object of this class is represented internally as an integer representing the number of days since a particular "origin" date. The as.Date () function converts text into objects of class Date in two ways. First, it can convert an integer number of days since the origin into a date. The usual origin date in R is January 1, 1970, or, unambiguously, "1970-01-01." In this example, we show how a vector of integers can be converted into a Date object.

```
> (dvec <- as.Date (c(0, 17250:17252),
                    origin = "1970-01-01"))
[1] "1970-01-01" "2017-03-25" "2017-03-26" "2017-03-27"
```

Notice that the value 0 is converted into the origin date, "1970-01-01." If we are given integer dates, we need to know what the origin is supposed to be. This concern arises when reading data in from the Excel spreadsheet program. Excel uses integer dates, but the origins are different between Windows and Mac, and Excel mistakenly treats 1900 as a leap year. We describe this in more detail in Section 6.5.2 when we describe reading data in.

The second conversion that as.Date() can perform is to convert text-based representations such as "7/4/17" or "July 4, 2017," using a format string that describes the way the input text is formatted. Each piece of the format string that starts with % identifies one part of the date or time; other pieces represent characters such as space, comma, /, or - between pieces of the input text. For example, %B matches the name of the month and %a matches the name of the day of the week. The most important pieces of the format are %d for day of the month, %m for the month, and %y and %Y for two- and four-digit year, respectively. (Two-digit years between 69 and 99 are assumed to be twentieth-century ones starting with 19, and the rest, twenty-first-century ones.) The help page for as.Date() refers us to the help page for strptime(), which lists all of the possibilities. For example, this command uses the format string "%B %d, %Y" to convert text dates such as "September 20, 2016" into a Date object.

```
> as.Date (c("Feb 29, 2016", "Feb 29, 2017",
            "September 30, 2017"), format = "%b %d, %Y")
[1] "2016-02-29" NA           "2017-09-30"
```

Notice that the format string had to contain the same pattern of spaces and comma that the input text had. R was able to read both the three-letter abbreviation Feb and the full name September – but it produced an NA for Feb 29, 2017 which was not a legitimate date.

The names of the days of the week, and the months of the year, are set by the computer's locale (see Section 1.4.6). By changing locales R can be made to read in days or months in other languages, as well, which is useful when data comes from international sources. In this example, we have some dates in which the month has been given in Spanish. By changing the locale we can read these in; then by re-setting the locale we can use as.character() to convert them into English.

```
> sp.dates <- c("3 octubre 2016", "26 febrero 2017",
              "5 mayo 2017")
> as.Date (sp.dates, format = "%d %B %y")
[1] NA NA NA
# Not understood in English locale; use Spanish for now
```

```
> Sys.setlocale ("LC_TIME", "Spanish")
[1] "Spanish_Spain.1252"                # Setting was successful
> (dts <- as.Date (sp.dates, format = "%d %B %Y"))
[1] "2016-10-03" "2017-02-26" "2017-05-05"
> Sys.setlocale ("LC_TIME", "USA")   # Change back
[1] "English_United States.1252"      # Setting was successful
> as.character (dts, "%d %B %Y")
[1] "03 October 2016"   "26 February 2017" "05 May 2017"
```

3.6.2   Common Operations on Date Objects

There are a number of convenience functions to manipulate date objects. The months () and weekdays () functions act on Date objects and return the names of the corresponding months and days of the week. Each has an abbreviate argument that defaults to FALSE; when set to TRUE these arguments produce three-letter abbreviations. In this example, we show examples of these convenience functions.

```
> d1 <- as.Date ("2017-01-02")
> d2 <- as.Date ("2017-06-15")
> weekdays (c(d1, d2))
[1] "Monday"   "Thursday"
> months (c(d1, d2))
[1] "January" "June"
> months (c(d1, d2), abbreviate = TRUE)
[1] "Jan" "Jun"
> quarters (c(d1, d2))
[1] "Q1" "Q2"
```

There is no function to extract the numeric day, month, or year from a Date object. These operations are performed using the format () function, which calls format.Date () to produce character output that can then be converted to numeric using as.numeric (). The elements of the format string are like those that are used in as.Date (). This example shows how to extract some of those pieces from a vector of Date objects – but, again, note that the output of format () is text.

```
> format (c(d1, d2), "%Y")
[1] "2017" "2017"
> format (c(d1, d2), "%d")
[1] "02" "15"
> format (d1, "%A, %B %m, %Y")
[1] "Monday, January 01, 2017"
```

The final command shows a more sophisticated formatting operation, using a format string like the one in as.Date ().

It is permitted to use decimals in a Date object to represent times of day. If you want to create a date object to represent 1:00 p.m. on July 29,

2015, as.Date(16645 + 13/24, origin = "1970-01-01") will
return a numeric, non-integer object that can be used as a date. However,
as.Date("2017-07-29 13:00:00") produces a Date that is represented
internally by the integer 17,376 – the time portion is ignored. Moreover
non-integer parts are never displayed and can even be truncated by some
operations. When times of day are required, it is a better idea to use a POSIXt
object (Section 3.6.4).

3.6.3 Differences between Dates

Very often we need to know how far apart two dates are. The difference between
two Date objects is not a date; it is instead a period of time. In R, one of
these differences is stored as a difftime object. Some functions, such as
mean() and range(), handle difftime objects in the expected way. Others, such as hist() (to produce a histogram) or summary(), fail or produce
unhelpful results. Normally, we will convert difftime objects into numeric
items with as.numeric(). Be careful, though: the units that R uses for the
conversion can depend on the size of the difference, whereas for data cleaning we almost always want to use one consistent choice of unit. Therefore, it
is a good habit, when converting difftime objects to numbers, to specify
units = "days" (or whichever unit we want) explicitly. In this example,
which continues the one above, we show addition on dates plus an example of
a difftime object.

```
# Date objects are numeric; we can add and subtract them
> d1 + 30
[1] "2017-07-02"
> (d <- d2 - d1)
Time difference of 13 days # an object of class difftime
> as.numeric (d)             # convert to numeric, in days
[1] 13
> units (d)
[1] "days"
> as.numeric (d, units = "weeks")
[1] 1.857143
```

In the last pair of commands, we saw that as.numeric() produced an output in days by default, the units being revealed by the units() command.
We can also set the units of a difftime object explicitly, with a command
like units(d) <- "weeks", or use the difftime() function directly, like
difftime(d2, d1, units = "weeks").

3.6.4 Dates and Times

If you don't need to do computations with times – only with dates – the Date
class will be enough, at least back to 1752, when Britain switched from the Julian

to the Gregorian calendar. If you need to do computations on times, there is a second set of objects that are stronger at storing and computing those. These are named POSIXct and POSIXlt objects, after the POSIX set of standards. Collectively, these two types of objects are called POSIXt objects. POSIXt objects measure the number of seconds (possibly with a decimal part) since the beginning of January 1, 1970 using Coordinated Universal Time (UTC), which is identical to Greenwich Mean Time (GMT). (Technically, the POSIX standard does not include leap seconds, a vector of which is given by R's built-in .leap.seconds variable. This has never affected us.)

The POSIXlt object is implemented as a list, which makes it easy to extract pieces; the POSIXct object acts more like a number, which makes it the choice for storing as a column in a data frame. We start with an example of a POSIXlt number. It prints out in a character string, but it behaves like a list. One unusual feature is that, to see the names of the list, you need to unlist() the object first. For example,

```
> (start <- as.POSIXlt("2017-01-17 14:51:23"))
[1] "2017-01-17 14:51:23 PST" # R has inferred time zone PST
> unlist(start)
   sec    min   hour   mday    mon   year   wday   yday
  "23"   "51"   "14"   "17"    "0"  "117"    "2"   "16"
 isdst   zone gmtoff
   "0"  "PST"     NA
```

Here start really is a list, and we can extract components in the usual way, with a dollar sign or double brackets (but, although you can use its names, names(start) is NULL, and you cannot extract a subset of components with single brackets). Notice also that the first day of the month gets number 1, but the first month of the year, January, carries the number 0, and that the year element counts the number of years since 1900. The advantage of a list is that, given a vector of POSIXlt objects named date.vec, say, you can extract all the months at once with data.vec$mon – but again, January is month 0 and December is month 11. Weekdays are given in the list by wday, with 0–6 representing Sunday through Saturday, respectively. The weekdays() function from above, and the other Date functions, also work on POSIXt objects – but be aware that the results are displayed in the locale of the user. Notice that the time zone above, PST, is deduced by our computer from its locale. The help for DateTimeClasses gives more information on the niceties of time zones, many of which are system specific.

Although we can use the weekdays(), months(), and quarters() functions on POSIXct objects, we extract other components, such as years or hours, via the format() function, as we did for Date objects. This is slightly less efficient than the list-type extraction from a POSIXlt object, but we recommend using POSIXct objects where possible, because we have encountered unexpected behavior when changing time zones with POSIX1t objects.

It is worth noting that although a POSIXt object may have a time, a time is not required. When a Date object is converted into a POSIXt object, the resulting object is given a time of 00:00 (i.e., midnight) in UTC. A vector of POSIXt objects that are all at midnight display without the time visible, but they do contain a time value. When a POSIXt object is converted to a Date object, the time is truncated.

3.6.5 Creating POSIXt Objects

R's as.POSIXct() and as.POSIX1t() functions convert text that is unambiguously formatted into POSIXt objects just as as.Date() does. Here the date can be followed by a 24-hour clock time like 17:13:14 or a 12-hour time with an AM/PM indicator. More usefully, perhaps, these functions allow the use of a format string such as the one used by as.Date(). This format string, documented in the help for strptime(), allows times, time zones, and AM/PM indicators, attributes that are also accepted by as.Date(). Often we discard time information, since we are only interested in dates, but sometimes discarding time information can lead to incorrect conclusions. In this example, we construct two POSIXct objects that represent the same moment expressed in two different time zones.

```
> (ct1 <- as.POSIXct ("Mar 31, 2017 10:26:08 pm",
        format = "%b %d, %Y %I:%M:%S %p"))
[1] "2017-03-31 22:26:08 PDT"
> (ct2 <- as.POSIXct ("2017-04-01 05:26:08", tz = "UTC"))
[1] "2017-04-01 05:26:08 UTC"
> as.numeric (ct1 - ct2, units = "secs")
[1] 0
```

The first date, ct1, is not given an explicit time zone, so the system selects the local one (shown here as PDT). In the second example, we explicitly provide the UTC indicator with the tz argument. The as.numeric() command shows that the two times are identical. There are a few confusing properties of POSIXt objects. All the objects in a vector of length >1 will be displayed with the local time zone, and their weekdays() and months() will be, too. For a single object, though, these functions refer to the time zone of the object, although, as this example shows, there is a complication.

```
> c(ct1, ct2)
[1] "2017-03-31 22:26:08 PDT" "2017-03-31 22:26:08 PDT"
> weekdays (c(ct1, ct2))
[1] "Friday" "Friday"
> weekdays (ct2) #
[1] "Saturday"
```

```
> weekdays (c(ct2))
[1] "Friday"
```

The top command shows that the vector of dates is displayed in our locale. That date refers to a moment that was on a Friday locally. When weekdays () acts on ct2 by itself, though, it shows that that moment was on a Saturday in Greenwich. In the final command, the c () causes ct2 to be converted to local time, where its date falls on a Friday.

To explicitly convert the time zone of a POSIXct object, you can set its tzone attribute, with a command like attr(ct1, tzone = "UTC"), or, equivalently, with tzone = "GMT"; see the help for Sys.timezone() for a way to determine the names of time zones. (The approach for POSIXlt objects is more complicated and we do not discuss it here.) Note that when POSIXct objects are converted to Date objects, they are rendered in UTC, so as.Date(ct1) and as.Date(ct2) both produce dates with value "2017-04-01".

The format string that is passed to as.POSIXct() allows for a lot of flexibility in the way dates are formatted. This example shows how you might convert R's own date stamp, produced by the date() function, into a POSIXct object and then a Date object.

```
> (curdate <- date())
[1] "Wed Sep 21 00:36:47 2016"
> (now <- as.POSIXct (curdate,
                      format = "%A %B %d %H:%M:%S %Y"))
[1] "2016-09-21 00:36:47 PDT" # POSIXct object
> as.Date (now)
[1] "2016-09-21"
```

As long as the format of the dates in your data is consistent, it will probably be possible to read them in using as.POSIXct(). In some cases, dates may appear with extraneous text. If the contents of the text is known exactly, the text can be matched. For example, the string Wednesday, the 17th of March, 2017 at 6:30 pm can be read in with the format string "%A, the %dth of %B, %Y at %I:%M %p". But this formatting will fail for the 21st or the 22nd or if the input string ends with p.m. (with periods). In cases where there is variable, extraneous text, you may have to resort to manipulating the text strings using the tools in Chapter 4.

3.6.6 Mathematical Functions for Date and Times

Since Date and POSIXt objects are numeric, many functions intended to work on numeric data also work on these date objects. In particular, range (), max (), min (), mean (), and median () objects in R. all produce vectors of date objects. The `diff()` function computes differences between adjacent elements in a vector, so `diff(range(x))` produces the range of dates in the vector `x` as a `difftime` object. The `summary()` function acts on a vector of date objects, producing an object that is slightly different from a vector of dates but still usable. You can also tabulate `Date` and `POSIXct` objects with `table()` – but `table()` does not work on the list-like `POSIXlt` objects.

The `seq()` function can also be used to generate a sequence of dates. This is useful for generating the endpoints of "bins" for histograms or other summaries. As we mentioned, `Date` objects are implemented in units of days, so a sequence of `Date` objects one unit apart has values 1 day apart by default. However, `POSIXt` objects are in units of seconds, so a sequence of `POSIXt` objects one unit apart are 1 second apart. One way to create a sequence of `POSIXt` objects representing consecutive days is to use `by = 86400`, since there are 86,400 seconds in a day. However, R has a better approach. When called with a vector of `Date` or `POSIXt` objects, the `seq()` function invokes one of the functions, `seq.Date()` or `seq.POSIXt()`, that is smarter about date objects. These functions let you use the `by` argument with a word like `"hour"`, `"day"` and so on. An additional value `"DSTday"` (for `POSIXt` only) ignores daylight saving time to produce the same clock time every day. In this example, we generate some sequences of `Date` and `POSIXt` objects. Notice that R suppresses times for `POSIXt` dates when all of the times in the vector are midnight.

```
> seq (as.Date ("2016-11-04"), by = 1, length = 4)
[1] "2016-11-04" "2016-11-05" "2016-11-06" "2016-11-07"
# Create and save a POSIXct object, for convenience
> ourPos <- as.POSIXct ("2016-11-04 00:00:00")
> seq (ourPos, by = 1, length = 3)
[1] "2016-11-04 00:00:00 PDT" "2016-11-04 00:00:01 PDT"
[3] "2016-11-04 00:00:02 PDT"
> seq (ourPos, by = "day", length = 3)
[1] "2016-11-04 PDT" "2016-11-05 PDT" "2016-11-06 PDT"
> seq (ourPos, by = "day", length = 4)
[1] "2016-11-04 00:00:00 PDT" "2016-11-05 00:00:00 PDT"
[3] "2016-11-06 00:00:00 PDT" "2016-11-06 23:00:00 PST"
> seq (ourPos, by = "DSTday", length = 4)
[1] "2016-11-04 PDT" "2016-11-05 PDT" "2016-11-06 PDT"
[4] "2016-11-07 PST"
> seq (ourPos, by = "month", length = 4)
[1] "2016-11-04 PDT" "2016-12-04 PST" "2017-01-04 PST"
[4] "2017-02-04 PST"
```

In the top example, we see a sequence of `Date` objects 1 day apart (as specified by `by = 1`). That same specification produces `POSIXt` dates 1 second apart.

Using by = "day" moves the clock by 24 hours, but since the Pacific Time Zone, where these examples were generated, switched from daylight saving to standard time on November 6, 2016, the old time of midnight standard time was advanced 24 hours to 11 p.m. standard time. With by = "DSTday" the clock time is preserved across days. The final example shows how we can advance 1 month at a time – the help for seq.POSIXt() shows how these functions adjust for the case when advancing by month starting at January 31, for example.

Differences between two POSIXt objects, like differences between Date objects, are represented by difftime objects in R. Here, though, you need to be even more careful to specify the units when converting the difftime object to numeric. This example shows how neglecting that specification can cause problems.

```
> d1 <- as.POSIXct ("2017-05-01 12:00:00")
> d2 <- as.POSIXct ("2017-05-01 12:00:06") # d1 + 6 seconds
> d3 <- as.POSIXct ("2017-05-07 12:00:00") # d1 + 6 days
> (d2 - d1) == (d3 - d1)
[1] FALSE # expected
> as.numeric (d2 - d1) == as.numeric (d3 - d1)
[1] TRUE # possibly unexpected
```

Here the d2 − d1 difference has the value 6 seconds, while the d3 − d1 difference has the value 6 days. The units are preserved in the difftime objects but discarded by as.numeric(). It is a good practice to always specify units = "days" or whatever your preferred unit is, whenever you convert a difftime object to a numeric value.

3.6.7 Missing Values in Dates

Dates of different classes should not be combined in a vector. It is always wise to use an explicit function to force all the elements of a date vector to have the same class. This also applies to missing values in date objects – they need to be of the proper class. In this example, we combine an NA with the d1 date from above, using the c() function. The c() function can call a second function depending on the class of its first argument – c.Date(), c.POSIXct() or c.POSIXlt().

```
> c(d1, NA)
[1] "2017-05-01 12:00:00 PDT" NA
> c(NA, d1)
[1]          NA 1493665200
> c(as.POSIXct (NA), d1)
[1] NA                       "2017-05-01 12:00:00 PDT"
> c(NA, as.Date (d1))
[1]     NA 17287
```

The first command succeeds, as expected, because `c.POSIXct()` is able to convert the `NA` value into a `POSIXct` object. In the second command, though, `c()` sees the `NA` and does not call a class-specific function. Instead, it converts both values to numeric. The resulting second element is the number of seconds since the `POSIXt` origin date. The way around this is to explicitly specify an `NA` value of class `POSIXct`, as in the third command. The final command shows that this problem exists for `Date` objects as well – here, `d1` is converted into the number of days since the origin date. The lesson is that you should ensure that every date element, even the `NA` ones, in your vector has the same class.

3.6.8   Using Apply Functions with Dates and Times

Often a data set will arrive as a data frame with a series of dates in each row. These might be dates on which a phenomenon is repeatedly recorded – monthly manpower data, for example, or payment information. If an operation needs to be performed on each row – say, finding the range of the dates in each one – it is tempting to use `apply()` on such a data frame. As with earlier examples (Section 3.5), this will not succeed – even (perhaps surprisingly) if the data frame's columns are all `Date` or all `POSIXct`. A better approach is to operate on each row via the `lapply()` or `sapply()` functions. Here we show an example of a data frame whose columns are both `Date` objects.

```
> date.df <- data.frame (
        Start = as.Date (c("2017-05-03", "2017-04-16")))
> date.df$End <- as.Date (c("2018-06-01", "2018-02-16"))
> date.df
        Start       End
1 2017-05-03 2018-06-01
2 2017-04-16 2018-02-16
> apply (date.df, 1, function (x) x[2] - x[1])
Error in x[2] - x[1] : non-numeric arg. to binary operator
```

Here, the `apply()` function converts the data frame to a character matrix. (Why it does not convert it to a numeric one is not clear.) So the mathematical operation fails. One way to apply the function to each row is via `sapply()`, as in this example:

```
> sapply (1:2, function (i)
                as.numeric (date.df[i,2] - date.df[i,1],
                    units = "days"))
[1] 394 306
```

Using `sapply()` to index the rows, we can compute each difference in days in a straightforward way. In general, you will need to pay attention when dealing with data frames of dates row by row.

3.7 Other Actions on Data Frames

It is a rare data cleaning task that does not involve manipulating data frames, and one very common operation is to combine two data frames. There are essentially three ways in which we might want to combine data frames: by columns (i.e., combining horizontally); by rows (i.e., stacking vertically); and matching up rows using a key (which we call *merging*). The first two of these are straightforward and the third is only a little more complicated. In this section, we describe these tasks, as well as some other actions you can perform on data frames. We show some more detailed examples in Chapter 7.

3.7.1 Combining by Rows or Columns

When we talk about "combining data frames by columns," we mean combining them side by side, creating a "wide" result whose number of columns is the sum of the numbers of columns in the things being combined. We have seen the cbind() function, which is the preferred function for joining matrices. We can also supply two data frames as arguments to the data.frame() function and R will join them. Both cbind() and data.frame() can incorporate vectors and matrices in its arguments as well – but they will convert characters to factors unless you explicitly provide the stringsAsFactors = FALSE argument. R is prepared to recycle some inputs, but it is best if the things being combined have the same numbers of rows.

Recall that a data frame needs to have column names, and that we (almost) always want these to be distinct. If two columns have the same name, R will use the make.names() function with the unique = TRUE argument to construct a set of distinct names. If three data frames each have a column named a, for example, the result will have columns a, a.1, and a.2. It is always a good idea to examine the set of column names for duplication (perhaps using intersection() as in Section 2.6.3) to ensure that you know what action R will take.

Combining data frames by rows means stacking them vertically, creating a "tall" result whose number of rows is the sum of the numbers of rows in the things being combined. The rbind() function combines data frames in this way. We can only operate rbind() on things with the same number of columns; moreover, the columns need to have the same names, but they need not be in the same order; R will match the names up. You will almost always want the columns being joined to be of the same sort – numeric with numeric, character with character, POSIXct with POSIXct, and so on – otherwise, R will convert each column to a common class. We usually check the classes explicitly and recommend you pass the stringsAsFactors = FALSE argument to rbind(). If we have two data frames called df1 and df2, we start by comparing the names, using code like this:

```
> n1 <- names (df1)
> n2 <- names (df2)
> all (sort (n1) == sort (n2)) # should be TRUE
```

We sort the names of each data frame to account for the fact that they might be out of order. Next, we extract the class of each column. The results, c1 and c2 as follows, will often be vectors, although they might be lists if some columns produce a vector of length 2 or more. (This will be the case if any columns are POSIXct objects.) We compare these two objects as in this example:

```
> c1 <- sapply (df1, class)
> c2 <- sapply (df2, class)
> isTRUE (all.equal (c1, c2[names (c1)])) # should be TRUE
```

Notice that we re-order the names of c2 so that they match the order of the names of c1. The all.equal() function compares two objects and returns TRUE if they match, and a small report (a vector of character strings) describing their differences if they do not. This report is useful, but to test for equality in, for example, an if() statement, the isTRUE() function is useful. This function produces TRUE if its argument is a single TRUE, as returned by all.equal() when its arguments match, and FALSE if its argument is anything else, like the character strings produced by all.equal() when its arguments differ.

If the data frames being combined have the usual unmodified numeric row names, R will adjust them so that the resulting row names go from 1 upward, but if there are non-numeric or modified row names, R will try to keep them, again deconflicting matches to ensure that row names are distinct.

When combining a large number of data frames, the do.call() function will often be useful. This function takes the name of a function to be run, and a list of arguments and runs the function with those arguments. For example, the command log(x = 32, base = 2) produces the result 5, because $\log_2(32) = 5$. We get the exact same result with the command do.call("log", list(x = 32, base = 2)). Notice that the arguments are specified in the form of a list. This mechanism allows us to combine a large number of data frames in a fairly simple way. Suppose we have a list of data frames named list.of.df (such a list arises frequently as the output from lapply()). Extracting the individual data frames from the list can be tedious, but we can rbind() them all with a command like do.call ("rbind", list.of.df) (assuming the data frames meet the rbind() criteria). If the data frames are not already on a list, we can construct such a list with a command like list(first.df, second.df, ...).

3.7.2 Merging Data Frames

Merging is a more complicated and powerful operation. In the usual type of merging, each data frame has a "key" field, typically a unique one. The merge()

matches up the keys and produces a data frame with one row per key, with all of the columns from both of the data frames. There are three main complications here: what to do when keys are present in one data set but not in the other, what to do when keys are duplicated, and what to do when keys match only approximately.

The action when keys are present in one data set, but not in the other, is controlled by the all.x and all.y arguments, both of which default to FALSE. For this purpose, x refers to the first-named data set and y to the second. By default, the result of the merge has one row for each key that appears in both x and y (except when there are duplicated keys). Database users call this an "inner join." When all.x = TRUE and all.y = FALSE, the result has one row for each key in x (this is a "left join"). Columns of the corresponding keys that do not appear in y are filled with NA values. Naturally, the converse is true when all.x = FALSE and all.y = TRUE – the result has one row for each key in y and the result has NAs for those columns contributed from x for those keys that did not appear in y. When all.x = TRUE and all.y = TRUE, the result has one row for every key in either x or y (this is an "outer join"). In this example, we merge two small data sets to show the behavior brought about by all.x and all.y.

```
> (df1 <- data.frame (Key = letters[1:3], Value = 1:3,
    stringsAsFactors = FALSE))
  Key Value
1  a     1
2  b     2
3  c     3
> (df2 <- data.frame (Key = c("a", "c", "f"),
    Origin = 101:103, stringsAsFactors = FALSE))
  Key Origin
1  a    101
2  c    102
3  f    103
> merge (df1, df2, by = "Key")                    # inner join
  Key Value Origin
1  a     1    101
2  c     3    102
> merge (df1, df2, by = "Key", all.x = TRUE)      # left join
  Key Value Origin
1  a     1    101
2  b     2     NA
3  c     3    102
> merge (df1, df2, by = "Key", all.y = TRUE)      # right join
  Key Value Origin
1  a     1    101
```

```
2   c      3     102
3   f     NA     103
> merge (df1, df2, by = "Key", all.x = TRUE,
                              all.y = TRUE)    # outer join
   Key Value Origin
1   a     1     101
2   b     2      NA
3   c     3     102
4   f    NA     103
```

The behavior of merge() when keys are duplicated is straightforward, but it is rarely what we want. It is best to remove rows with duplicate keys, or to create a new column with a unique key, before merging. The number of rows produced by merge() when there are duplicates is the number of pairs of keys that match between the two data frames. In this example, we establish some duplicated keys and show the behavior of merge in the left join case.

```
> (df3 <- data.frame (Key = c("b", "b", "f", "f"),
           Origin = 101:104, stringsAsFactors = FALSE))
   Key Origin
1   b    101
2   b    102
3   f    103
4   f    104
> merge (df1, df3, by = "Key", all.x = TRUE)
   Key Value Origin
1   a     1      NA
2   b     2     101
3   b     2     102
4   c     3      NA
```

Here the merge produces one row every time a key in df1 matches a key in df3 – even if that happens more than once – in addition to producing rows for every key that does not match. If df1 had included two rows with the Key value of b, as df3 does, then the result would have had four rows with Key value b.

The issue of matching when keys that match only approximately is a thornier one. This arises when matching on people's names, for example, since these are often represented in slightly different ways – think about the slightly differing strings "George H. W. Bush," "George HW Bush," "George Bush 41," and so on. The adist() and agrep() functions (see also the discussion of grep() in Section 4.4.2) help find keys that match approximately, but this sort of "fuzzy matching" (also called "entity resolution" or "record linkage") is beyond the scope of this book.

3.7.3   Comparing Two Data Frames

At some point you will have two versions of a data frame, and you will want to know if they are identical. "Identical" can mean slightly different things here. For example, if two numeric vectors differ only by floating-point error, we would probably consider them identical. If a character vector has the same values as a factor, that might be enough to be identical, but it might not. The identical() function tests for very strict equivalence and can be used on any R objects. It returns a single logical value, which is TRUE when the two items are equal. The help page notes that this function should usually be applied neither to POSIXlt objects nor, presumably, to data frames containing these. This is partly because two times might represent the same value expressed in two different time zones.

The all.equal() function described above compares two objects but with slightly more room for difference. The tolerance argument lets you decide how different two numbers need to be before R declares them to be different. By default, R requires that the two data frames' names and attributes match, but those rules can be over-ridden. Moreover, two POSIXlt items that represent the same time are judged equal. When two items are equal under these criteria, all.equal() returns TRUE. Since the return value of all.equal() when its two arguments are not equal is a vector of text strings, one correct way to compare data frames a and b for equality is with isTRUE(all.equal (a, b)).

3.7.4   Viewing and Editing Data Frames Interactively

R has a couple of functions that will let you edit a matrix, list, or data frame in an interactive, spreadsheet-like form. The View() function shows a read-only representation of a data frame, whereas edit() allows changes to be made. The return value from the edit() function can be saved to reflect the changes. A more dangerous option is provided by data.entry(); changes made by that function are saved automatically. If you use these functions to clean your data, of course, your steps will not be reproducible, and we strongly recommend using commented scripts and functions, which we describe in Chapter 5.

3.8   Handling Big Data

The ability to acquire, clean, handle, and model with big data sets will surely become more and more important in coming years. From its beginning, R has assumed that all relevant data will fit into main memory on the machine being used, and although the amount of memory installed in a computer has certainly grown over time, the size of data sets has been growing much faster. Handling data sets too big for the computer is not part of this book's focus, but in the following section we lay out some ideas for dealing with data sets that are just too big to hold in memory.

Given data that requires more storage than main memory can provide, we often proceed by breaking the data into pieces outside of R. For text data we use the command-line tools provided by the bash program (Free Software Foundation, 2016), a widespread command interpreter that comes standard on OS X and Linux systems and which is available for Windows as well. Bash includes tools such as `split`, which breaks up a data set by rows; `cut`, which extracts specific columns; and `shuf`, which permutes the lines in a file (which helps when taking random samples). These tools provide the ability to break the data into manageable pieces.

Another approach for manipulating large data, this time inside R (in main memory), was noted in Section 2.7. R has support for "long vectors," those whose lengths exceed $2^{31} - 1$, but these are not recommended for character data. Moreover, they are vectors rather than data frames, so the long vector approach does not mirror the data frame approach.

Sometimes the data can fit into memory, but the system is very slow performing any actions on it. In this case, the `data.table` packages might be useful; it advertises very fast subsetting and tabulation. Unfortunately, the syntax of the calls inside the `data.table` package is just foreign enough to be confusing. We will not cover the use of `data.table` in this book. If specific actions are slow, we can often gain insight by "profiling," which is where we determine which actions are using up large amounts of time. The "Writing R Extensions" manual has a section on profiling (Section 3) that might be useful here.

Other ways to speed up computations include compiling functions and running in parallel. We discuss these and other ways to make your functions faster in Section 5.5.

There are several add-in packages that provide the ability to maintain "pointers" to data on disk, rather than reading the data into main memory. The advantage of this approach is that the size of objects it can handle is limited only by disk storage, which can be expected to be huge. In exchange, of course, we have to expect processing to be much slower because so much disk access can be required. Packages with this approach include bigmemory (Kane *et al.*, 2013) and its relatives, and ff (Adler *et al.*, 2014) . The tm package (Feinerer *et al.*, 2008) does something similar for large bodies of text.

R is so popular in the data science world that there are many other programs, including big data storage mechanisms, for which R interfaces are available. This allows you to use familiar R commands to access these other mechanisms without having to understand the details of those programs. In this way, you can keep your data in a relational database or some storage facility that uses, for example, distributed memory for efficient retrieval. These approaches are beyond the scope of this book, but we have some discussion of acquiring data from a relational database in Chapter 6.

3.9   Chapter Summary and Critical Data Handling Tools

Matrices are important in many mathematical and statistical contexts, but they do not play an important role in data cleaning. However, learning about matrices makes learning about data frames more natural. Data frames also have the attributes of lists, so we have discussed lists as well in this chapter. But the important type of object in this chapter, and in R generally, is the data frame.

Data frames are often created by reading data in from outside R. We can also create them directly by combining vectors, matrices, or other data frames with the `cbind()`, `rbind()`, or `merge()` functions. We can add a character vector to a data frame with the dollar-sign notation, but whenever we supply a character vector as a column to be added to a data frame via `data.frame()` or `cbind()`, we need to specify the `stringsAsFactors = FALSE` argument.

Once our data has been placed into a data frame (say, one called `data1`), we often start by recording the classes of each column in a vector, using a command like `col.cl <- sapply(data1, function(x) class(x)[1])`. We use the function shown here rather than simply using the `class()` function, as we did earlier, to account for columns with a vector of two or more classes – usually these would be columns with one of the date classes like `POSIXct`. Keeping the names `data1` for the data and `col.cl` for the vector of classes in this example, we use commands such as these as part of our data cleaning process:

- `table(col.cl)` to tabulate the column classes. Often we will have an expectation that some proportion of the columns will be numeric, or that we will have, say, exactly 10 date columns. This is a good starting point to see if the data frame looks as we expect.
- `sapply(data1, function(x) sum(is.na(x)))` to count missing values by column. If the number of columns is large, we would often use `table()` on the result of the `sapply()` call to see if there are a few columns with a large number of missing values. It is also interesting if many columns report the same number of missing values. For example, if there are 56 different columns each with exactly 196 missing values, we might hypothesize that those are the very same 196 records in every column – and investigate them. In some cases, we might also count the number of negative values or values equal to 99 or some other "missing" code. Instead of the function above, then, we might substitute `function (x) sum (x < 0, na.rm = TRUE)` or something analogous.
- `sapply(data1[,col.cl == "numeric"], range)` to compute the ranges of numeric columns in a search for outliers or anomalies. If some columns have class "integer" we will need to address those as well, perhaps

using `col.cl %in% c("numeric", "integer")`. We might have to add the `na.rm = TRUE` argument, and we might also use other functions here such as `mean()`, `median()`, or `sd()`.

• `sapply(data1, function(x) length(unique(x)))` to count unique values by column. Since these numbers will count `NA` values, we might instead use `function(x) length(unique(na.omit(x)))`.

The `apply()` family functions provide a lot of power, but they need to be exercised carefully on data frames. The `apply()` function itself converts the data frame to a matrix first, and should only be used if all the columns of a data frame are of the same type. `Sapply()` tries to return a vector or matrix if it can, so if the return elements are of different classes they will often be converted. We suggest using `lapply()` unless you know that one of the other functions will succeed.

Another important focus of this chapter was on date (and time) objects. Although `Date` and `POSIXct` objects are implemented inside R in a numeric fashion, they are not quite numeric items in the usual ways. Similarly, while the `POSIXlt` object has some numeric features, it is best thought of as a list. So we deferred description of these objects until this chapter. Date and time data take up a lot of energy in the data cleaning process because the number of formats is large and variable and because of complications such as time zones and date arithmetic.

4

R Data, Part 3: Text and Factors

A lot of data comes in character ("string") form, sometimes because it really is text, and sometimes because it was originally intended to be numeric but included a small number of non-numeric items such as, for example, the word "Missing." Almost every data cleaning problem requires manipulating text in some way, to find entries that include particular strings, to modify column names, or something else. In this chapter, we describe some of the operations you can perform on character data. This includes extracting pieces of strings, formatting numbers as text, and searching for matches inside text.

However, there are really two ways that character data can be stored in R. One is as a vector of character strings, as we saw in Chapter 2. The tools we mentioned above are primarily for this sort of data. A second way text can appear in R is as a *factor*, which is a way of storing individual text entries as integers, together with a set of character labels that match the integers back to the text. Factors are important in many R modeling functions, but they can cause trouble. We discuss factors in Section 4.6.

One consideration has become much more important in recent years: handling text from alphabets other than the English one. We are very often called on to deal with text containing accented characters from Western European languages, and increasingly, particularly as a result of data from social media sources, we find ourselves with text in other alphabets such as Cyrillic, Arabic, or Korean. The Unicode system of representing all the characters from all the world's alphabets (together with other symbols such as emoji) is implemented in R through encodings including the very popular UTF-8; Section 4.5 discusses how we can handle non-English texts in R.

A Data Scientist's Guide to Acquiring, Cleaning, and Managing Data in R, First Edition.
Samuel E. Buttrey and Lyn R. Whitaker.
© 2018 John Wiley & Sons Ltd. Published 2018 by John Wiley & Sons Ltd.
Companion website: www.wiley.com/go/buttrey/datascientistsguide

4.1   Character Data

4.1.1   The `length()` and `nchar()` Functions

The length of a character vector is, as with other vectors, the number of elements it has. In the case of a character vector, you also might want to know how many characters are in each element. We use the `nchar()` function for that. Remember that some characters require two keystrokes to type (see Section 1.3.3 for a discussion), but they still count as only one character. In this example, we construct a character vector and observe how many characters each element has.

```
> (planets <- c("Mercury", "Venus", NA, "Mars"))
[1] "Mercury" "Venus"    NA          "Mars"
> length (planets) # Four elements
[1] 4
> nchar (planets)  # Count characters
[1]   7   5 NA   4
```

Notice that the number of characters in the missing value is itself missing. In older versions of R (through 3.2), `nchar()` reported the lengths of missing values as 2 – as if those entries were made up of the two characters NA. Starting with version 3.3, returning NA for that string's length is the default, though the older behavior can be requested by passing the `keepNA = FALSE` argument.

4.1.2   Tab, New-Line, Quote, and Backslash Characters

There are a few characters in R that need special treatment. We discussed this in Section 1.3.3, but it is worth repeating that if you want to enter a tab, a new-line character, a double quotation mark, or a backslash character, it needs to be "protected" – we say "escaped" – by a backslash. The leading backslash does not count as a character and is not part of the string – it's just a way to enter these characters that otherwise would be taken literally. As an example, consider entering into R this text: She wrote, "To enter a 'new-line,' type "\n" ." Normally, of course, we enclose text in quotation marks, but here R will think that the character string ends at the quotation mark preceding To. To remedy that, we escape the two inner double quotation marks. (Alternatively, we could enclose the entire quote in single, instead of double quotation marks. Then we would have to escape the two inner single quotation marks.) Moreover, the backslash is a special character. It, too, needs to be escaped. So to enter our quote into an R object, we need to type this:

```
> (quo <-
      "She wrote, \"To enter a 'new-line,' type \"\\n\".\"")
[1] "She wrote, \"To enter a 'new-line,' type \"\\n\".\""
```

```
> nchar (quo)
[1] 47
> cat (quo, "\n")
She wrote, "To enter a 'new-line,' type "\n"."
```

Notice the length of the string as given by nchar (). Even though it takes 52 keystrokes to type it in, there are only 47 characters in the string. There is no real difference between single and double quotes in R; if you create a string with single quotes, it will be displayed just as if it had been created with double quotes.

The backslash also escapes hexadecimal (base 16) and Unicode entries. Hexadecimal values describe entries in the ASCII table that converts binary values into text ones. For example, if you type "\x45", R returns the value from the ASCII table that has been given value 45 in base 16 (69 in decimal): the upper-case E. Passing the string "\x45" to nchar () returns the value 1. Unicode entries can be one or more characters, and arguments to nchar () help control what that function will return in more complicated examples. We talk more about Unicode in Section 4.5.

4.1.3 The Empty String

In an earlier chapter (Section 2.3.2), we saw that some vectors have length 0. We could create a character vector of length 0 with a command like character(0). However, something that is much more common in text handling is the empty string, which is a regular character string that does not happen to have any characters in it. This is indicated by "", two quote characters with nothing between them. That empty string has length () 1 but nchar () 0. Often the empty string will correspond to a missing value but not always. It is very common to see empty strings when, for example, reading data in from spreadsheets. In our experience, spreadsheets will sometimes produce empty strings, and other times produce strings of spaces (e.g., sometimes, when all the other entries in a column are two characters long, the empty cells of the spreadsheet may contain two spaces). Naturally, these different types of empty or blank strings will need to be addressed in any data cleaning task.

One area of confusion is when using table () on a character vector. The names () of the table will always be exactly right, but since those names are displayed without quotation marks, leading spaces are impossible to see.

```
> vec <- c (" ", " ", "", "    ", "", "2016", "",
            " 2016", "2016", "     ")
> table (vec)
vec
                    2016  2016
       3     2     2     1     2
> names (table (vec))
[1] ""       " "        "     "   " 2016" "2016"
```

In this example, we have items that are empty, items that consist of one space and three spaces, and items that look like 2016 but sometimes with a leading space.

The output of the table() function is not enough to determine the values being tabulated because of the leading spaces. We need the names() function applied to the table (or, equivalently, something like unique(vec)) to determine what the values are.

The nzchar() is a fast way to determine whether a string is empty or not; it returns TRUE for strings that have non-zero length and FALSE for empty strings (think of "nz" as indicating "non-zero").

4.1.4 Substrings

Another action we perform frequently in data cleaning is to extract a piece of a string. This might be extracting a year from a text-formatted date, for example, or grabbing the last five characters of a US mailing address, which hold the ZIP code. The tool for this is the substring() function, which takes a piece of text, an argument first giving the position of the first character to extract, and an argument last that gives the last position. The last argument defaults to 1 million, so unless your strings exceed that length, last can be omitted when we seek the end of a string. For example, to extract characters three and four from a string named dt containing "2017-02-03", we use the command substring (dt, 3, 4); the result is the string "17". (If the string has fewer than three characters, the empty string is returned.) To extract the final five characters we could use substring(dt, nchar(dt) - 4). This extracts characters 6–10 from a string of length 10, characters 21–25 from a string of length 25, and so on.

The substring() function works on vectors, so substring(vec, nchar(vec) - 4) will produce a vector the same length as vec, giving the last five (or up to five) characters of each of its entries. In this example, the first argument was a numeric vector, and in general both first and last may be vectors. This lets us use substring() to pull out parts of each element in a string vector depending on its contents (e.g., "all the characters after the first parenthesis").

We can exploit this vectorization to use substring() to break a string into its individual characters. The command substring(a, 1:nchar(a), 1:nchar(a)) does exactly that, just as if we had called substring(a, 1, 1), substring(a, 2, 2), and so on. Another, slightly more efficient, way to break a string into its characters is mentioned below under strsplit() (Section 4.4.7).

One of the strengths of substring() is that it can be used on the left side of an assignment operation. For example, to change the last two letters of each month's name to `"YZ"`, you could do this, using R's built-in `month.name` object, as we do in this example.

```
> new.month <- month.name
> substring (new.month, nchar (new.month) - 1) <- "YZ"
> new.month
 [1] "JanuaYZ"    "FebruaYZ"  "MarYZ"    "AprYZ"
 [5] "MYZ"        "JuYZ"      "JuYZ"     "AuguYZ"
 [9] "SeptembYZ"  "OctobYZ"   "NovembYZ" "DecembYZ"
```

4.1.5 Changing Case and Other Substitutions

R is case-sensitive, and so we often need to manipulate the case of characters (i.e., change upper-case letters to lower-case or vice versa). The `tolower()` and `toupper()` functions perform those operations, as does the equivalent `casefold()` function, which takes an argument called `upper` that describes the direction of the intended change (`upper = TRUE` means "change to upper case," with `FALSE`, the default, indicating "change to lower case"). Note that case-folding works with non-Roman alphabets in which that operation is defined, such as Cyrillic and Greek. The help page for these functions describes a more complicated approach that can capitalize the first letter in each word, which is particularly useful for multi-word names such as "kuala lumpur" or "san luis obispo."

A more general substitution facility is provided by the `chartr()` ("character translation") function. This takes two arguments that are vectors of characters, plus a string, and it changes each character in the first argument into the corresponding character in the second argument.

4.2 Converting Numbers into Text

Numbers get special treatment when they are converted into text because R needs to decide how they should be formatted. As we have seen earlier, R formats entries in a numeric vector for display, but that formatting is part of the print-out, not part of the vector, and the formatting can change when the vector changes. In this section, we describe some of the details of those formatting choices. We also describe how R uses scientific notation, and how you can create categorical versions of numeric vectors.

4.2.1 Formatting Numbers

Often it is convenient to represent a series of numbers in a consistent format for reporting. The primary tools for formatting are `format()` and `sprintf()`. `Format()` provides a number of useful options, particularly for lining up decimal points and commas. (The European usage, with a comma to denote the start of the decimal and a period to separate thousands, is also supported.) Of course, formatting strings nicely in R doesn't guarantee that those strings will line up nicely in a report; that will depend on which font is used to display the formatted strings. Still, `format()` is a fast and easy way to format a set of numbers in a common way. Important arguments are `digits`, to determine the number of digits, `nsmall` to determine the number of digits in the "small" part (i.e., to the right of the decimal point), `big.mark` to determine whether a comma is used in the "big" part, `drop0trailing`, which removes trailing zeros in the small part, and `zero.print`, which, if TRUE, causes zeros to be printed with spaces. (You can also specify an alternate character like a dot, which might be useful when most entries are zero.)

This example shows some of these arguments at work.

```
# Seven digits by default, decimals aligned
> format (c(1.2, 1234.56789, 0))
[1] "   1.200" "1234.568" "   0.000"
# Add comma separator
> format (c(1.2, 1234.56789, 0), big.mark=",")
[1] "   1.200" "1,234.568" "   0.000"
# Currency style, blank zeros
> format (c(1.2, 1234.56789, 0), digits = 6, nsmall=2,
          zero.print=F, width=2)
[1] "   1.20" "1234.57" "        "
```

In the last example, the `digits` and `nsmall` arguments had to be chosen carefully in order to produce exactly two digits to the right of the decimal point. (The `nsmall` argument describes the minimum, not the maximum, number of digits to be printed.) There are a few formatting tasks, including incorporating text and adding leading zeros, that `format()` is not prepared for, and these are handled by `sprintf()`.

The `sprintf()` function takes its name from a common function in the C language (the name evokes "string print, formatted"). This powerful function is complicated, and we just give a few examples here. The important point about `sprintf()` is the format string argument, which describes how each number is to be treated. (In R fashion, the format string can be a vector, in which case either that argument or the numerics being formatted may have to be recycled in the manner of Section 2.1.4.) A format string contains text, which gets reproduced in the function's output (this is useful for things such as dollar signs) and conversion strings, which describe how numbers and other variables should appear in that output. Conversion strings start with a percent sign and contain some optional modifiers and then a conversion character, which describes the manner of object being formatted. Although `sprintf()` can produce hexadecimal values and scientific notation (see the following discussion) with the proper conversion characters, the two most useful are i (or d) for integer values, f for double-precision numerics, and s for character strings.

So, for example, `sprintf("%f", 123)` formats 123 as a double precision using its default conversion options and produces the text `"123.000000"`, while `sprintf("%f", 123.456)` produces `"123.456000"`.

Much of the power in `sprintf()` comes from the modifiers. Primary among these are the field width and precision, two numbers separated by a period that give the minimum width (the total number of characters, including sign and decimal point) and the number of digits to the right of the decimal points, respectively. Other modifiers include the 0, to pad with leading zeros; the space modifier, which leaves a space for the sign if there isn't one (so that negative and positive numbers line up), and the + modifier, which produces plus signs for positive numbers. So, to continue the example, the format string in `sprintf("%9.1f", 123.456)` asks for a field width of 9 and a precision of 1, and the result is the nine-character string `"    123.5"`. The command `sprintf("%09.1f", 123.456)` asks for leading zeros and therefore produces `"0000123.5"`. The items to be formatted, and even the format string itself, can be vectors. This vectorization makes it straightforward to insert numbers into sentences like this:

```
costs <- c(1, 333, 555.55, 123456789.012)
# Format as integers using %d
> sprintf ("I spent $%d in %s", costs, month.name[1:4])
[1] "I spent $1 in January"     "I spent $333 in February"
[3] "I spent $555 in March"     "I spent $123456789 in April"
```

In this example, each element of `costs` and `month.name[1:4]` is used, in turn, with the format string.

The format strings are very flexible. We show two more examples here.

```
# Format as double-precision (%f) with default precision
> sprintf ("I spent $%f in %s", costs, month.name[1:4])
[1] "I spent $1.000000 in January"
[2] "I spent $333.000000 in February"
[3] "I spent $555.550000 in March"
[4] "I spent $123456789.012000 in April"
# Format as currency, without specifying field width
> sprintf ("I spent $%.2f in %s", costs, month.name[1:4])
[1] "I spent $1.00 in January"
[2] "I spent $333.00 in February"
[3] "I spent $555.55 in March"
[4] "I spent $123456789.01 in April"
```

One final feature of `sprintf()` is that field width or precision (but not both) can themselves be passed as an argument by specifying an asterisk in the format conversion string. This allows fine-tuning of the widths of output, which is useful in reporting. Suppose we wanted all four output strings from the last example to have the same length. We can compute the length of the largest number in costs (after rounding to two decimal points) and supply that length as the field width, as seen in this example.

```
> biggest <- max (nchar (sprintf ("%.2f", costs)))
> sprintf ("I spent $%*.2f in %s",
            biggest, costs, month.name[1:4])
[1] "I spent $        1.00 in January"
[2] "I spent $      333.00 in February"
[3] "I spent $      555.55 in March"
[4] "I spent $123456789.01 in April"
```

Although sprintf() is complicated, it is very handy for at least one job – generating labels that look like 001, 002, 003, and so on. The command sprintf("%03d", 1:100) will generate 100 labels of that sort.

4.2.2 Scientific Notation

Scientific notation is the practice of representing every number by an optional sign, a number between 1 and 10, and a multiplier of a power of 10. The choice that R makes to put a number into scientific notation depends on the number of significant digits required. For example, the number 123,000,050 is written 1.23e+08, but 123,000,051 is written 123000051. When one number in a vector (or matrix) needs to be represented in scientific notation, R represents them all that way, which can be helpful or annoying, depending on the job at hand. In this example, we show some of the effects of the way R displays numbers in scientific notation. Notice that the rules are slightly different for integer and for floating-point values.

```
> 100000              # Big enough to start scientific notation
[1] 1e+05
> c(1, 100000)        # Both numbers get scientific notation
[1] 1e+00 1e+05
> c(1, 100000, 123456)     # R keeps precision here
[1]      1 100000 123456
> as.integer (10000000 + 1)
[1] 10000001              # Integers are a little different
```

There is no easy way to change scientific notation for a single command. The R option scipen controls the "crossover" points between regular ("fixed") and scientific notation, which depends on the number of characters required to print the vector out. (This, in turn, depends on the number of digits R is prepared to display, which depends on the digits option.) Set options(scipen = 999) to disable all scientific notation, and options(scipen = -999) to require scientific notation everywhere – but don't forget to set it back to the default value of 0 as needed. (As with other options() calls, the value of scipen is re-set when you close and re-open R.) An alternative is to use the `format()` command with the `scientific = FALSE` option. This example shows the `format()` command at work on a large number.

```
> format (10000000)
[1] "1e+07"              # scientific notation
> format (100000000, scientific = FALSE)
[1] "100000000"
```

Notice that, like `sprintf()`, `format()` always produces a character string, which makes further numeric computation difficult.

4.2.3   Discretizing a Numeric Variable

Very often we construct a discretized, categorical version of a numeric vector with just a few levels for exploration or modeling purposes (we sometimes call this procedure "binning"). For example, we might want to convert a numeric vector into a categorical with levels "Small," "Medium," and "Large." The natural tool for this in R is the `cut()` function. The arguments are the vector to be discretized, the breakpoints, and, optionally, some labels to be applied to the new levels. The result of a call to `cut()` is a factor vector; we discuss factors in Section 4.6, but for the moment we will simply convert the result back to characters. In this example, we start with a numeric vector and bin them into three groups. We will set the boundary points at 4 and 7.

```
> vec <- c(1, 5, 6, 2, 9, 3, NA, 7)
> as.character (cut (vec, c(1, 4, 7, 10)))
[1] NA          "(4,7]"    "(4,7]"    "(1,4]"    "(7,10]"  "(1,4]"
[7] NA          "(4,7]"
```

The `cut()` function has some distracting quirks. By default, intervals do not include their left endpoint, so that in this example, the value 1 does not belong to any interval. This produces the NA in element 1 of the output; the second, of course, arises from the missing value in `vec`. The `include.lowest = TRUE` argument will force the leftmost breakpoint to belong to the leftmost bin. In this example, the number 1 would be found in the leftmost bin if `include.lowest = TRUE` were specified. Alternatively, the `right = FALSE` argument makes intervals include their left end and exclude their right (in which case `include.lowest = TRUE` actually refers to the largest of the breakpoints). In this example, any values larger than 10 would have produced NAs as well. This requires that you know the lower and upper limits of the data before deciding what the breakpoints need to be.

If the exact locations of the breakpoints are not important, `cut()` provides a straightforward way to produce bins of equal width or of approximately equal counts. The first is accomplished by specifying the `breaks` argument as an integer. In this case, cut () assigns every non-missing observation (even the lowest) to one of the bins. For bins of approximately equal counts, we can compute the quantiles of the numeric vector and use those as breakpoints. The following two examples show both of these approaches on a set of 100 numbers generated from R's random number generator with the standard normal distribution. We use the set.seed() function to initialize the random number generator; if you use this command your generator and ours should produce the same numbers. First we pass breaks as an integer to produce bins of approximately equal width.

```
> set.seed (246)
> vecN <- rnorm (100)
> table (cut (vecN, breaks = 5))
  (-3.18,-1.94]  (-1.94,-0.709]  (-0.709,0.522]
             2              21              52
  (0.522,1.75]    (1.75,2.99]
            20              5
```

In the following example, we use R's quantile() function to compute the minimum, quartiles and maximum of the vecN vector. (Other choices are possible through the use of the probs argument.) Once the quantiles are computed we can pass them as breakpoints to produce four bins with approximately equal counts – but, as before, cut () produces NA for the smallest value unless include.lowest = TRUE – and by default, table () omits NA values.

```
> quantile (vecN)
         0%          25%          50%          75%         100%
-3.17217563  -0.61809034  -0.06712505   0.45347704   2.98469969
> table (cut (vecN, quantile (vecN)))  # lowest value omitted
  (-3.17,-0.618]  (-0.618,-0.0671]   (-0.0671,0.453]
              24                25               25
  (0.453,2.98]
            25
> table (cut (vecN, quantile (vecN), include.lowest = TRUE))
  [-3.17,-0.618]  (-0.618,-0.0671]   (-0.0671,0.453]
              25                25               25
  (0.453,2.98]
            25
```

Notice how supplying include.lowest = TRUE changed the first bin from a half-open interval (indicated by the label starting with ()) to a closed one (label starting with [). In general, the default labels are somewhat unwieldy – a character value like " (-0.618,-0.0671] " will be difficult to manage. The cut () function allows us to pass in a vector of text labels using the labels argument.

4.3   Constructing Character Strings: Paste in Action

Character strings arise in data we bring in from other sources, but very often we need to construct our own. The primary tool for building character strings is the `paste()` function, plus its sibling `paste0()`. In its simplest form, `paste()` sticks together two character vectors, converting either or both, as necessary, from another class into a character vector first. By default R inserts a space in between the two. For example, `paste("a" ,"b")` produces the result `"a b"` while `paste(1 == 2, 1 + 2)` evaluates the two arguments, converts them to character (see Section 2.2.3) and produces `"FALSE 3"`.

   In practice, we prefer to control the character that gets inserted. We want a space sometimes, for example, when constructing diagnostic messages, but more often we want some other separator, in order to construct valid column names, for example. The `sep` argument to `paste()` allows us to specify the separator. Very often in our work we use a period, by setting `sep = "."`, or no separator at all, by setting `sep = ""`. In the latter case, we can also use the `paste0()` function, which according to the help file operates more efficiently in this case.

   What really gives `paste()` its power is that it handles vectors. If any of its arguments is a vector, `paste()` returns a vector of character strings, recycling (Section 2.1.4) shorter ones as needed. This gives us great flexibility in constructing sets of strings. For example, the command `paste0("Col", LETTERS)` produces a vector of the strings `"ColA"`, `"ColB"`, and so on, up to `"ColZ"`.

   A final useful argument to `paste()` is `collapse`, which combines all the strings of the vector into one long string, using the separator specified by the value of the `collapse` argument. Common choices are the empty string `""`, which joins the pieces directly, and the new-line and tab characters, when formatting text for output to tables.

   `Paste()` is such a big part of character manipulation in R that we think it important to show a few examples of how it works and where it can be useful.

4.3.1   Constructing Column Names

When a data frame is constructed from data without header names, R constructs names such as `V1` and `V2`. Normally, we will want to replace these with meaningful names of our own, but in big data sets the act of typing in those names is tedious and error-prone. Moreover it is often true that the names follow a pattern – for example, we might have a customer ID followed by 36 months of balance data from 2016 to 2018, followed by 36 months of payment data for the same years. One way to generate those latter

72 names is through the outer() function. This function operates on two vectors and performs another function on each pair of elements from the two vectors, producing a matrix of results. For example, outer(1:10, 1:10, "*") produces a 10 × 10 multiplication table. The command outer(month.abb, 2016:2018, paste, sep="."), similarly, produces a matrix. In this example, we show the first few rows of that matrix using the head() command.

```
> head (outer (month.abb, 2016:2018, paste, sep = "."), 3)
        [,1]         [,2]         [,3]
[1,]  "Jan.2016"  "Jan.2017"  "Jan.2018"
[2,]  "Feb.2016"  "Feb.2017"  "Feb.2018"
[3,]  "Mar.2016"  "Mar.2017"  "Mar.2018"
```

To construct column labels with Bal. on the front, we can simply paste that string onto the elements of the matrix. Remember that paste() converts its arguments into character vectors before operating, so the result of this operation is a vector of column labels, as shown in this example, where again we show only a few of the elements of the result.

```
> myout <- outer (month.abb, 2016:2018, paste, sep = ".")
> paste0 ("Bal.", myout) [1:3]
[1] "Bal.Jan.2016" "Bal.Feb.2016" "Bal.Mar.2016"
```

So to construct a vector with all 73 desired names, we could use a single command as in this example.

```
newnames <- c("ID", paste0 ("Bal.", myout),
                    paste0 ("Pay.", myout))
```

We note that outer() is not very efficient. For very big data sets, we might create separate vectors from the year part and the month part, and then paste them together. Suppose that the balance and payment values alternated, so the first two columns gave balance and payment for January 2016, the next two for February 2016, and so on. Then a straightforward way to construct the labels using paste() is by repeating the components as needed, with rep(), and then pasting the resulting vectors together:

```
# 2 values x 12 months x 3 years
part1 <- rep (c("Bal", "Pay"), 12 * 3)
# Double each month, repeat x 3
part2 <- rep (rep (month.abb, each = 2), 3)
part3 <- rep (2016:2018, each = 24)
newnames <- c("ID", paste (part1, part2, part3, sep = "."))
```

The task in this example could actually have been done more easily with expand.grid(). This function takes, as arguments, vectors of values and produces a data frame containing all combinations of all the values.

Since the output is a data frame, for many purposes you will want to specify `stringsAsFactors = FALSE`. The next step is to use `paste()` on the columns of the data frame. We use `paste()` regularly and in many contexts.

4.3.2 Tabulating Dates by Year and Month or Quarter Labels

Often we want to summarize vectors of dates (Section 3.6) across, for example, years, months, or calendar quarters. An easy way to do this is by pasting together identifiers of year and month, then using `table()` or `tapply()` to compute the relevant numbers of interest. We use `paste()` here because the built-in `months()` and `quarters()` functions do not produce the year as well (and the `format()` function does not extract quarters). In this example, we first generate 600 dates at random between January 1, 2015 and December 31, 2016 (a period of 731 days) and then tabulate them by quarter.

```
> set.seed (2016)
> dts <- as.Date (sample (0:730, size = 600),
                  origin = "2015-01-01")
> table (quarters (dts)) # Shows calendar quarter
 Q1  Q2  Q3  Q4
134 153 151 162
```

To combine both year and quarter, we can use `substring()` to extract the years, then paste them together with the quarters. (We could also have extracted the years with `format(dts, "%Y")`.) We put the years first in these labels so that the table labels are ordered chronologically. In this example, we paste the year and quarter, and then tabulate.

```
> table (paste0 (substring (dts, 1, 4), ".",
                 quarters (dts)))
2015.Q1 2015.Q2 2015.Q3 2015.Q4 2016.Q1 2016.Q2 2016.Q3
     72      71      75      81      62      82      76
2016.Q4
     81
```

To add months to the years, we could call the `months()` function and once again use `paste()` to combine the year and month information. Alternatively, we can use `format()` directly, as in this example. Notice, however, that `table()` sorts its entries alphabetically by name.

```
> (mtbl <- table (format (dts, "%Y.%B")))
   2015.April    2015.August  2015.December ...
           24             23             24 ...
```

To put these entries into calendar order explicitly, we can use `paste0()` to construct a vector of names to be used as an index. Then we can use that index to re-arrange the entries in the `mtbl` table. We show that in this example.

```
> (month.order <- paste0 (2015:2016, ".", month.name))
 [1] "2015.January"    "2016.February"   "2015.March" ...
> mtbl [month.order]
   2015.January  2016.February      2015.March ...
            24              21             27 ...
```

4.3.3   Constructing Unique Keys

Often we need to construct a single column that uniquely labels each row in a data frame. For example, we might have a table with one row for each customer in every month in which a transaction took place. Neither customer number nor month is enough to uniquely identify a transaction, but we can construct a unique key by pasting account number, year, and month. In this example, we would probably use a two-digit numeric month here and put year before month. That way an alphabetical ordering of the keys would put every customer's transactions together in increasing date order.

4.3.4   Constructing File and Path Names

In many data processing applications, our data is spread out over many files and we need to process all the files automatically. This might require constructing file names by pasting together a path name, a separator like /, and a file name. R can then loop over the set of file names to operate on each one. As an example, one way to get the full (absolute) file names of all the files in your working directory is by combining the name of the directory (retrieved with getwd()) and the names of the files (retrieved with list.files()). The command paste(getwd(), list.files(), sep = "/") produces a character vector of the absolute file names of files in the working directory. This is not quite the same as the output from list.files(full.names = TRUE); we discuss interacting with the file system in more detail in Section 5.4.

4.4   Regular Expressions

A *regular expression* is a pattern used in a tool to find strings that match the pattern. The patterns can be very complicated and perform surprisingly sophisticated matches, and in fact entire books have been written about regular expressions. While we cannot cover all the complexities of regular expressions in this book, we can make you knowledgeable enough to do powerful things.

We use regular expressions to find strings that match a rule, or set of rules, called a *pattern*. For example, the pattern a matches strings that include one or more instances of a anywhere in them. The pattern a8 matches strings with a8, with no intervening characters. Most characters, such as a and 8 in this example, match themselves. What gives regular expressions their power is the ability to add certain other characters that have special meaning to the pattern. The exact set of special characters differs across the different kinds of regular expression, but as a first example, the character ^ means "at the start of a line," and $ means "at the end of a line." So the pattern ^The matches every string that starts with The; end$ matches every string that ends with end, and ^No$ matches every string that consists entirely of No. By default, patterns are case-sensitive, but shortly we will see how to ignore case.

4.4.1 Types of Regular Expressions

The details of regular expressions differ from one implementation to the next, so a regular expression you write for R may not work in, for example, Python or another language. Actually, R supports two sorts of regular expressions: one is POSIX-style (named for the same POSIX standards group that gave us the POSIXt date objects), and the other is Perl-style, referring to the regular expressions used in the Perl language. (Specifically, if you need to look this up somewhere, the POSIX style incorporates the GNU extensions and the Perl style comes via the PCRE library.) By default, POSIX regular expressions are used in R.

4.4.2 Tools for Regular Expressions in R

There are three primary tools for regular expressions in R: grep() and its variants, regexpr() and its variants, and sub() and its variants. These three are similar in implementation. We start by describing grep() in some detail. The grep() function takes a pattern and a vector of strings, and returns a numeric vector giving the indices of the strings that match the pattern. With the value = TRUE argument, grep() returns the matching strings themselves. The related function grepl() (the letter l on the end standing for "logical") returns a logical vector with TRUE indicating the elements that match. In this example, we look through R's built-in state.name vector to find elements with the capital letter C.

```
> grep ("C", state.name)
[1]   5   6   7  33  40
> grep ("C", state.name, value = TRUE)
[1] "California"      "Colorado"          "Connecticut"
[4] "North Carolina" "South Carolina"
> grep ("^C", state.name, value = TRUE)
[1] "California"  "Colorado"    "Connecticut"
```

The first call to grep() produces a vector of indices. These five numbers show the locations in state.name where strings containing C can be found. With value = TRUE, the names of the matching states are returned. In the final example, we search only for strings that start with C.

Several other arguments are also important. First, the `ignore.case` argument defaults to `FALSE`, but when set to `TRUE`, it allows the search to ignore whether letters are in upper- or lower-case. Second, setting `invert = TRUE` reverses the search – that is, `grep()` produces the indices of strings that do not match the pattern. (The `invert` argument is not available for `grepl()`, but of course you can use `!` applied to the output of `grepl()` to produce a logical vector that is `TRUE` for non-matchers.) Third, `fixed = TRUE` suspends the rules about patterns and simply searches for an exact text string. This is particularly useful when you know your pattern, and also it has a special character in it – such as, for example, a negative amount indicated with parentheses, such as `($1,634.34)`. To continue an earlier example, `grep("^The", vec)` finds the entries of `vec` that start with the three characters `The`, whereas `grep("^The", vec, fixed = TRUE)` finds the entries that include the four characters `^The` anywhere in the string.

A fourth useful argument is `perl`, which, when set to `TRUE`, leads the `grep` functions to use Perl-type regular expressions. Perl-type regular expressions have many strengths, but for this development we will describe the default, POSIX style. Finally, all of these regular expression functions permit the use of the `useBytes` argument, which specifies that matching should be done byte by byte, rather than character by character. This can make a difference when using character sets in which some characters are represented by more than one byte, such as UTF-8 (see Section 4.5).

4.4.3 Special Characters in Regular Expressions

We have seen how `^` and `$` match, respectively, the beginning and end of a line. There are a number of other special characters that have specific meanings in a regular expression. In order for one of these special characters to be used to stand for itself, it needs to be "protected" by a backslash. We talk more about the way backslashes multiply in R regular expressions in the following section.

Table 4.1 lists the special characters in R's implementation of POSIX regular expressions. Many implementations of regular expressions work on lines of text in a file, so we use the word "line" here synonymously with "element of a character vector."

4.4.4 Examples

In this section, we show our first examples of using regular expressions to locate matching strings. Remember that, by default, `grep()` gives the indices of the matching strings; pass `value = TRUE` to get the strings themselves and use `grepl()` to get a logical indication of which strings match. In these functions, a string matches or does not – there is no notion of the position within a string where a match takes place. The tool for that is `regexpr()`, described

Table 4.1 Special characters in R (POSIX) regular expressions

Char	Name	Purpose	Example
		Matching characters	
.	Period	Match any character	t.e matches strings with tae, tbe
			t9e, t;e, and so on, anywhere
[ ]	Brackets	Match any character	t[135]e matches t1e, t3e, t5e;
		between them	t[1-5]e matches t1e, t2e, ..., t5e,
			but note: [a-d] might mean [abcd]
			or [aAbBcCdD], depending on your
			computer. See "character ranges"
^	Caret	(i) Start of line	^L matches lines starting with L
		(ii) "Not" when appear-	t[^h]e matches lines containing t,
		ing first in brackets	then something *not* an h, then e
$	Dollar	End of line	the$ matches lines ending with the
|	Pipe	"Or" operator	th|sc matches either th or sc
( )	Parentheses	Grouping operators	
\\	Backslash	Escape character	See text
		Repetition characters	
{ }	Braces	Enclose repetition operators	(a|b){3} matches lines with three (a or b)'s in a row, for example, aba, bab, ...
,	Comma	Separate repetition operators	j{2,4} matches jj, jjj, jjjj
*	Asterisk	Match 0 or more	ab* matches a, ab, abb, ...
+	Plus	Match 1 or more	ab+ matches ab, abb, abbb, ...
?	Question mark	Match 0 or 1	ab? matches a or ab

in Section 4.4.5. We start by creating a vector of strings that contain the string sen in different cases and locations.

```
> sen <- c("US Senate", "Send", "Arsenic", "sent", "worsen")
> grep ("Sen", sen)              # which elements have "Sen"?
[1] 1 2
> grep ("Sen", sen, value = TRUE)      # elements with "Sen"
[1] "US Senate" "Send"
> grep ("[sS]en", sen, value = TRUE)   # either case "S"
[1] "US Senate" "Send"       "Arsenic"   "sent"      "worsen"
> grep ("sen", sen, value = TRUE,      # upper or lower-case
        ignore.case = T)
```

```
[1] "US Senate" "Send"        "Arsenic"    "sent"       "worsen"
> grep ("^[sS]en", sen, value = T)       # start "Sen" or "sen"
[1] "Send" "sent"
> grep ("sen$", sen, value = T)          # end with "sen"
[1] "worsen"
```

The first grep() produces the indices of elements that match the pattern – this is useful for extracting the subset of items that match. The second grep() uses value = TRUE to returns the element themselves. These simple examples start to show the power of regular expressions. That power is multiplied by the ability to detect repetition, as we see next.

Repetition

The second part of Table 4.1 describes some repetition operators. Often we seek not a single character, but a set of matching characters – a series of digits, for example. The regular expression repetition operator ? allows for zero or one matches, essentially making the match optional; the * allows for zero or more, and the + operator allows for one or more matches. So the pattern 0+ matches one or more consecutive zeros. Since the dot character matches any character, the combination .+ means "a sequence of one or more characters"; this combination appears frequently in regular expressions. We also often see the similar pattern .* for "zero or more characters." The following example shows how we can match strings with extraneous text using repetition operators. We start by creating a vector of strings, and our goal is to find elements of the vector that start with Reno and are followed at some point later in the string by a ZIP code (five digits).

```
> reno <- c("Reno", "Reno, NV 895116622", "Reno 911",
            "Reno Nevada 89507")
> grep ("Reno.+[0-9]{5}", reno, value = TRUE)
[1] "Reno, NV 895116622" "Reno Nevada 89507"
```

Here, the .+ accounts for any text after the o in Reno and the [0-9]{5} describes the set of five digits. It is tempting to add spaces to your pattern to make it more readable, but this is a mistake; the regular expression will then take the spaces literally and require that they appear. Notice that the nine-digit number was also matched by the {5} repetition, since the first five of the nine digits satisfy the requirement.

We end this section with a more complicated example. Here, we search for strings with dates in the form of a one- or two-digit numeric day, a month name (as a three-letter abbreviation), and a four-digit year number, when there might be text between any of these pieces. This example shows the text to be matched.

```
> dt <- c("Balance due 16 Jun or earlier in 2017",
          "26 Aug or any day in 3018",
          "'76 Trombones' marched in a 1962 film",
```

```
"4 Apr 2018", "9Aug2006",
"99 Voters May Register in 20188")
```

The pieces of the regular expression to detect the dates are these. First, we can have leading text, so `.*` will match that if it is present. Second, `[0-3]?[0-9]` matches a one-digit number (since the first digit is optional, as indicated by the ?) or a two-digit number less than 40. Next, there is (optional) additional text, followed by a set of month names. The month-related part of the pattern looks like `(Jan|Feb|Mar...|Dec)`, where the pipes denote that any month will match and the parentheses make this a single pattern. (The abbreviations in the pattern will match a full name in the text.) Finally, we match some more additional text, followed by four digits that have to start with a 1 or a 2. We construct the month-related part of the pattern first by using `paste()` with the `collapse` argument.

```
> (mo <- paste (month.abb, collapse = "|"))
[1] "Jan|Feb|Mar|Apr|May|Jun|Jul|Aug|Sep|Oct|Nov|Dec"
> re <- paste0 (".*[0-3]?[0-9].*(", mo, ").*[1-2][0-9]{3}")
> grep (re, dt, value = TRUE)
[1] "Balance due 13 Jun or earlier in 2017"
[2] "26 Aug or any day in 2018"
[3] "9Aug2006"
[4] "99 Voters May Register in 20188"
```

Notice that the `mar` in `marched` does not match the month abbreviation `Mar`. However, the `99` in the final string matches the day portion of our pattern. That is because the `[0-3]` is optional; the first 9 matches in the `[0-9]` pattern and the second, in the `.*` pattern. Moreover, the five-digit year `20188` in that string matches the pattern `[1-2][0-9]{3}` because its first four digits do. We see how to refine this example later in the section – but regular expressions are tricky!

The Pain of Escape Sequences

Special characters give regular expression much of their power. But sometimes we need to use special characters literally – for example, we might want to find strings that contain the actual dollar sign $. A dollar sign in a pattern normally indicates the end of a line; to use it literally in a pattern it needs to be "escaped" with a backslash. So in order for the regular expression "engine" to look for a dollar sign, we need to pass it the pattern `\$`. But remember that to type a backslash into R, we need to type *two* backslashes, since R also uses the backslash as the character that "protects" certain other characters (in strings like `\n` for new-line). That is, we have to type `\\$` in R so that the engine can see `\$` and know to search for a dollar sign. In this example, we create a vector of character strings and search for a dollar sign among them. Remember that $ matches the end of a string. In the first `grep()` command below, the pattern $ matches every element in the vector that has an end – all of them.

```
> vec <- c("c:\\temp", "/bin/u", "$5", "\n", "2 back: \\\\")
> grep ("$", vec)              # Indices of elements with ends
[1] 1 2 3 4 5
> grep ("\$", vec, value = TRUE)
Error: '\$' is an unrecognized escape...
> grep ("\\$", vec, value = TRUE)
[1] "$5"
```

The pattern \\$ looks to R as if we are constructing a special "protected" character such as \n or \t. Since there is no such character in R, we see an error. The next command produces the elements of vec that contain dollar signs since value = TRUE; in this case, the only element that matches is $5.

Other special characters also need to be escaped. To search for a dot, use \\.; to search for a left parenthesis, use \\(, and so on. The "pain" of this section's title refers to searching for the backslash itself. Since a backslash is represented as \\, and we need to pass two of them to the engine, the pattern for finding backslashes in a string is \\\\. This looks like four characters, but it's actually two (as nchar ("\\\\") will confirm). The first tells the regular expression engine to take the second literally.

Backslashes are fortunately pretty rare in text, but they do arise in path names in the Windows operating system. In this example, we show how we can locate strings containing the backslash character.

```
> grep ("\\", vec)
Error in grep("\\", vec) :
 invalid regular expression '\', reason 'Trailing backslash'
> grep ("\\\\", vec, value = TRUE)          # elements with \
[1] "c:\\temp"    "2 back: \\\\"
> grep ("\\\\\\\\", vec, value = TRUE)       # two backslashes
[1] "2 back: \\\\"
```

In the first command, the backslash \\ in valid in R, but because the regular expression engine uses the backslash as well, it expects a second character (like $ in our example above). When no second character is found, grep() produces an error. The second example shows the elements of vec that contain a backslash. Notice that the \n character in position 4 is a single character. The backslash depicts its special nature but is not part of the actual character. The final pattern matches the string with two backslashes.

The fixed = TRUE argument can alleviate some of the pain when searching for text that includes special characters. In this example, we repeat the searches above using fixed = TRUE.

```
> grep ("\\", vec, value = TRUE, fixed = TRUE)          # one \
[1] "c:\\temp"    "2 back: \\\\"
> grep ("\\\\", vec, value = TRUE, fixed = TRUE)         # two \
[1] "2 back: \\\\"
```

As a final example in this section, we show how we can use the pipe character | to find elements of vec with either forward slashes or backslashes.

```
> grep ("\\\\|/", vec, value = TRUE)
[1] "c:\\temp"     "/bin/u"     "2 back: \\\\"
> grep ("\\|/", vec, value = TRUE, fixed = TRUE)
character(0)
```

In the first command, we found strings containing either a backslash (\\\\) or forward slash (/), the two separated by the pipe character indicating "or." In the second command, we used fixed = TRUE to look for strings containing the literal text \ | / in that order – and of course none was found.

Character Ranges and Classes

We saw earlier how we can match ranges of digits by enclosing them in square brackets as [0-9]. This extends to other sets of characters. For example, we might want to match any of the lower-case letters, or any punctuation character, or any of the letters A–G of the musical scale. It is easy to specify a range of characters using square brackets and a hyphen, so [a-z] matches a lower-case letter and [A-G] matches an upper-case musical note. To match musical notes given in either case, we can combine a range with the pipe character: [A-G] | [a-g] matches any of those seven letters in either case. To include a hyphen in the pattern, put it first or last in the brackets. (You can also put an opening square bracket in a set or range, but to include a closing square bracket, you will need to escape it so that the set isn't seen as ending with that character.) So, for example, the range [X-Z] matches "any of the letters X, Y or Z," and includes Y, whereas the set [XZ-] matches "any of X, Z, or hyphen" and does not.

We can negate a character class or range by preceding it with the caret character ^. So the set [^XZ-] matches any characters other than X, Z, or hyphen. Notice that the caret must be inside the brackets; outside, it matches the start of the line as we saw above. A caret elsewhere than the first character is interpreted literally – that is, it matches the caret character.

There is a predefined set of *character classes* that makes it easy to specify certain common sets. These include [:lower:], [:upper:], and [:alpha:] for lower-case, upper-case, and any letters; [:digit:] for digits; [:alnum:] for alphanumeric character (letters or numbers); [:punct:] for punctuation; and a few more (see the help pages). Notice that the name of the class includes the square brackets; to use these in a regular expression they need to be enclosed in another set of square brackets. So, for example, the pattern [[:digit:]] matches one digit, and [^[:digit:]] matches any character that is not a digit. We start this example by showing how to identify strings that include, or do not include, upper-case letters.

```
> vec <- c("1234", "6", "99 Balloons", "Catch 22", "Mannix")
> grep ("[[:upper:]]", vec, value = TRUE)   # any upper-case
```

```
[1] "99 Balloons" "Catch 22"    "Mannix"
> grep ("[^[:upper:]]", vec, value = TRUE)  # any non-upper
[1] "1234"        "6"           "99 Balloons" "Catch 22"
[5] "Mannix"
> grep ("^[^[:upper:]]+$", vec, value = TRUE) # no upper
[1] "1234" "6"
```

The first grep() uses the [:upper:] character class to identify strings with at least one upper-case character in them. It is tempting to think that the second regular expression, [^[:upper:]], will find strings consisting only of non-upper-case characters, but as you can see the result is something different. In fact, this pattern matches every string that has at least one non-upper-case character. The last example shows how to identify strings consisting entirely of these characters – we specify that a sequence of one or more non-upper-case characters (i.e., [^[:upper:]] followed by +) should be all that can be found on the line (i.e., between the ^ and the $).

Some classes are so commonly used that they have aliases. We can use \d for [:digit:] and \s for [:space:], and \D and \S for "not a digit," "not a space." (Here, "space" includes tab and possibly other more unusual characters.) This makes it easy to, for example, find strings that contain no digits at all, as we see in this example.

```
> grep ("^[^[:digit:]]+$", vec, value = TRUE) # long way
[1] "Mannix"
> grep ("^\\D*$", vec, value = TRUE)         # shorter
[1] "Mannix"
```

Word Boundaries

Often we require that a match take place on a word boundary, that is, at the beginning or end of a word (which can be a space or related character such as tab or new-line, or at the beginning or end of the string). Word boundaries are indicated by \b, or by the pair \< and \>. The characters that are considered to go into a word include all the alphanumeric (non-space) characters. Recall our earlier example where we tried to locate strings with dates included – such as, for example, "4 Apr 2018". Our earlier effort inadvertently matched a year with the value 20188. Using the word-boundary characters, we can specify that, in order to match, a string must include a word with exactly four digits. This example shows how that might be done.

```
> (newvec <- grep ("\\<\\d{4}\\>", dt, value = TRUE))
[1] "Balance due 16 Jun or earlier in 2017"
[2] "26 Aug or any day in 3018"
[3] "'76 Trombones' marched in a 1962 film"
[4] "4 Apr 2018"
> grep (mo, newvec, value = TRUE)
[1] "Balance due 16 Jun or earlier in 2017"
```

```
[2]  "26 Aug or any day in 3018"
[3]  "4 Apr 2018"
```

In the first command, we found strings that contained words of exactly four dig-its and saved the result into the new item `newvec`. The second command then searched for the month string in that new vector. We did not look for the days in this example, but in practice we very often use multiple passes (sometimes with `invert = TRUE`) in order to extract the set of strings we need. It may be more computationally efficient to call `grep()` only once for any problem, but that may not be the fastest route overall.

4.4.5   The `regexpr()` Function and Its Variants

While `grep()` identifies strings that match patterns, the `regexpr()` function is more precise: it returns the location of the (first) match within the string – that is, the number of the first character of the match. We can use this information to not only identify strings that contain numbers but also extract the number itself. This example shows the result of calling `regexpr()` with a pattern that looks for the first stand-alone integer in each string. It is not enough to extract a set of digits because that would match strings such as `11-dimensional` or `B2B`. Word boundaries provide the mechanism for specifying an integer, as seen here:

```
> (regout <- regexpr ("\\<\\d+\\>", dt))
[1] 13   1   2   1 -1   1
attr(,"match.length")
[1]  2   2   2   1 -1   2
attr(,"useBytes")
[1] TRUE
```

The `regexpr()` function returns a vector (plus some other information we describe as follows). The vector, which starts with `13`, shows the number of the character where the first integer begins. For example, the number `16` in the first element of `dt` appears starting at the 13th character in that string, the number `26` starts in the 1st character of the second element, and so on. The `-1` in the fifth position indicates that string does not contain an integer as a word.

The function also returns attributes, extra pieces of information attached to its output. The `match.length` attribute in this case gives the length of the match – so the first element is 2 because the integer in the first string is two characters long; the fourth is 1 because the integer in the fourth string is one character long. (We will not need the `useBytes` attribute.) We could extract the `match.length` vector using the `attr()` function, and then use `sub-string()` to extract the numbers in the strings. But a more convenient alter-native is provided by `regmatches()`, which takes the initial string and the output of `regexpr()` and performs the extraction for us, as in this example.

```
> regmatches (dt, regout)
[1] "13" "26" "76" "4"  "99"
```

There are five entries in this vector because only five of the strings contained integers. (The -1 values in the original vector remind you of which strings did not produce values here.)

Finding All Matches

The regexpr() function finds the first instance of a match in a vector of strings. To find all the matches is only a little more complicated. We use the gregexpr() function, the g evoking "global." The return value of gregexpr() is a list, not a vector, because some strings may contain many integers. However, regmatches() works on this return value just as it does for regexpr(). In this example, we extract all of the integers from each of our strings in one command.

```
# Note that some output from this command is suppressed
> (gout <- gregexpr ("\\<\\d+\\>", dt))
[[1]]
[1] 13 34
attr(,"match.length")
[1] 2 4
...
[[2]]
[1]  1 22
attr(,"match.length")
[1] 2 4
...
[[6]]
[1]  1 27
attr(,"match.length")
[1] 2 5
...
> regmatches (dt, gout)
[[1]]
[1] "13"   "2017"

[[2]]
[1] "26"   "2018"

[[3]]
[1] "76"   "1962"

[[4]]
[1] "4"    "3018"

[[5]]
character(0)
```

```
[[6]]
[1] "99"    "20188"
> matrix (as.numeric (unlist (regmatches (dt, gout))),
          ncol = 2, byrow = TRUE)
      [,1]  [,2]
[1,]   13  2017
[2,]   26  2018
[3,]   76  1962
[4,]    4  3018
[5,]   99 20188
```

Here, the result of the call to regmatches () is a list of length 6, one for each string in the original dt. The fifth entry in the list is empty because the fifth entry of dt had no integers that were words. The final command shows one way you might form the list into a two-column numeric matrix, a useful step on the way to constructing a data frame. A second approach would use do.call () and rbind ().

Greedy Matching

By default, regular expression matching is "greedy" – that is, matches are as long as possible. As an example consider using the pattern \\d.*\\d to find a digit, zero or more characters, and a second digit in the string "4 Apr 3018". You might expect the regular expression engine to find the string "4 Apr 3", but in fact it gathers as much as possible: "4 Apr 3018", stopping at the last 8. Adding a question mark makes the match "ungreedy" (or "lazy") – so that \\d.*?\\d produces "4 Apr 3".

4.4.6 Using Regular Expressions in Replacement

In addition to finding matches, R has tools that allow you to replace the part of the string that matches a pattern with a new string. These are sub (), which replaces the first matching pattern, and gsub (), which replaces all the matching patterns. The replacement text is not a regular expression. For example, here is a vector of four character strings. In the first example, we replace the first lower-case i with the number 9. In the second, we replace the first instance of either i or I with 9, and in the last, we replace all instances of either one with 9.

```
> (mytxt <- c("This is", "what I write.",
              "Is it good?", "I'm not sure."))
[1] "This is" "what I write." "Is it good?" "I'm not sure."

> sub ("i", "9", mytxt)      # replace first i with 9
[1] "Th9s is" "what I wr9te." "Is 9t good?" "I'm not sure."

> sub ("[iI]", "9", mytxt)   # replace first (i or I) with 9
[1] "Th9s is" "what 9 write." "9s it good?" "9'm not sure."
```

```
> gsub("[iI]", "9", mytxt)    # replace all (i or I) with 9
[1] "Th9s 9s" "what 9 wr9te." "9s 9t good?" "9'm not sure."
```

Sometimes the text being matched is needed in the replacement. This can sometimes be done very neatly using "backreferences." When a regular expression is enclosed in parentheses, its matching strings get labeled by integers and can be re-used in the replacement string by referring to them as \1, \2, and so on – of course, to be typed into R as \\1, \\2, and so on. In this example, we are given names in the form "Firstname Lastname" and asked to produce names of the form "Lastname, Firstname."

```
> folks <- c("Norman Bethune", "Ralph Bunche",
                "Lech Walesa", "Nelson Mandela")
> sub ("([[:alpha:]]+) ([[:alpha:]]+)", "\\2, \\1", folks)
[1] "Bethune, Norman" "Bunche, Ralph"   "Walesa, Lech"
[4] "Mandela, Nelson"
```

The first argument to the sub() command gave the pattern: a series of one or more letters (captured as backreference 1), a space, and another series of letters (backreference 2). The replacement part gives the second backreference, then a comma and space, and then the first backreference. We note that this task is more complicated with people whose names use three words, since sometimes the second word is a middle or maiden name (as with John Quincy Adams or Claire Booth Luce) and sometimes it is part of the last name (Martin Van Buren, Arthur Conan Doyle) – and of course some people's names require four or more words (Edna St Vincent Millay, Aung San Suu Kyi).

4.4.7 Splitting Strings at Regular Expressions

It is common to want to split a string whenever a particular character occurs. This is more or less the opposite of the paste() operation. For example, in our work we often construct a unique key to identify each of our observations, using paste(). We might combine a company identifier, transaction identifier, and date, with a command like key <- paste (co.id, tr.id, date, sep = "-"). Of course, in this example, the sep = "-" argument specifies a hyphen as the separator.

At a later time, it might be necessary to "unpaste" those keys into their individual parts. The strsplit() function performs this duty. In this example, strsplit(key, "-") produces a list with one entry for each string in key. Each entry is a vector of parts that result when the key is broken at its hyphens; so if one key looked like 00147-NY-2016-K before the split, the corresponding entry in the output of strsplit() would be a vector with four elements (and no hyphens). If the key had two hyphens in a row, there would have been an empty string in the output vector. In this example, we show the effect of strsplit() on several keys constructed using hyphens.

```
> keys <- c("CA-2017-04-02-66J-44", "MI-2017-07-17-41H-72",
            "CA-2017-08-24-Missing-378")
> (key.list <- strsplit (keys, "-"))
[[1]]
[1] "CA"    "2017" "04"   "02"    "66J"   "44"

[[2]]
[1] "MI"    "2017" "07"   "17"    "41H"   "72"

[[3]]
[1] "CA"       "2017"    "08"     "24"      "Missing" "378"
```

In cases like these, where the number of pieces is the same in every key, it is common to construct a matrix or data frame from the parts. We saw a similar example using the output of regmatches() in an earlier section. Here, we construct a character matrix in the same way. We can then use data.frame() to make the matrix into a data frame, although the columns of the latter will be character unless you then convert them explicitly.

```
> matrix (unlist (key.list), ncol = 6, byrow = TRUE)
     [,1]  [,2]    [,3]  [,4] [,5]      [,6]
[1,] "CA" "2017" "04" "02" "66J"     "44"
[2,] "MI" "2017" "07" "17" "41H"     "72"
[3,] "CA" "2017" "08" "24" "Missing" "378"
```

Note that the alternative do.call("rbind", key.list) produces the same character matrix.

Unlike the sep argument to paste(), which is a character string, the second argument to strsplit() can be a regular expression. The strsplit() function also accepts the fixed, perl, and useBytes arguments as the other regular expression operators do. Because that second argument can be a regular expression, extra work is required to split at periods. The command strsplit(key, ".") produces a split at *every* character, since the period can represent any character, so it returns an unhelpful vector of empty strings. The command strsplit(key, "\\.") or its alternatives, strsplit(key, "[.]") or strsplit(key, ".", fixed = TRUE) will split at periods. Remember that the output of strsplit() is always a list, even if only one character string is being split.

4.4.8   Regular Expressions versus Wildcard Matching

The patterns used in regular expressions are more complicated, and more powerful, than the sort of *wildcard matching* that many users will have seen as part of a command-line interpreter. In wildcard matching, the only special characters are *, meaning "match zero or more characters," and ?, meaning "match exactly one character." So, for example, the wildcard-type pattern *an? matches any string that includes an followed by exactly one more character. R does not use wildcard matching, but it does allow you to convert a wildcard pattern, which R calls a "glob," into a regular expression, by means of the glob2rx() function. For example, glob2rx("*an?") produces "^.*an.$". Notice the ^ and $ sign; glob2rx() adds those by default, but they can be omitted with the trim.head = TRUE and trim.tail = TRUE arguments.

4.4.9 Common Data Cleaning Tasks Using Regular Expressions

Regular expressions make it possible to do many complicated things to text, specific to your particular problem and data. There are a few operations, though, that seem to be called for in a lot of data cleaning tasks. In these sections, we describe how to do some of these.

Removing Leading and Trailing Spaces

One frequent need in text handling is removing leading and trailing spaces from text. The regular expression "^ *" matches any string with leading spaces, while " *$" matches one with trailing spaces. To match either or both of these, we combine them with the pipe character, and use gsub() instead of sub() since some strings will have both kinds of matches – as in this example.

```
> gsub ("^ *| *$", "", c(" Both Kinds ", "Trailing    ",
                        "Neither", "    Leading"))
[1] "Both Kinds" "Trailing"    "Neither"    "Leading"
```

Here, the embedded space inside "Both Kinds" does not match – it is neither leading nor trailing – and is not deleted. The command gsub(" ", "", vec) will remove all spaces in every element of vec.

Converting Formatted Currency into Numeric

We see something similar in formatted currency amounts such as $12,345.67. Here, we need to remove the currency symbol and the comma before converting to numeric. If the only currency sign we expected to encounter was the dollar sign, we might do this:

```
> as.numeric (gsub ("\\$|,", "", "$12,345.67"))
[1] 12345.67
```

Recall that the as.numeric() will accept and ignore leading and trailing spaces. More generally, we might delete any non-numeric leading characters like this:

```
> as.numeric (gsub ("^[^0-9.]|,", "", "$12,345.67"))
[1] 12345.67
> as.numeric (gsub ("^[^[:digit:]]|,", "", "$12,345.67"))
[1] 12345.67
```

In this example, the first ^ indicates "a string that starts with · · ·." The [^0-9.] bracketed expression starts with a ^, meaning "not," so that part means "anything except a number or a dot." The |, sequence says "or a comma," so the regular expression will find any leading non-numeric (and non-period) characters, as well as any commas anywhere, and delete them all.

Removing HTML Tags

Occasionally, we come across text formatted with HTML tags. These are instructions to the browser regarding display of the material, so, for example, Bold formats the word "Bold" in bold face. Other tags indicate headings, delineate cells of tables, paragraphs, and so on. It can be useful to strip out all of the formatting information as a first step toward processing the text. Every tag starts with the angle bracket < and ends with >. So, given a character string txt, the command gsub("<.*?>", "", txt) will delete all the brackets (the < and > are treated literally) and all the text between any pair (here, the .* indicates "zero or more characters" and the ? instructs the engine to match in a lazy way).

Converting Linux/OS X File Paths to R and Windows Ones

The Windows file system uses the backward slash, \, to separate directories in a file path, whereas Linux and Mac operating systems use the forward one, /. Suppose we are given a Linux-style path like /usr/local/bin, and we want to switch the direction of the slashes. The command gsub("/", "\\\\", "/usr/local/bin") will produce the desired result. To make the change in the other direction, the command gsub("\\\\", "/", "\\usr\\local\\bin") will convert Windows path separators to Linux ones. As an alternative in this case, we can specify the matching pattern exactly with a command like gsub("\\", "/", "\\usr\\local\\bin", fixed = TRUE).

4.4.10 Documenting and Debugging Regular Expressions

Regular expressions are complicated, and debugging them is hard. It is annoying (and time-consuming) to try to fix a regular expression that you know is wrong, but you're not sure why. It is worse to have one that is wrong and not knowing it. There are online aids to diagnosing problems with regular expressions that we have found useful. An Internet search will turn up a number of helpful sites – but make sure that the site you find describes the regular expression type (POSIX with GNU extensions or PCRE) that you use. Because regular expressions are complicated, be sure to document them as well as you can. Write out the patterns you expect to match and the rules you use to match them.

4.5   UTF-8 and Other Non-ASCII Characters

4.5.1   Extended ASCII for Latin Alphabets

Up until now we have implicitly been dealing only with the "usual" characters, those found on a keyboard used in English-speaking countries. The starting point for the way characters are displayed is ASCII, a table that gives characters and the corresponding standard digital representations. ASCII provides representations of only 128 characters, many of which are unprintable "control" characters, such as tab, new-line, or the command to ring the bell of an old-fashioned teleprinter. Much of the text we handle in our work is of this sort, but ASCII does not include codes for letters with accents or other diacritical marks, required for many Western European languages. Every computer today honors a much broader character set, often based on a standard named `latin1`, but realized in slightly different ways by different manufacturers. For example, Windows uses its own "Win-1252" table, which includes some characters not found in `latin1`, such as the Euro currency symbol and the curly "smart quotes," and Apple OS X uses a table called "Mac OS Roman." Each character has a hexadecimal representation – for example, the upper-case E with a circumflex, Ê, has code `ca`, and typing `"\xca"` into R (with quotation marks because this is text) will produce that character. The `\x` is used to introduce hexadecimal notation in R, and it is case-sensitive – `\X` may not be used – but the hexadecimal digits themselves are not case-sensitive. Entering text in hexadecimal is different from entering numeric values in hexadecimal. Typing `0xca` produces the number whose hexadecimal value is `ca`, that is, the number 202. Typing `"\xca"` produces the character whose code in the ASCII table is `ca`, that is, Ê.

Characters represented by their hexadecimal codes can be used just like regular characters, as arguments to `grep()` or other functions. (They can also be entered in other, different ways that depend on your computer and keyboard.) Almost all of these characters will display on your screen, depending on which fonts you have installed. One exceptional character is the so-called null character, which has code `00` (following the convention that every character requires two hexadecimal digits). This character is not permitted in R text; if needed nulls can be held in objects of class `raw`, but they should be avoided. In Chapter 6, we describe how you can skip null characters when reading data from outside sources.

The Windows and OS X character codes generally coincide. The one commonly encountered character for which the two disagree is the Euro currency symbol, €, which was introduced after the `latin1` standard was decided. In the Win-1252 table, the symbol has hexadecimal value `80`, whereas in OS X, it has `db`.

4.5.2 Non-Latin Alphabets

Of course, the need for standardization goes beyond the Euro sign. Increasingly, with the availability of data from social media data and other sources, analysts need methods to read, store, and process characters from very different languages such as Chinese, Arabic, and Russian. The computing communities have settled on Unicode, which is a system that intends to describe all the symbols in all the world's alphabets. Unicode values are shown in R by preceding them with \U (or \u, but the upper-case U is more general). Unicode includes ASCII as a subset. For example, the lower-case letter k has an ASCII and Unicode representation as the hexadecimal value 6b, so typing "\U6b" or "\U006B" into R will produce a lower-case k. As with other hexadecimal encodings, Unicode characters may be in either case.

As a non-Latin example, the two Chinese characters "中国" represent the word "China" in (simplified) Chinese. These cannot be represented in ASCII, but their Unicode representations are (from left) "\U4E2D" and "\U56FD", and these values can be entered (inside quotation marks) directly in R, as in this example:

```
> "\U4e2d\U56fd"
[1] "中国"                    # If fonts permit
> nchar ("\U4e2d\U56fd")
[1] 2                         # Two characters...
> nchar ("\U4e2d\U56fd", type = "bytes")
[1] 6                         # ...requiring six bytes in UTF-8
```

There are several ways to represent Unicode, but the most popular, particularly in web pages, is UTF-8. In this encoding, each character in Unicode is represented by one or more bytes. For our purposes, it is not important to know how the encoding works, but it is important to be aware that some characters, particularly those in non-European alphabets, require more than one byte. In the example above, the two Chinese characters take up six bytes in UTF-8.

Depending on your computer, its fonts, and the windowing system, the Chinese characters may not appear. Instead, you might see the Unicode representation (such as \U4e2d), an empty square indicating an unprintable character, an empty space, or even, on some computers, some seemingly garbled characters such as "ä¸å". Sometimes these characters indicate the latin1 encoding, but on some computers the very same representation will be used for UTF-8. You can ensure that the computer knows these characters are UTF-8 by examining their encoding (the following section). The important point is that the display of UTF-8 characters can be inconsistent from one machine to the next, even when the encodings are correctly preserved. We talk about reading and writing UTF-8 text in Section 6.2.3.

4.5.3   Character and String Encoding in R

Handling Unicode in R requires knowledge of one more detail, which is "encoding." R assigns an encoding to every element in a character vector (and different elements in a vector may have different encodings). ASCII strings are unencoded (so their encoding is marked as unknown); strings with latin1 characters (but no non-Latin Unicode) are encoded as latin1 and strings with non-Latin Unicode are encoded as UTF-8. The Encoding() function returns the encoding of the strings in a vector and iconv() will convert the encodings. In the following first example, we create a latin1 string and look for the à character using regexpr(). The search succeeds whether the regular expression is entered in latin1 style (as "\xe0"), Unicode style (as "\Ue0", or directly with the keyboard. In each case, the à is found in location 9 as we expect.

```
> (yogi <-  "It's d\xe9j\xe0 vu all over again.")
[1] "It's déjà vu all over again."
> Encoding (yogi)
[1] "latin1"
> c(regexpr ("\xe0", yogi), regexpr ("\ue0", yogi),
    regexpr ("à", yogi))
[1] 9 9 9
```

Different encodings only cause problems in the rare cases where the Win-1252 and Mac OS Roman pages disagree with Unicode, and the primary example of this issue is, again, the Euro sign. In this example, we create a string containing the Euro sign using the Windows value "\x80" (to repeat this example with OS X, use "\xdb"). We then use grepl() to check to see if the sign is found in the string. R encodes the string as latin1 when it sees the non-ASCII character. Here, the Euro sign in the latin1 string is not matched by the Unicode Euro, but after the string is converted into UTF-8, the Unicode Euro is matched.

```
> (bob <- "bob owes me \x80123")
[1] "bob owes me €123"
> Encoding (bob)
[1] "latin1"
> (euro <- "\U20ac")                    # Assign Unicode Euro
[1] "€"
> Encoding (euro)
[1] "UTF-8"
> grepl (euro, bob)                     # Is it there?
[1] FALSE
> (bob <- iconv (bob, to = "UTF-8"))    # Convert to UTF-8
[1] "bob owes me €123"
> grepl (euro, bob)                     # Is it there?
[1] TRUE
```

Notice that iconv() has no effect on strings that contain only ASCII text. These will continue to have encoding "unknown."

UTF-8 is vital for handling non-European text. Although the display is not always perfect, R is usually intelligent about handling UTF-8 once it is read in. UTF-8 text behaves as expected in regular expressions, paste() and other string manipulation tools. R's functions to read from, and write to, files also support the notion of encoding in UTF-8 and other formats. We talk more about reading and writing UTF-8 in Chapter 6.

We have noted that the display of UTF-8 strings can be unexpected on some computers (at least, for some characters). Even on computers equipped with the correct fonts, though, an issue arises when UTF-8 characters are part of a data frame. When the print() function is applied to a data frame, it calls the print.data.frame() function, which in turns calls format(). This later, though, reacts poorly to UTF-8, often converting it into a form like <U+4E2D>. In this example, we create a data frame with those Chinese characters and show the results of printing the data frame.

```
> data.frame (a = "\U4e2d\U56fd", stringsAsFactors = FALSE)
                a
1 <U+4E2D><U+56FD>
```

Here, the data.frame() command produced a data frame whose one entry was two characters. The data frame, as displayed by the print.data.frame() function, shows the <U+4E2D>-type notation. Despite the display, the underlying values of the characters are unchanged – as seen in the next command.

```
> data.frame (a = "\U4e2d\U56fd",
              stringsAsFactors = FALSE) [1,1]
[1] "中国"
```

R shows the expected result because print() is being called on a vector, not a data frame.

Sometimes, UTF-8 is inadvertently saved to disk in the <U+4E2D> form as literal characters – < followed by U, and so on. At the end of the chapter, we show one way to reconstruct the original UTF-8 from this representation.

4.6 Factors

4.6.1 What Is a Factor?

A *factor* is a special type of R vector that looks like text but in many cases behaves like an integer. Factors are important in modeling, but they often cause trouble in data entry and cleaning. In this section, we describe how factors are created, how they behave, and how to get them to do what you want them to do.

Factors arise in several ways. You can create a factor vector from some other vector using the `factor()` or equivalent `as.factor()` function; this will often be a final step, after data cleaning has been completed and modeling is about to start. Factors are also created automatically by R when constructing data frames, or when character vectors are added into data frames, with the `data.frame()` or `cbind()` functions (Sections 3.4 and 3.7.1), or when reading data into R from other formats (Section 6.1.2). In both of these cases, the behavior can be changed through a function argument or global option.

Factors are useful in a number of places in R but particularly in modeling. They provide a natural and powerful way of representing categorical variables in a statistical model. However, we recommend that you only turn character vectors into factors when all the data cleaning is finished and it is time to start modeling. Chapter 7 shows a complete data cleaning example in depth and there we ensure that our character data starts out and remains as character. Still, it is important to understand how factors work in R.

Think of a factor as having two parts. One part is the set of possible values, the "levels." In a manpower example, the levels of a factor named "Gender" might be "Male" and "Female," and perhaps a third called "Not Recorded." The second part is a set of integer codes that R uses to represent and store the levels. These codes start at 1 and go up. By default, R assigns codes to levels alphabetically – so in this example, "Female" would be represented by 1, "Male" by 2, and "Not Recorded" by 3. The `class()` of a factor vector is `factor`, showing its special nature, but the `mode()` of a factor vector is `numeric`, and the `typeof()` is `integer`, referring to the underlying codes that R stores. The advantage of this representation is efficiency: in a data set of a million observations, it is clearly much more efficient to store a million small integers than to store millions of copies of longer strings.

4.6.2   Factor Levels

Once a set of levels is defined for a factor, it is resistant to change. If you try to change a value of one of the elements of a factor vector to a new value that is not already a level, R sets that value to NA and issues a warning. Conversely, if you remove all the elements with a particular value from the vector, that value is still one of the levels. In this example, we create a factor whose levels are the three colors of a traffic light.

```
> (cols   <- factor (c("red", "yellow", "green", "red",
                        "green", "red", "red")))
[1] red     yellow green   red     green   red     red
Levels: green red yellow
> table (cols)
 green    red yellow
    2      4      1
```

We can tell that the result is showing factor levels, rather than character strings, because there are no quotation marks and because R also prints out the levels themselves. Notice that the levels consist of the unique values in the vector, sorted alphabetically, and that the `table()` command performs as expected on the factor vector. The `levels` and `labels` arguments to the `factor()` function control the setting and ordering of the factor's levels. In the following example, we show what happens when we exclude the elements whose values are green from the vector.

```
> cols[cols != "green"]
[1] red     yellow red     red     red
Levels: green red yellow
> table (cols[cols != "green"])
 green    red yellow
     0      4      1
```

In this example, we see that the green level is still present in the vector, even though none of the elements in the vector have that value. Moreover, the `table()` command acknowledges the empty level. This can be annoying when many levels are empty, but it can also be helpful when, for example, levels are months of the year and some sources omit some months. In this case, tables constructed from the different sources can be expected to line up nicely.

Another way in which factor levels are resistant to change is shown in this example, where we try to change the value yellow to amber. We start by making a copy of cols called cols2.

```
> cols2 <- cols
> cols2[2] <- "amber"
Warning message:
In `[<-.factor`(`*tmp*`, 2, value = "amber") :
  invalid factor level, NA generated
> cols2
[1] red    <NA> green red    green red    red
Levels: green red yellow
```

This assignment failed because amber is not one of the levels of the factor vector cols2. It would have been okay to assign to the yellow element of our vector the value green or red because those levels existed in the factor. But trying to assign a new value, such as amber, generates an NA. Notice how that NA is displayed with angle brackets, as <NA>, to help distinguish it from a legitimate level value of NA.

The `levels()` function shows you the set of levels in a factor, and you can use that function in an assignment to change the levels. Here, we show how we might have changed the yellow level to have a different label.

```
> levels(cols)
[1] "green"  "red"     "yellow"
> levels(cols)[3] <- "amber"
> cols
[1] red    amber green red    green red    red
Levels: green red amber
```

This operation changes only the level labels; the underlying integer values are not changed. Here, then, the labels are no longer in alphabetical order. We often want to control the order of the levels in our factors; a good example is when we tabulate a factor whose levels are the names of the months. By default, the levels are set alphabetically (April, then August, and so on, up to September) – this affects the output of the table() function (and more, like the way plots are laid out). The order of the levels can be specified in the original call to the factor() function, and we can re-order the levels using another call to factor(), as in this example:

```
> levels(cols)
[1] "green" "red"    "amber"
> factor (cols, levels = c("red", "amber", "green"))
[1] red    amber green red    green red    red
Levels: red amber green
```

In this example, we changed the level through use of the factor() function. To repeat, assigning to the levels() function changes only the labels, not the underlying integers. The following example shows one common error in factor handling, which is assigning levels directly.

```
> (bad.idea <- cols)
[1] red    amber green red    green red    red
Levels: green red amber
> levels(bad.idea) <- c("red", "amber", "green")
> bad.idea
[1] amber green red    amber red    amber amber
Levels: red amber green
```

Here, the elements of bad.idea that used to be red are now amber. If you use this approach, make sure this is what you wanted.

The feature of R that causes more data-cleaning problems than any other, we think, is this: *Factor values are easy to convert into their integer codes but we almost never want this*. In the following section, we see an example of how having a factor can produce unexpected results.

4.6.3 Converting and Combining Factors

To convert a factor f to character, simply use as.character(f). Actually, the help files tell us that it is "slightly more efficient" to use levels(f)[f].

Here, the interior [f] is indexing the set of levels after converting f, internally, to its underlying integer codes. Usually, we use the slightly less efficient approach because we think it is easier to read. R's conversion of factors to integers can be useful when exploited carefully; this arises more often in plotting than in data cleaning.

When a factor f has text labels that look like integers, it is tempting to try to convert it directly into a numeric vector using as.numeric(). This is almost always a mistake; convert levels to numeric *only* after first converting to character. This example shows how this conversion can go wrong. We start by creating a factor containing levels that look numeric, except that one of the values in the vector (and therefore one of the levels of the factor) is the text string Missing. This factor is intended to give the indices of elements to be extracted from the vector src.

```
> wanted <- factor (c(2, 6, 15, 44, "Missing"))    # indices
> src <- 101:200                     # vector to extract from
> as.numeric (wanted)                # ...but this happens
[1] 2 4 1 3 5
> src[wanted]
[1] 102 104 101 103 105
```

When wanted is created, its text labels ("2", "6", ..., "Missing") are stored, together with its integer codes. By default, these are assigned according to the alphabetical order of the labels; so "15" gets level 1, "2" gets level 2, "44" gets level 3, and so on. When we enter src[wanted], R uses these integer codes to extract elements from src. If we actually want the 2nd, 6th, 15th, and so on elements of src, we have to convert the elements of wanted to character first, and then to numeric, as in this example.

```
> src[as.numeric (as.character (wanted))]
[1] 102 106 115 144   NA
Warning message:
NAs introduced by coercion
```

Here, the warning message is harmless – it indicates that the text Missing could not be converted to a numeric value.

One time that the behavior of factors can be helpful is when we need to convert text into numeric labels for whatever reason. For example, given a character vector sex containing the values "F" and "M", we might be called on to produce a numeric vector with 0 for "F" and 1 for "M". In this case, factor(sex) creates a factor with levels 1 and 2; as.numeric (factor(sex)) creates an integer vector with values 1 and 2; and therefore as.numeric(factor(sex)) - 1 produces a numeric vector with values 0 and 1.

It is surprisingly difficult to combine two factor vectors, even if they have the same levels. R will convert both vectors to their underlying integer codes before combining them. Our recommendation is to always convert factors to characters before doing anything else to them. There is one happy exception, though, when two or more data frames containing factors are being combined with rbind() (Section 6.5). Other than in this case, however, combining factor vectors will usually end badly. We recommend converting factors into character, combining, and then, if necessary, calling factor() to return the new vector to factor form.

4.6.4 Missing Values in Factors

Like other vectors, factors may have missing values. Missing values look like NA values in most vectors, but in factors they are represented by <NA> with angle brackets. This level is special and does not prevent you from having a real level whose value is actually <NA>, but you should avoid that. (Analogously, it's permitted to have the string value "NA", and it is a good idea to avoid that, too.) Values of a factor that are missing have no level. In this example, we create a vector with missing values, and also with values that are legitimately "NA" and "<NA>".

```
> (f <- factor (c("b", "a", "NA", "b", NA, "a", "c",
                  "b", NA, "<NA>")))
 [1] b     a     NA    b     <NA> a     c     b     <NA> <NA>
Levels: <NA> a b c NA # alphabetized by default
> table (f, exclude=NULL)
<NA>     a     b     c    NA <NA>
   1     2     3     1     1     2
levels (f)
[1] "<NA>"  "a"     "b"     "c"     "NA"
```

The levels() function makes no mention of the true missing values, since they do not have a level. The first <NA> in the output of table() describes the final element of the vector, whereas the last <NA> refers to the two items that really were missing. Clearly there is a possibility of confusion here.

When elements of a factor vector are missing, the addNA() function can be used to add an explicit level (which is itself NA) to the factor. More often we want to replace the NA values with an explicit level so that, for example, those entries are accounted for in the result of table(). In this example, we show one way to add such a level.

```
> (f <- factor (c("b", "a", NA, "b", "b", NA, "c", "a")))
 [1] b     a     <NA> b     b     <NA> c     a
Levels: a b c
> f <- as.character(f)                # Convert to character
> f[is.na (f)] <- "Missing"           # Replace missings
```

```
> (f <- factor (f))              # Re-factorize
[1] b       a       Missing b       b       Missing c       a
Levels: a b c Missing
```

Here, the factor is converted to character, missing values replaced by a value like Missing, and then the vector converted back to factor.

4.6.5   Factors in Data Frames

Factors routinely appear in data frames, and, as we have mentioned, they are important in R modeling functions. Factors inside data frames act just like factors outside them (except sometimes when printing, as we saw with Chinese characters in an earlier example) – they have a fixed set of levels and they are represented internally as integers. A few points should be noticed here. First, as we mentioned above, R is not good at combining factor vectors on their own, but when data frames containing factors are combined with rbind(), R creates new factors from the factors in the input, extending the set of levels to include all the levels from both data frames. The set of levels is formed by concatenating the two initial sets; the levels are not re-sorted. (If a column is factor but its corresponding column in another data frame is character, then the resulting combined column will have the class of the column in the first data frame passed to rbind().) Second, applying functions to the rows of a data frame containing factors can produce unexpected results. We discuss applying functions to the rows of a data frame in Section 3.5 and the concerns there apply even more to data frames containing factor levels. Our recommendation is to not use apply() functions on data frames, particularly with columns of different types. Instead, use sapply() or lapply() on columns. If you need to process rows separately, loop over the rows with a command like lapply (1:nrow(mydf), function(i) ...) where your function operates on mydf[i,], the *i*th row of the data frame mydf.

4.7   R Object Names and Commands as Text

4.7.1   R Object Names as Text

In some data cleaning problems, a large set of related objects need to be created or processed. For example, there might be 500 tables stored in disk files, and we want to read them all into R, saving them in objects with names such as M2.2013.Jan, M2.2013.Feb, ⋯, and M2.2016.Dec. Or, we might have data frames named p001, p002, ⋯, p100 and we want to run a function on each one. It is easy enough to construct the set of names using paste() and sprintf() (see Section 4.2.1). But there is a distinction between the name "p001" (a character string with four characters) and the R object p001 (a data frame). The R command `get()` accepts a character string and returns the object with that name. (If there is no object by that name, an error is produced; the related function `exists()` can test to see whether such an object exists, and `get0()` allows a value to be specified in place of the error.)

One place where `get()` is useful is when examining the contents of your workspace. The `ls()` command returns the names of the objects there; by using `get()` in a loop we can apply a function to every object in the workspace. For example, the `object.size()` function reports the size of an object in your workspace in bytes (by default). This function operates on an object, not a name in character form. So often we do something like this: first, we produce the set of names of the objects of interest, perhaps with a command like `projNames <- ls(pattern = "^projA")` to identify all the names of objects that start with `projA`. Then, the command `sapply(projNames, function(i) object.size(get(i)))` passes each name to the function, and the function uses `get()` to produce the object itself and report its size. The result is a named vector of the sizes of every object in the workspace whose name starts with `projA`.

The complement of `get()` is `assign()`. This takes a name and a value and creates a new R object with that name and value. Be careful; it will over-write an existing object with that name. Assigning is useful when each iteration of a loop produces a new object. In the following example, we use a `for()` loop to create an item named `AA` whose value is 1, one named `BB` with value 2, and so on, up to an object `ZZ` with value 26. (We used double letters here to avoid creating an item `F` that might conflict with the alias for `FALSE`.)

```
> for (i in 1:26)
      assign (paste0 (LETTERS[i], LETTERS[i]), i, pos = 1)
> get ("WW")                    # Example
[1] 23
# Remove the 26 new objects from the workspace
> remove (list = grep ("^[A-Z]{2}$", ls (), value = T))
```

The final command uses a regular expression to remove all items in the workspace whose names start (`^`) with a letter (`[A-Z]`) that is repeated (`{2}`) and then come to an end (`$`). The `remove()` and `rm()` commands operate identically. Notice the `pos = 1` argument to `assign()`. At the command line this has no effect. Inside a function it creates a variable in your R workspace, not one local to the function. We discuss the notions of global and local variables in Section 5.1.2.

4.7.2   R Commands as Text

It is also possible to construct R commands as text and then execute them. Suppose in our earlier example that we have objects `p001, p002, ⋯, p100` and we want to run a function `report()` on each one, producing results `res001`,

···, res100. We could use the get() and assign() approach from above, like this:

```
nm <- paste0 ("p", sprintf ("%03d", 1:100))      # Object names
res <- paste0 ("res", sprintf ("%03d", 1:100))# Result names
for (i in nm) {                                  # Begin loop
    result <- report (get (i))                   # Run function
    assign (res[i], result, pos=1)
}
```

But it is easy to think of more complicated examples where each call is different. Perhaps the caller needs to supply the month and year associated with a file as an argument, or perhaps each call requires an additional argument whose name also varies. In these cases, it can be useful to construct a vector of R commands using, say, paste0(), and then execute them. This requires a two-step process: first the text is passed to parse() with the text argument, to create an R "expression" object; then the eval() function executes the expression. For example, to compute the logarithm of 11 and assign it to log.11 we can use the command eval(parse(text = "log.11 <- log(11)")). After this command runs, our R workspace has a new variable called log.11 whose value is about 2.4.

Imagine having objects p001, p002, ..., p100 and also q001, q002, ..., q100, and suppose we wanted to run res001 <- report(p001, q001), res002 <- report(p002, q002) and so on. It is simple to construct a set of 100 character strings containing these commands:

```
> num <- sprintf ("%03d", 1:100)          # 001, 002, etc.
> pnm <- paste0 ("p", num)
> qnm <- paste0 ("q", num)
> rnm <- paste0 ("res", num)
> cmd <- paste0 (rnm, " <- report (", pnm, ", ", qnm, ")")
> cmd[45]                                  # as an example
[1] "res045 <- report (p045, q045)"
```

Now all 100 reports can be run with the command eval(parse(text = cmd)). This approach can both save time and cut down on the errors associated with copying and modifying dozens – or hundreds – of similar lines of code.

As a final example, we encountered a problem with some UTF-8 data (Section 4.5), which we solved with regular expressions (Section 4.4) and eval(). Under some circumstances, UTF-8 can be saved to disk as ASCII in a form like "<U+4E2D><U+56FD>" – that is, with a literal representation of <, U, +, and so on. To convert this into "real" UTF-8, we used regular expressions and the gsub() command to delete each > and to replace each <U+ with \U. Of course, + and \ are special characters and will need to be escaped. Then we surrounded the entire result in quotation marks. The resulting string

contains what we might have typed in at the R command line, and when it is executed with `parse()` and `eval()`, the UTF-8 characters are produced, as in this example:

```
> inp <- "<U+4E2D><U+56FD>"              # ASCII (not UTF-8)
> (out <- gsub (">", "", inp))           # remove > chars
[1] "<U+4E2D<U+56FD"
> (out <- gsub ("<U\\+", "\\\\U", out))  # change <U+ to \U
[1] "\\U4E2D\\U56FD"
> (out <- paste0 ("\"", out, "\""))      # add quotes
[1] "\"\\U4E2D\\U56FD\""
> eval (parse (text = out))

[1]"中国"
```

4.8   Chapter Summary and Critical Data Handling Tools

This chapter discusses character data, which forms an important part of almost every data cleaning project. Even if you have very little data in text form you will need to be proficient at handling text in order to modify column names or to operate on multiple files across multiple directories. This chapter includes discussion of these important R tools:

- The `substring()` function, which extracts a piece of a string as identified by the starting and ending positions. This function and the others in this chapter are made more powerful by the fact that they are vectorized, so they can operate on a whole set of strings as once.
- The `format()` and `sprintf()` functions, which help convert numeric values into nicely-formatted strings. `Sprintf()` in particular provides a powerful interface for formatting values into report-like strings. Also handy here is the `cut()` function, which lets us convert a numeric variable into a categorical one for reporting or modeling.
- The `paste()` and `paste0()` functions. These combine strings into longer ones in a vectorized way. We use the `paste` functions in every data cleaning project.
- Regular expression functions. These functions (`grep()` and `grepl()`, `regexpr()` and `gregexpr()`, `sub()` and `gsub()`, and `strsplit()`) use regular expressions to find, extract, or replace parts of strings that match patterns. The power of regular expressions comes from the flexibility that the patterns provide. Regular expressions form a big subject, but we find that even a limited knowledge of them makes data cleaning much easier and more efficient.

- Tools for UTF-8. UTF-8 describes a particular, popular encoding of the set of Unicode characters. More and more data cleaning problems will involve non-Roman text and R provides tools for handling these strings.
- Factors. Factors are indispensable in some modeling contexts in R, and they provide for efficient storage of text items. In data cleaning tasks, however, they often get in the way. Remember to convert factors, even ones that look numeric, into character before converting the result into numeric.
- The `get()` and `assign()` functions. These let us manipulate R objects by name, even when the name is held in an R object. This can make some repetitive tasks much simpler. The combination of `parse()` and `eval()` lets us construct R commands and execute them – again, allowing us to execute sequences of commands once we have created them with `paste()` and other tools.

5

Writing Functions and Scripts

Functions and scripts are two methods by which we can do repetitive tasks easily. They have similar goals, but they operate in different ways. In our work, we use both, and every data cleaning project will require that you create functions or scripts – probably both but almost certainly scripts, since R already has lots of functions to perform lots of necessary tasks – and, of course, we have met many of these in earlier chapters.

Writing functions is more difficult than writing scripts because there are strict rules about what functions can do and how they operate. In contrast, a script is very often just a saved set of commands that you typed in to accomplish a particular task. Of course, the commands you type in are themselves calls to R's built-in functions, and sometimes you need to do something for which no function has been written. In that case, you may have to write your own. In this chapter, we describe what functions and scripts do and their relative strengths.

5.1 Functions

A *function* is a special R object. If you have made it this far in the book, you probably know a lot about how functions work. But we want to repeat some of the details here, to make clear the important points that will come up when you start writing your own. A function's text starts with the reserved word `function`, then it has its list of arguments inside parentheses, and then it has the body of the function enclosed in braces. If the body is only one line, the braces are unnecessary, but we recommend that you use them anyway. For example, suppose you needed a function that takes the numbers x and y as input and returns the value $\sqrt{x} + y$. If x is negative, the value of $\sqrt{x}$ is not defined, so the function issues a warning and returns NA. In the following code, we define this function and assign it to an R object named `funk`. Notice that in the function "declaration" (where the arguments are specified), the `y` argument is given the default value of 2. If no value is entered for `x`, the function will fail, because `x`

A Data Scientist's Guide to Acquiring, Cleaning, and Managing Data in R, First Edition.
Samuel E. Buttrey and Lyn R. Whitaker.
© 2018 John Wiley & Sons Ltd. Published 2018 by John Wiley & Sons Ltd.
Companion website: www.wiley.com/go/buttrey/datascientistsguide

has no default value, but if no value is entered for y, the default value of 2 is used. This code shows the definition of the function.

```
> funk <- function (x, y = 2) {
# Example function to compute sqrt (x) + y
# Arguments: x, numeric;
#            y, numeric
    if (x < 0) {
        warning ("Negative number cannot be funk-i-fied")
        return (NA)
    }
    return (sqrt(x) + y)
}
> funk (x = 9, y = 3)              # run with x = 9, y = 3
[1] 6
```

In the final command we run the function, passing in both arguments explicitly. Just typing the name funk, without parentheses, causes R to print out the function itself. Notice that our function includes some comments. In this case, we have listed the arguments together with their types. It is important to document all of your functions, even the ones you only plan to use yourself. In addition to the arguments, this documentation might include the date, version number, author, or other relevant information.

There are several aspects to a function, and you will need to understand all of them to use functions properly. These include the arguments (information passed into the function), the return value (information computed and returned), and side effects (actions by the function beyond simply computing the return value). This section describes the different pieces of an R function.

5.1.1 Function Arguments

An *argument* is a value passed to a function. The aforementioned funk function has two arguments named x and y. R functions may have as many arguments as needed (or none at all). Arguments may be vectors or data frames or lists or functions or any other R object. This means that if you develop a function, particularly for other users, the first thing it should do is to ensure that the arguments are of the types expected by the user. For example, the funk function checks to see that the argument x is a non-negative number. But what happens if the user passes a data frame or a character string or a list? The function developer needs to detect these unexpected inputs and stop gracefully. We discuss error handling in Section 5.3.

Argument Matching

When a user calls a function, he or she may specify the arguments by name. In this case, R knows unambiguously which input goes with which argument.

So, in our example, the call `funk(x = 4, y = 1)` will produce the result 3, and so too will the call `funk(y = 1, x = 4)`. The user may also specify arguments without naming them. In this case, R matches arguments in the call to arguments in the function declaration by position. Since `funk` listed x before y, the call `funk(9, 3)` is equivalent to `funk(x = 9, y = 3)`.

Arguments are matched by partial names in a way similar to the way that the elements of a list can be matched by an unambiguous substring (see Section 3.3.1). If a function g has arguments `dimension`, `data`, and `subset`, for example, the user may specify s, su, or sub to supply the `subset` argument. An argument d is ambiguous and will produce an error, but da would suffice to supply the `data` argument. While this is permitted, we recommend using full names where possible. This enhances readability and lessens the chance of confusion if a function is updated later to include more arguments.

If some arguments are named and others are not, named arguments are matched by name and the others by position. In the example of the previous paragraph, the call `g(data = 2, 5, 3)` will assign 2 as the `data` argument, then 5 as the `dimension` argument, and then 3 as `subset`. In interactive work we often match arguments by position, but when constructing code we plan to save, re-use, distribute or archive we try to specify arguments by name.

The Ellipsis

Some functions are defined with one special argument, the ellipsis (. . .). This is R's mechanism for allowing functions to accept variable numbers of arguments. The ellipsis captures all of the arguments that are not otherwise matched and presents them to the function as a list. One complication is that the names of function arguments defined after the ellipsis may not be abbreviated. For example, the `table()` function takes the ellipsis as its first argument; this allows us to pass as many vectors as needed into the function. Subsequent arguments include the `exclude` and `usaNA` arguments described in Section 2.5. In this example, we show what happens when one of those names is abbreviated.

```
> table (c(1, 1, 2, 3, 1, NA, 2, 1), use = "always")
Error in table(c(1, 1, 2, 3, 1, NA, 2, 1), use = "always") :
  all arguments must have the same length
> table (c(1, 1, 2, 3, 1, NA, 2, 1), useNA = "always")
   1    2    3 <NA>
   4    2    1    1
```

In the first command, `table()` sees two vectors to tabulate. The `use` argument is insufficient to act as the `usaNA` instruction, so it is treated as an input vector of length 1 (with the value `"always"`). Unable to create a two-way table from vectors of different lengths, `table()` produces an error. In the second command, the complete name successfully indicates the action to perform with the NA. We can examine the arguments of table () using the args () function, as follows:

```
> args (table)
function (..., exclude = if (useNA == "no") c(NA, NaN),
            useNA = c("no", "ifany", "always"),
            dnn = list.names(...), deparse.level = 1)
NULL
```

This output shows that the ellipsis precedes the useNA argument in the definition. Therefore, the name useNA needs to be specified in its entirety.

Very often the ellipsis is one of the final arguments in the function definition. This has two consequences. First, arguments defined after the ellipsis must be matched by name exactly. If not – if you supply an argument whose name is not in the declaration – that argument will often "fall into" the ellipsis and be ignored. For example, when you type the name of a data frame at the command line, R invokes a particular function called print.data.frame (). This function takes an argument called digits that specifies the precision of the printing of numeric columns – but this argument is defined only after the ellipsis, so its name must be matched exactly. Specifying digit = 3, for example, has no effect – the name digit does not match an argument exactly, so the argument digit = 3 is given to the ellipsis, which ignores it. In this example, we construct a data frame and then use print.data.frame () to display it.

```
> (newdf <- data.frame (a = c(1, 2.345)))
      a
1 1.000
2 2.345
> print.data.frame (newdf, digits = 2)
    a
1 1.0
2 2.3
> print.data.frame (newdf, digit = 2)
      a
1 1.000
2 2.345
```

Here, the mis-typed argument name digit has had no effect on the output, but no error or warning is produced. This points up the importance of comparing the output you see to what you expect. Similarly, arguments that are unmatched are often ignored in functions with the ellipsis; in this example, we show how a made-up argument name does not produce an error or warning in print.data.frame () – but it does in the log () function, which is defined with no ellipsis.

```
> print.data.frame (newdf, NOTANARGUMENT = 1)
```

```
        a
1 1.000
2 2.345
> log (newdf)                              # this is valid, but...
        a
1 0.0000000
2 0.8522854
> log (newdf, NOTANARGUMENT = 1)              # ...this is not.
Error in log(newdf, NOTANARGUMENT = 1) :
  unused argument (NOTANARGUMENT = 1)
```

In this example, we used the print.data.frame() function to print a data frame. However, we could have just used print(); R will detect that the object being printed is a data frame and use the appropriate printing function. We saw this in Section 4.5.3. This practice of having "generically" named functions such as print() call functions specific to a data type is an example of "object-oriented programming." In this approach, the class of an object being operated on helps to determine the operation being performed. We have seen other examples of this behavior earlier in the book. For example, we saw how seq() calls seq.POSIXt() in Section 3.6.6. We talk a little more about object-oriented programming in Section 5.6.3.

Most commonly ellipses are used for function that will call other functions and pass arguments down to the function being called. For example, lots of functions that we write draw plots using the plot() function. The plot() function accepts dozens of possible arguments reflecting the values of "graphical parameters" such as colors, line sizes, typefaces, and axes. Rather than prepare our plot function for every possible argument, we will often create a function similar to the following one.

```
myplot <- function (x, y, ...) {
# Do stuff here
    plot (x, y, ...) # Call plot()
}
```

In this example, any arguments after x and y are passed to plot() just as they were supplied by myplot(), in the same order with the same names. If we needed access to the individual arguments passed in the ellipsis, we could capture those arguments with a command such as mylist <- list(...) and use mylist like any other R list. In this example, we examine the arguments passed to our function myplot() to see if the argument xlab is among them, and, if so, print it.

```
> myplot <- function (x, y, ...) {
    mylist <- list (...) # grab extra arguments
    plot (x, y, ...) # Call plot()
    if (any (names (mylist) == "xlab"))
        cat ("xlab was supplied as ", mylist$xlab, "\n")
  }
```

```
> myplot (1:5, 1:5, xlab = "Plot of x vs y")
xlab was supplied as   Plot of x vs y
```

Modifying an argument and passing it along as part of the ellipsis requires some thought. Suppose our standard required that *x*-axis labels always be in upper case. To modify the value of the xlab argument, the easiest way is to add the x and y arguments to mylist, and then to invoke the plot () function via do.call (plot, mylist). We rarely need to do this, but for advanced users we give here an example of how it might be done.

```
myplot <- function (x, y, ...) {
    mylist <- list (...) # grab extra arguments
    if (any (names (mylist) == "xlab"))
        mylist$xlab <- casefold (mylist$xlab, upper = TRUE)
    mylist$x <- x; mylist$y <- y
    do.call (plot, mylist)
}
```

Missing Arguments

Sometimes users do not pass an argument, because it is optional, because they are satisfied with the default value, or by mistake. The missing () function returns TRUE if an argument is missing. If an argument named arg has not been supplied and has no default value, then any reference to arg in the code, other than a call to the missing (arg) function, will produce an error. Here, missing (arg) will produce TRUE and the code can then determine what action to take. When used inside a function, the missing () function should be used only near the beginning of a function (since, e.g., if arg gets assigned in the code, then missing (arg) will subsequently be FALSE). An argument that is not passed explicitly is considered to be missing even if it has a default value.

5.1.2   Global versus Local Variables

A *local variable* is one that exists only inside your function. All of the variables inside your function are local. That is, when the function starts, it creates a special area of memory where local variables are stored and manipulated, and when the function ends, that area of memory (and the variables in it) is destroyed. Other variables are *global*; most often global variables are in your workspace. The R variables in the workspace that are supplied as values to the function are untouched (but see "side effects," as follows). This example demonstrates how workspace values passed to a function are unchanged.

```
> new <- function (a = 5) {
    a <- a + 1
    cat ("a is now", a, "\n")
    return (a)
  }
```

```
> a <- 11
> new (a)
a is now 12
[1] 12
> a
[1] 11
```

The value of the global variable a in the workspace is 11 before the call and 11 after. The local a, inside the function, changes, but that change has no effect on the global one. Another way to say this is that R uses the "call by value" approach. (In one alternative scheme, "call by reference," the item passed into the argument is a reference to the global variable, so changes to the reference produce changes in the global variable.) There are some packages that implement "call by reference" in R, and this approach can bring efficiencies, but discussion of this strategy is beyond the scope of this book.

It is possible to access global variables directly from inside a function, simply by referring to them by name. We might use system-defined global variables such as pi or letters, in our functions, but you should avoid using your own workspace objects directly in your functions. The objects in your workspace can change, and in any case such a function would not be usable by another user. Instead, pass into the function all of the values it will need as arguments. The one exception to this informal rule is when writing a function to be used by a one-time application of apply() or its relatives, when operating on, for example, the rows of a data frame. Recall from Section 3.5 that it is unwise to use apply() directly on a data frame's rows. In that section, we operated on the rows of a data frame named dd with code such as sapply(1:nrow(dd), function (x) any (dd[i,] == 1)). Although the embedded function uses the workspace variable dd, this approach is powerful and convenient.

As a side observation, note the cat () statement designed to print out some text and the value of a in the aforementioned example. At the command line, you can simply type a to have the system print its value. Inside a function, though, a line with only a on it has no effect – the value of a is evaluated, which in more complicated examples might require some processing, but nothing is assigned or printed. To print a value to the screen from inside a function, use cat () or print () explicitly.

5.1.3 Return Values

The most important thing functions do is to produce a *return value*, which is the results of the computation done by the function. In R, a function always produces one return value, so if you want to compute different things inside a function, and return them, you have to combine them into a vector, matrix, data frame, or list. A function returns whatever is inside the first call to return ()

that it encounters; if there isn't a call to `return ()`, the function returns whatever the last line it executes produces. You can hide a function's return value with the `invisible ()` command, but every function has an output. If you assign the output of a function with an invisible return value, that value is preserved in the usual way.

Side Effects

Functions can do other things beyond producing return values. These things are called *side effects*. One important side effect is to produce graphics. It is also possible to change global variables with a function, separate from the return value (see the discussion of `assign ()` in Section 4.7.1), and indeed sometimes R modifies global variables without using the return value, intentionally. For example, the `fix ()` function (Section 5.1.4) creates and modifies functions, and the `edit ()` function (Section 3.7.4) modifies data frames and other R objects. We do *not* recommend changing global variables in your code.

A third, more benign, side effect is to print out information for debugging purposes. This is very handy, particularly when the function needs to run hundreds or thousands of times. We talk more about debugging in Section 5.3.

Another common side effect is to write files to the disk. These might be text files with data in them, they might be tables of results, they might be graphics, or something else. We discuss the ways to get data out of R in Chapter 6.

Side effects can be good or bad. It is important to recognize when one of your functions produces a side effect. Such a function might even behave differently at a different time, or on another machine.

When a Function Produces Errors or Warnings

A function that has been successfully created or edited is always syntactically correct. However, functions can still produce errors, either because the inputs were unexpected, or because you tried to read a file that didn't exist, because R encountered an NA for which it was unprepared, or R tried to perform arithmetic on a character vector, or for one of many other reasons. When an error results, an error message is produced and the function terminates. Local variables are lost and no return value is produced. However, any side effects produced by code before the error occur.

Sometimes, functions produce warnings rather than errors. A function that produces warnings will nonetheless return a value. Still, unless you're sure you understand the cause of the warnings, we recommend that you not ignore them. We talk more about errors, warnings, and debugging in Section 5.3.3.

Cleaning Up

When a function completes, there might be a few bookkeeping-type tasks that remain before the result can be returned. For example, files or other connections (Chapter 6) might need to be closed, graphics devices reset, and warnings re-armed. Moreover, we usually want these actions performed even if the function exits prematurely because of an error. The `on.exit()` function allows you to specify one or more expressions to be evaluated however the function ends. We show an example in Section 6.2.6.

5.1.4 Creating and Editing Functions

It is possible to type a function in at the command line, but this is almost never practical. Instead, R provides a simple interface to one of your system's editing programs to allow you to create and edit functions. The R function is called `fix()`. You can create a new function `newf` by entering `fix(newf)` and the editor will appear with an empty function skeleton that looks like this:

```
function ()
{
}
```

If the function `newf` already exists, the `fix(newf)` command will open the existing function for editing. The exact editor that R uses depends on what is available on your system and its name can be displayed by `options()$editor`. When you are done editing, exit the editor. In Windows, with the default editor, you can do that by clicking the red X in the top right and choose "Yes" to keep modifications; in OS X's default, click the red dot in the top left and choose "Save." Do not choose "Save As" from the File menu. In Linux using the default "vi" editor, type `:wq` to save and quit, or `:q!` to exit without saving your changes. Other editors may require different keystrokes, of course. If you asked for modifications to be saved, R checks to see if the new version of the function has no errors and, if so, saves it so that the function is ready to use.

   If R detects that errors have been introduced, it will produce an error message that, apart from the details, might look something like this:

```
Error in .External2(C_edit, name, file, title, editor) :
  unexpected symbol occurred on line 3
 use a command like
 x <- edit()
 to recover
```

The second line contains the meat of the error message: the cause (in this case, "unexpected symbol," but many other choices are possible) and the location (here, line 3). The last part of the error message is a specific instruction that is unclear to many R beginners. It says that to resume editing the flawed function `newf`, we should enter the command `newf <- edit()`. The `edit()` command, without any argument, edits the function most recently operated on; here this command re-edits our `newf` function. If our modifications produce a valid function, that function is saved to the object `newf`. Otherwise, the next error detected will be reported, and we can enter `newf <- edit()` to edit the function once again. You will need to produce an error-free version of your function before R will save it. `Edit()` without an argument always operates on the most recently edited function. We recommend using it only immediately after encountering an editing error and otherwise using `fix()`.

Reading and Writing Functions to and from Disk

It is easy to store functions in readable text files, so this is a natural way to save and distribute them. We prefer to save functions using the `dump()` command. `Dump()` creates a disk file with the exact text of your function (including comments, blank lines, and UTF-8). The first argument to `dump()` is a vector of the names of the items to be dumped. The second argument gives the name of the disk file to be created. For example, to dump a single function named `newf` to a file named `newf.txt`, you can use the command `dump("newf", "newf.txt")`.

Importantly, `dump()` also adds an assignment line at the top of the disk file – so if you dump a function named `newf`, the first line of the file looks like `newf <-`; the second line starts with `function` and begins the function definition.

Once a function is on disk, it can be read back into R using the `source()` command. This command reads disk files containing R code and executes the code in your R session. In this example, the command `source("newf.txt")` will read the file and re-create the function in your workspace with its original name. This will over-write an R object named `newf` if one exists.

It is equally possible to call `dump()` with a vector of names of R objects. This vector can include the names of lists, data frames, or other R objects as well as functions. So, this is one quick way to transport a set of objects from one machine or user to another.

However, `dump()` is not equipped to handle certain complicated objects. The `saveRDS()` function (the letters RDS evoke "R data serialization") takes an object and produces a binary disk file with all of that object's data and attributes. Each call to `saveRDS()` applies to exactly one R object. So, for example, `saveRDS(myobj, "newfile")` produces a disk file named `"newfile"` with a binary representation of the R object `myobj`. The complementary action is performed by `readRDS()`: in this case, `readRDS("newfile")` returns the object just as it was saved. Note that `readRDS()` does not replace the existing `myobj`; instead, it simply returns the object. You can assign the return value with a command such as `newobj <- readRDS("newfile")`, which will create a new object `newobj` that is identical to the original `myobj`.

The `save()` function operates on sets of objects. We call it by passing the names of objects (in quotation marks) rather than passing the object itself.

The resulting file should be readable by R on any machine or operating system. (Make sure that the two machines share the same character set, like UTF-8.) Moreover, the file can be compressed at the time it is created. The complement of `save()` is `load()`; this function reads in a file created by `save()` and re-creates the items specified at the time the file was created. An important distinction between `load()` and `readRDS()` is that with `load()`, all the objects are automatically re-created with their original names. This means that R will over-write any existing objects with those names.

5.2   Scripts and Shell Scripts

A script is a text file that contains R commands and possibly other lines as well. We like to differentiate between two sorts of these text files: files we call *scripts* and files we call *shell scripts*. (The word "shell" here refers to a command line, like Terminal on OS X or `cmd.exe` on Windows. Admittedly, these two names are more similar than perhaps they should be.) A script is just a text file with stuff in it. New scripts are created through the File | New script (or New Document) dialog, and existing ones can be opened under File | Open script (or Open Document). A script file will contain R commands, but it might also contain comments, musings, invalid pieces of code you plan to fix someday, or other notes. In normal, interactive usage, the script will be visible in a separate window. You can run the line that the cursor is sitting on with control-R (command-R in OS X), or highlight a few lines with the mouse and run those, also with control-R, or run the entire script using "Run all" from the "Edit" menu. (Those who prefer keyboard commands can run an entire script using control-A to select all the lines, and then control-R to run them.) After you modify a script you can save the updated version however your system requires.

We use scripts to store a lot of our commands, and we often run them bit by bit, interactively, a few lines at a time. Running lines from a script is not like running a function. Instead it is like typing commands, one at a time, into the console. There are no "local" variables in a script; every assignment is made immediately in the global workspace. If you run several lines of a script at once, and one produces an error, R will still attempt to run all the others. (In contrast, remember, when a function encounters an error, it quits.)

A script can also be run, all at once, like a function, through the `source()` command we described earlier (Section 5.1.4). In this case, like a script run interactively, there are no local variables. An error terminates a script being run via `source()`, and only the commands prior to the error are executed. Also as with a function, if you want to print intermediate results to the screen during a script file being `source()`-d, you need to explicitly call `cat()` or `print()` inside the script. A script to be run in this way is often a good product to deliver to another R user; you can deliver the data as one part (perhaps using one of the techniques in Chapter 6) and a script to read or manipulate it, make computations, draw pictures, or anything else as another. In fact, we sometimes deliver several scripts for performing the different tasks of the project, together with one parent or "wrapper" script that allows the user to invoke all of the other scripts in the proper order. The scripts for the extended exercise in Chapter 8 operate in this way, with a wrapper that can invoke a number of other scripts. These scripts and the wrapper can be found in the `cleaningBook` package.

Ordinary scripts are good for developing techniques to handle data, or for tasks that will only be done one or two times. A shell script is useful in a production environment where a specific task needs to be performed every day, for example – frequently and automatically. A shell script is also a text file, but it is a unit intended to be run all at once by R or another program, not as part of an interactive session but from an outside "shell" program. In this way, a shell script is like a script to be run via `source()`. The difference is that a script is run from within R, either interactively or via `source()`, whereas a shell script is run from a command line without having to open R.

A particular version of the R program called "Rscript" (included when you acquire R) runs shell scripts. Shell scripts differ from regular scripts in that the very first line will always look like `#!Rscript`. Those first two characters, `#!`, are sometimes whimsically called "shebang" or "hash bang." They indicate that this line is a comment (the `#`), but that it's a very special sort of comment that may only be placed on line 1 of the script (the `!`). The `Rscript` after the shebang tells the operating system that the file that contains it is filled with commands intended to be executed by `Rscript`. Lots of other programs, besides `Rscript`, also support shell scripts, so you might see files that start `#!python` or `#!ruby` or something else.

One note here is that the operating system needs to know how to find the `Rscript` program. Generally, the set of folders the operating system will search is set by the `PATH` environment variable (see Section 5.4.2 for a discussion of environment variables). If the `PATH` has not been set to include the folder that holds the `Rscript` program, the first line of the shell script will need to specify the complete path to `Rscript`. For example, on one of our Linux machines, a shell script might start with the line `#!/usr/bin/Rscript`.

It is common for details – information about, say, input files, output location, numbers of replications, and so on – to be passed into the shell script via environment variables. An alternative, perhaps more R-like, mechanism is given by the `commandArgs()` function, which produces a vector of the arguments passed to `Rscript` at the time it was called. Either approach requires that the shell script know where to look for the information it needs, of course, whereas with an interactive script this information will often be entered by the user at the command line.

Once `Rscript` reaches the end of a shell script, it stops and control returns to the command-line interface from which it was started. Normally, the point of the shell script will be to produce some output files, graphics, or informative messages. You can also have the shell script modify the contents of your R workspace, but this is not the default and we avoid it because it feels messy. The command `Rscript --help` will show you some of the options available when running shell scripts.

5.2.1 Line-by-Line Parsing

If you use scripts, you will probably some day copy a piece of a function into a script window and run it from there. Remember that a function is an entire unit, but a script is a sequence of lines. This distinction can cause problems. Suppose that you have some code like this:

```
if (i > 100)
    x <- x + 200
else
    x <- x - 200
```

In a function, this will do just what you think it will; it will look at the value of i and use that to decide what to do with x. In a script, this code will fail. Here's why: remember, the script executes line by line. The first line is clearly incomplete, so R waits for the second line. At the end of the second line, the script interpreter has seen an entire R expression, and it executes it. If i is > 100 then x is set to x + 200. Now it comes to the third line and it thinks a new expression has started with an else that has no paired if. Executing a script is just like typing the lines of the script into the console.

In this example, you would have to use braces to "protect" the else. In the following code, the second line doesn't end the expression because there is still an open brace.

```
if (i > 100) {
    x <- x + 200
} else {
    x <- x - 200
}
```

The choice of whether to construct a function or script is a personal one. As we have said, functions operate on local variables, so there is less danger of them over-writing items in your global workspace or of them creating unnecessary copies of large data sets. Moreover, R examines functions for errors before saving them. However, functions are difficult to transport and need to be run all at once, not in pieces. Scripts are less formal; they can be run bit by bit and passed around as simple text files. However, they only create global variables, over-writing the existing objects with the same name in the process.

5.3 Error Handling and Debugging

At some point, sad to say, your function or script will fail unexpectedly or produce unexpected results. You will need to debug it. Debugging is a difficult task; there are many more ways to do something wrongly than there are to do it correctly, and it is difficult to anticipate all the possible ways your function might be called. Still, there are several ways to approach debugging, with different levels of complexity. This section describes some of these approaches, from least to most complicated.

5.3.1 Debugging Functions

`cat()` Statements

The easiest way to debug is to insert `cat()` statements into your code at strategic locations, to print out intermediate results. Of course it's difficult to know in advance what the best locations will be. If your function is failing with an error message, then of course you want your `cat()` to be higher up than the place where you think the error takes place. We recommend labeling your `cat()` statements, particularly if you insert several, to display where in the program they are placed and what the program is about to do. So, for example, you might have `cat()` statements that look like the following:

```
cat ("A: Start setup, i is", i, " dim (X):", dim (X), "\n")
cat ("B: Top of loop, xcount is", xcount, "\n")
cat ("C: End loop, result[1:3] is", result[1:3], "\n")
```

and so on. The `cat()` statements are easy to put in and take out (the labeling scheme helps ensure you remove them all), but for them to be informative, you must have selected the proper thing to display. We have sometimes found it useful to include an argument to the function being debugged that controls whether this diagnostic printing takes place. Conventionally, such an argument is called `verbose`. So some of our functions include a number of lines like, for example, `if(verbose) {cat("Now operating on file", fname, "\n")}`. The `verbose` argument might be logical, or it might be numeric, with higher numbers producing more detailed diagnostics.

A little note that writes a line every hundredth iteration or so can be very reassuring. The `%%` operator gives remainders, so if you have a loop variable named `i`, the line `if(i %% 100 == 0) cat(We're on rep", i, "\n")` will print a line when `i` is 100, 200, and so on.

There is a complication when using a function to print out intermediate diagnostic messages. For efficiency R uses *buffered output*, which means that it saves up a lot of these messages to deliver them all at once. For diagnostic purposes, we often want the messages to be shown as soon as they are generated; in these cases, we turn buffering off. In Windows, you can do that by right-clicking inside the console window (not on its title bar) and selecting "Buffered Output"; control-W will toggle its setting back and forth.

The `traceback()` Function

When an error occurs, your first question will often be where, exactly, the problem was. Although the line number is often printed, that might be unhelpful if the function that failed is nested inside a sequence of calls. A call to the `traceback()` function is often the first action to take when an error occurs. Its goal is to show the sequence of function calls that led to the error and it often (but perhaps not always) succeeds. We give a brief example in Section 5.3.3. The `recover()` function will help advanced users; it lists the set of calls and starts a browser session in the one that the user selects.

The `browser()` Function

The `browser()` function represents a big step forward in interactive debugging. When a function or script encounters a call to `browser()`, it pauses and produces a prompt like `Browse [1]`. (The `[1]` part indicates that this prompt arose from a function called at the command line; for a function called by a function it would be `[2]`, and higher numbers would indicate even more nesting of function calls.) At the browser prompt, you can type the name of an object to display it, enter other function calls, create local variables, and do other things you can do in a regular R session – but usually we use the browser to display or modify the values of variables in the function. There are a few commands you can issue to the browser: c means "continue" (i.e., resume running), s means "step" (go to the next statement, even if it's inside another function), n means "next" (i.e., go to the next statement, treating function calls as if they were one step), f means "finish this loop or function," and Q means "quit the browser." Since these are command names, if you need to print out the value of a variable named c or f or another of these, you need to do that explicitly with a command such as `print(c)`. It is also worth knowing that, inside a function, the `ls()` command shows you only the variables local to that function. To see the variables in the global workspace, specify `ls(pos = 1)`.

Just as we sometimes set up a `verbose` argument that allows the user to specify that diagnostic messages be printed out, it is sometimes valuable to add an argument such as `browse` that specifies where calls to `browser()` might be made. Ensure that this argument is `FALSE` by default if you give your code to other users, since the browser prompt has the potential to confuse them.

The `debug()` Function

Another mechanism for debugging expands on the `browser()` call. The `debug()` function labels a function as "to be debugged," so that, whenever the function is run, browsing starts at its top. The label persists until it is removed with `undebug()`; the `debugonce()` function imposes the label for only one run of the function. Debugging produces the browser prompt; it just saves you from having to include an explicit call to `browser()` in the text of the function.

5.3.2 Issuing Error and Warning Messages

Sometimes, you will want to stop your function early, perhaps because arguments of the wrong type were passed, or some value important to the computation is missing. Other times, you might want the function to produce a warning in the R style and then continue processing. The `stop()` and `warning()` functions and their relatives perform these tasks in R.

Producing Errors

`Stop()` stops the function and prints its argument to the console, so in a function called `funk`, the code `stop("Integer needed")` will produce the message `Error in funk() : Integer needed`. (Notice that no "new-line" character is needed in the error text.) Even if the function with the `stop()` was called from inside another function, control returns all the way out to the command line. (In the following section, we show how that behavior can be modified.)

One very common use of `stop()` is to test whether all the arguments are of the expected type. Our code often includes lines such as `if(!is.matrix (X)) stop("X must be matrix")`. If multiple strings need to be combined – often a good practice since it allows you to include diagnostic information in the messages – use `paste()` (Section 4.3) first.

An enhancement to `stop()` is provided by `stopifnot()`, which acts like `stop()` unless every one if its arguments evaluates to a vector of TRUE values. This makes it easy to handle a set of arguments at once, as well as the case where NAs are found inside a vector. Suppose we require that an argument b must be present, and contain elements that are greater than zero and also not missing. We could ensure that in a function with code such as `if(any(is.na (b)) || any(b < 0)) {stop("Illegal argument b")}` but we would need to have one line for each of the several arguments that had that requirement. Here we used the double-vertical bar version of OR so that R would stop evaluating if the first `any()` were TRUE. In this case, it would be easier to specify `stopifnot(b > 0)`. This function evaluates all its arguments with an implicit `all()` command, and calls `stop()` unless all its arguments are TRUE.

Here, if any element of b is negative or NA, the implicit `all()` command will return something other than TRUE, and the function would stop with the error message `Error: b > 0 is not TRUE`.

Warnings

In situations that do not require the function to stop entirely, you can issue a warning to your user. R has two functions with similar names that help you manage warnings: `warning()` and `warnings()`. Like `stop()`, the warning() function prints out text supplied by the function (often after a call to `paste()` to assemble some diagnostic information), but with `warning()` the function attempts to continue.

The exact behavior of warning messages is determined by the value of the warn option. This value can be displayed with a call to `options()$warn`. By default, `warn` has the value 0. This means that warnings are printed after control is returned to the command line. If there are fewer than 10 warnings, their text is printed out; if there are more than 10, a single message indicating how many messages are there is displayed. In that case, as the messages point out, the individual messages can be accessed with a call to the `warnings()` function. If `warn` is set to 1, with the command `options(warn = 1)`, warning messages appear as they are generated, instead of being saved up until control returns to the console. An even more rigorous choice is `warn = 2`, which causes any warning to be treated as an error. This is particularly useful in a debugging environment and we often choose this option. In your own use of R, you should investigate every warning until you are certain as to why it is being produced. We also recommend that you anticipate that your users will ignore your warnings – because they will.

One final choice of value for `warn` is possible; if `warn` is set to a negative value, all warnings will be suppressed. This is almost never a good idea, although we do know of one exception. We often run into a case where the contents of a character vector (say, `vec`) are mostly numeric, with a few non-numeric items that we are prepared to convert to NA. For example, `vec` might represent the number of days since a customer declared bankruptcy, and it might have the value `c("342", "1101", "Never", "615")`. A call to `as.numeric(vec)` will produce a warning ("NAs introduced by coercion") that should be ignored, and we do not like to produce warnings that we really do want our users to ignore. Happily, the `suppressWarnings()` function takes care of this by setting `warn` to −1 just long enough to execute the expression passed to it. In this case, the call `suppressWarnings(as.numeric(vec))` will produce a numeric vector with one NA – and no warning.

5.3.3 Catching and Processing Errors

An error, as we mentioned earlier, causes R to stop processing and return control to the command line, even if the error takes place in a nested stack of function calls. There are many circumstances where we would rather intercept the error processing, take some necessary action, and then resume processing. As R has evolved, the mechanisms for this have become more sophisticated, but the most basic of these mechanisms is the `try()` function. The `try()` function lets you "try" a call to an R expression. If the call fails, the return value is an object of class "try-error," whereas if it succeeds, the return value is the value of the call. As an example, consider a function a that computes the square of its argument. This function, as follows, issues an error if its argument is not supplied:

```
a <- function (arg1) {
    if (missing (arg1)) stop ("Missing argument in a!")
    return (arg1^2)
}
```

Now suppose we have a function b that calls a, but does so without checking to see whether the argument is supplied. In our example, b has parameters input (which defaults to 9) and offset, the latter of which is used as the input to a(). The b function then returns input + a (offset). This example shows the b function, and the result of its being run with no arguments as input.

```
# Compute input + a (offset)
> b <- function (input = 9, offset) {
    a.result <- a (offset)
    return (input + a.result)
  }
> b ()
Error in a(offset) : Missing argument in a!
```

The error took place inside a (), but control was returned to the command line immediately. If we had not known where the error occurred, we might have called traceback(). This example shows the result of that call.

```
> traceback ()
3: stop("Missing argument in a!") at #2
2: a(offset) at #3
1: b()
```

The output of traceback() is not always helpful or easy to read. We start at the bottom and work up. In this case, we can see that the error arose in a call to b(), which called a() at its line 3 (i.e., the third line of the b() function). The error took place at the second line of a().

In this next version of b(), we use try() to see whether the call to a() can be completed successfully. If it cannot, we issue a warning and set the value of offset to 3. This example shows an updated version of b() and the result of running it.

```
> b <- function (input = 9, offset) {
    a.check <- try (a.result <- a (offset))
    if (class (a.check) [1] == "try-error") {
        warning ("Call to a() failed; setting a.result = 3")
        a.result <- 3
    }
```

```
      return (input + a.result)
}
> b ()
Error in a(offset) : Missing argument!
[1] 12
Warning message:
In b() : Call to a() failed; setting a.result to 3
```

In this example, the function is completed, returning the value 12. The text of the error was still produced, though; this can be disconcerting to users, and it can be turned off with the `silent = TRUE` argument to the `try()` function. Indeed, with both `silent = TRUE` and no call to `warning()`, this error will be handled without notifying the user at all – which very well may *not* be what you want. Notice, by the way, that when we examine the class of the `a.check` variable, we use `class(a.check)[1]`. The `[1]` is there because lots of R objects have a vector of classes. Comparing that vector to the single value `"try-error"` will produce a warning, just the action we're hoping to avoid.

We have found `try()` to be particularly useful when we are relying on programs and files outside R's control. For example, if a call to an outside function fails, or if one in a series of files cannot be read in, we will usually want to trap the error, inform the user and continue processing. R also supplies more sophisticated error handling, which allow different treatments of errors and warnings, which allow functions to signal unusual conditions and other functions to interpret those signals, and which allow more control over restarting. A discussion of those is outside the scope of a book on data cleaning, but interested R programmers should start at the help page for `tryCatch()`.

5.4 Interacting with the Operating System

A function or script will very often need to interact with the operating system. For example, it might need to get a list of all the files in a particular directory whose names end in `.data` so it can process them. It might need to create a new sub-directory for results (this is an example of a "side effect"), and so on. A number of built-in functions manage R's access to the file system. As examples, we saw `dump()` and `source()` in Section 5.1.4 as ways to interact with files.

Many scripts – particularly those used for cleaning data – start by acquiring the data from an outside source such as a file or relational database. This is such an important part of the data cleaning process that we devote the following chapter (Chapter 6) to the topic of getting data into and out of R. In this section, we give a couple of examples of the different ways that R can interact with the operating system, separately from the chore of actually acquiring data from an outside source.

5.4.1 File and Directory Handling

By default, R presumes that the files it is dealing with are in the working directory. This is normally the directory from which R was started. So, a command such as `source ("myfile.txt")` is assumed to refer to a file in the working directory, and a command such as `cat (message, file = "output")` will likewise create a file in that directory. The `getwd()` command prints the working directory to the screen; the `setwd()` command allows you to change the working directory to a new location.

The `list.files()` command, with no arguments, will show you all the files in the working directory. This function has a large number of useful arguments. By default, only the file name, without the path, is returned. However, it is possible to list the files in a vector of directories, in which case the `full.names = TRUE` argument will return a path name (relative to the working directory) for each file. Full names are also useful when using the `recursive = TRUE` argument to find files in the working directory and all of its subdirectories. More important, perhaps, is the ability to select files that match a regular expression (Section 4.4). So, for example, the command `list.files("..", pattern = "xlsx*$", recursive = TRUE)` will list all files whose names end in `xls` or `xlsx` in any directory underneath the parent (`..`) of the working directory. OS X and Linux users may find the `ignore.case` argument useful as well, and other arguments control the inclusion of directories in the listing.

Beyond merely listing the files, we often want to determine something about their content. The `file.info()` command gives some information about a file – here, the full name will be needed for a file outside the working directory – and a series of commands with names such as `file.copy()`, `file.exists()` (to check for existence), and the slightly more dangerous `file.remove()` are also available. For directories there are the corresponding functions `dir.exists()` and `dir.create()` that, respectively, test for the existence of a directory and create one.

5.4.2 Environment Variables

An environment variable is a name and (single) value stored inside the operating system. These are available for programs to read and, in some cases, create or update. For example, on most systems, an environment variable named HOME holds the location of the user's home directory. When R starts, it reads a few existing variables (e.g., LC_ALL describes the locale – see Section 1.4.6) and creates a few of its own (e.g., R_HOME gives the directory where R is installed). Environment variables are case-sensitive in OS X and Linux and not in Windows, but it is conventional to use all upper case for variable names.

Environment variables provide a convenient way for one program to communicate with another. In R, the set of environment variables is available through the `Sys.getenv()` function, which returns a vector whose names and values are the names and values of all the variables in the environment. This list is often long and unwieldy, but you can specify particular variables to extract with a command such as `Sys.getenv("R_HOME")`. Variables can be created or updated with `Sys.setenv()`. So, for example, we might create a new environment variable named `REPS` with a command such as `Sys.setenv(REPS = 12)`. Now if R starts another program, R's environment will be available in that program, and in particular that program will be able to determine that the value `REPS` had been set to `"12"`. (Notice the quotation marks; environment values are always treated as text by R.) Environment variables are one way to pass information from "outside" into R in, for example, a shell script. Notice that a function that creates an environment variable is producing a side effect (see Section 5.1.3).

5.5 Speeding Things Up

Some functions are fast and some are slow. Sometimes functions are so slow that they keep you from doing what you need to do. The slow speed can be a function of things outside R's control – maybe a file is just very big, or is being fetched over a slow network connection – but it can also be a result of inefficient programming. In this section, we talk about how to measure a function's performance and then give a few ideas on how to speed things up.

5.5.1 Profiling

The process of measuring how much time and memory a function uses is called "profiling." The very simplest way of measuring how much time a function uses is with the `system.time()` function, which essentially reads the computer's clock at the beginning and end of a call to an R expression and reports the difference. While this is a useful measure, it does neither divide the time used into pieces attributable to each of the function's components nor address memory use.

R has a much more sophisticated profiling tool based on the `Rprof()` function. This can help you identify both the steps that use a lot of time and also the ones using a lot of memory. This function writes out a log file describing what R is doing 50 times a second, by default (and so these files can get big). After your function terminates, the `summaryRprof()` function can produce a report. The help page for `Rprof()` and the chapter of the online manual referenced there address this topic in detail. While profiling can be important in a production environment where a function is run thousands of times, we rarely find need of it in our more interactive functions for data cleaning that are only run a few times.

5.5.2 Vectorizing Functions

It is almost always useful to ensure that a function can act on vectors of any length as well as on single values. Moreover, using a vectorized function on a vector will almost always be more efficient than looping over the individual entries. Often vectorization will happen automatically, at least in part, because arithmetic functions such as + are themselves vectorized. However, the funk() function from the start of the chapter is not properly vectorized. The example in Figure 5.1 shows that function on the left (we have shortened the text of the warning) and a vectorized version on the right.

Here, the non-vectorized behavior was associated with the if (x < 0) statement that was part of error checking. In the vectorized version, we initialize the out vector with NAs, then fill only the values for which x is ≥ 0. As a technical note, the initial out is actually a logical vector because NAs are logical by default. The vector gets converted to a numeric as soon as the first numeric is stored in it, but if no x values are ≥ 0 this function will return a logical vector. If this were an issue, we would get around it by initializing out as as.numeric(rep(NA, length(x))).

One source of slow R code is inefficient looping. If it is possible to replace a for() or while() loop with a call to one of the apply functions, the result will almost always be faster. The apply functions use looping internally, too, but usually in a much more efficient way. Sometimes, replacing a for() loop will be difficult – for example, if the action to be taken on iteration i depends on the results from iteration $i - 1$. But we always try to vectorize our functions.

However, sometimes vectorization makes code harder to read and maintain. It is gratifying to produce a function that runs faster, but sometimes it is the total time taken to code, run, explain, and maintain that is the more important measure of quality. In the sort of large data sets we run into, with many more rows than columns, the critical point is to work hard to avoid looping over rows. Looping over columns is usually much less costly. Data in other formats (e.g., with many more than columns than rows) will need to be approached differently.

Non-vectorized	Vectorized
| ```
funk <- function (x, y = 2) {
    if (x < 0) {
        warning ("Neg(s)")
        return (NA)
    }
    return (sqrt(x) + y)
}
``` | ```
funk <- function (x, y = 2) {
    out <- rep (NA, length (x))
    if (any (x < 0)) warning ("Neg(s)")
        out[x >= 0] <- sqrt(x[x >0]) + y
    return (out)
}
``` |

Figure 5.1 Vectorized and non-vectorized code example.

5.5.3 Other Techniques to Speed Things Up

Vectorization is always the first thing to try when you need to speed up your R code. But sometimes a fully vectorized function is just not fast enough. The rest of this section suggests some avenues to try when looking for more speed from your R computations.

Compiling

One quick way to gain some speed is through compiling, which is the translation of R code (which, of course, looks something like English) into "byte code," which the machine can read much faster and more efficiently. Indeed almost all of the R's built-in functions have already been compiled into byte code; type the name of a function like q and you will see near the bottom a line with a byte-code address, like, for example, <bytecode: 0x00000000067c6368>. The built-in package compiler allows you to compile your own functions, either one at a time with cmpfun() for functions (or compile() for expressions), or package by package with compilePKGS(). Sometimes, compilation does not appear to speed things up, but it is easy to try. In this example, we show system.time() applied to a simple function, which, essentially, does nothing.

```
> dumb <- function (n = 100) {
    for (i in 1:n) {}
  }
> system.time (dumb (6e8))
   user  system elapsed
  33.48    0.23   33.71
```

The function dumb() takes no action, but in our example it does so six hundred million times. R required about 34 seconds for those operations, although the exact time can vary. The result of system.time() will depend greatly on how fast your computer is; we show our result as a baseline. (Our machine is fast. If you try this example, you might want to start with a smaller number.) In this case, anyway, compilation definitely helps. The following example shows the result of compiling the function (an operation that used 0.02 seconds of elapsed time) and then running it.

```
> dc <- cmpfun (dumb)
> system.time (dc (6e8))
   user  system elapsed
   7.33    0.00    7.34
```

In this example, we see a substantial savings from compiling – the compiled version required only 22% of the time required by the original. Another very useful approach is the "just-in-time" compilation enabled by a call to enableJIT(), with an integer argument describing the details of how the compilation should work. Specifically, `enableJIT(3)` performs as much compilation as possible. Once this call has been made, functions are compiled right before their first use (and stay compiled). In this way, you do not need to specify specific functions to be compiled – they all are – and this has the potential to result in substantial time savings. In practice, it sometimes happens that the time-consuming parts of your data cleaning tasks are being done inside built-in functions – and these will probably already have been compiled. On the other hand, there are very few drawbacks to compilation. To "uncompile" a function, edit it with `fix()` – or "deparse" it to convert it to text, and then convert it back into a function, with a command such as `dc <- eval(parse(text = deparse(dc, con-trol="useSource")))`.

Parallel Processing

An even greater gain in processing speed can sometimes be realized using parallel processing, which exploits the fact that modern computers almost all have multiple "cores" capable of more-or-less independent processing. The built-in package `parallel` allows control over the use of multiple cores. Using the `parallel` package requires three steps: first, a "cluster" of cores is created, possibly with the `makeCluster()` command. (Creating the cluster may take a few seconds, but it only needs to be done once per session.) Second, any necessary items from the global workspace need to be passed to the cluster via a call to `clusterExport()`. Finally, the cluster created in the first step is passed to one of the functions that knows how to exploit it. For example, the `parSapply()` function acts as a "parallel `sapply()`," running a function on the columns of a data frame, with different cores acting on different columns. The machine on which we wrote this book has 32 cores – we can determine this via a call to the `detectCores()` function – so in this example we set aside 24 of them to act as the cluster. Creating the cluster takes about 5 seconds in this example. Next we export the `dumb()` and `dc()` functions so that the cluster can use them, and then we run `parSapply()` to run 24 separate instances of each of these functions.

```
> detectCores () # after library (parallel)
[1] 32
> clust <- makeCluster (24)
> clusterExport (clust, c("dumb", "dc"))
> system.time (
        parSapply (clust, 1:24, function (i) dumb (6e8/24)))
   user   system elapsed
   0.00     0.00    2.29
> system.time (
        parSapply (clust, 1:24, function (i) dc (6e8/24)))
   user   system elapsed
   0.00     0.00     0.67
```

Because we were running 24 instances of our dumb() and dc() functions, we only needed to run 1/24th of the iterations within each instance. Notice the substantial time savings realized from running in parallel – even more so when running the compiled version of the function. Interestingly, functions inside a call to parSapply() are not automatically compiled even if enableJIT() has been called; you will need to compile them explicitly (or run them first, to get them to compile if enableJIT() has been set) and then export the compiled version to the cluster.

It is a good practice to stop the cluster with stopCluster() when parallel processing is complete, although the cluster will be stopped when R terminates.

Even More Speed

When even more speed is required, R can interface nicely with code that is compiled down to the machine level. Often this is code from somewhere else that was originally written in, say, C or Fortran. We run code like this all the time inside R, and in packages, without even knowing it. The ability to write this sort of code is perhaps more valuable for production environments requiring lots of specialized computation than for the sorts of data cleaning problems relevant to this book, and we will not discuss this here. The help pages for dyn.load() and .C(), and especially Chapter 5 ("System and foreign language interfaces") of the "Writing R Extensions" manual will be useful starting points. The Rcpp package provides another, cleaner approach to incorporating C++ code, and the paper of Eddelbuettel and Françcois (2011), and their web page, www.rcpp.org, together with that of Wickham, adv-r.had.co .nz/Rcpp.html, provide more details for the interested user.

5.6 Chapter Summary and Critical Data Handling Tools

This chapter discusses functions and scripts, two ways to automate actions in R. Every data cleaning task will generate one or more of these. Functions are self-contained but hard to transport. Unless you include a side effect (such as plotting or writing to a file) they operate on local variables and do nothing more than compute a return value. Scripts are easy-to-read text files that act as sets of commands – often including lots of function calls and even function definitions – just like those you type into the console (including commands that may not be valid). All variables in a script are global.

Important features of functions (and scripts) include the following:

- Function arguments are matched by name and by position. Names can often be abbreviated. One special argument is the ellipsis . . ., which allows the number of arguments to vary. However, names of arguments defined after the ellipsis cannot be abbreviated, and the ellipsis can "consume" arguments whose names are typed in error. It is important for you as the function developer – and as a user – to check the arguments carefully. The `missing()` function is useful here.

- A function has a return value. This can only be one R object, so if you need to return several items, put them into a list. If you do not want a function to return any value, end it with a call to `invisible()`.
- Side effects are when a function does something other than compute and return a value. Sometimes these are harmless, as when a function draws a plot, or necessary, as when a function reads in data from a disk file. Sometimes side effects are dangerous, as when a function changes or deletes an object in the global workspace. Avoid this sort of side effect.
- Functions can be saved to disk with `dump()` and restored with `source()`, or via `save()` and restored via `load()`. Scripts are saved as ordinary text files, but using `source()` on a script file causes its code to be run.
- Functions and scripts will have errors. Debugging is a substantial part of every development effort. We can debug with a simple method, such as inserting `cat()` statements, or via the more sophisticated interactive debugging tools `browser()` and `debug()`. Our functions can generate our own errors (and warnings), and these can be handled via `try()`. If a function produces an error or warning, be sure to find out why – but do not expect your users to behave similarly.
- Functions and scripts can access files and directories through ordinary R functions.
- To speed things up, try compiling your functions, either individually with `cmpfun()` from the `compiler` package, or via `enableJIT()`, which compiles every function it runs. For problems with large loops, you can achieve substantial gains in speed via parallel processing through the `parallel` package.

5.6.1 Programming Style

In any data cleaning project you should expect to deliver your functions and scripts, as well as your results. Your code should be neatly and consistently formatted. A number of proposed R style guides can be found on the Internet and inevitably they disagree. For example, one source suggests separating parts of an R object's names with underscores (as in `first_sub_total`) while another recommends never using underscores. R's code itself uses different schemes in different places. Make sure your names are meaningful – s is an uninformative name for a standard deviation, for example. The cost of typing longer variable names is less than the cost of debugging code later when you cannot remember what that variable was for.

Our recommendation is to select a style and stick with it. Most importantly, add comments to your code – more than you think you need. Use spacing – blank lines, spaces around operators, and indentation – for readability. For example, in our code we do not indent commands in a function that are not part of an `if()`, `for()`, or similar clause. Then, we indent four spaces for each such nested clause. Other programmers indent everything inside a function. On another point, consider including dates or version numbers in your functions and scripts.

It is as important to write readable code as it is to write efficient code. Tailor your style to your reader. For example, suppose you want to check whether a vector has a zero length. We would use an expression such as `if(length(x) == 0)` .... This shows clearly the two things being compared. Some programmers use the more cryptic `if(!length(x))` .... Here R computes the length, then converts it to a logical to be able to apply the `!` operator. If the length is 0, then `!0` produces `TRUE`. Even if this latter approach were marginally faster it would not be worth it.

5.6.2 Common Bugs

In this section, we mention a number of the bugs we see in our, and other people's, R code. Avoiding these bugs is a good start toward building useful, re-usable code.

- Many bugs arise from unexpected input, so when you prepare a function for someone else's use, you should consider testing the classes, sizes, and other attributes of input arguments to ensure they match what a function expects. Sometimes, the "unexpected" behavior is related to missingness, so if a computation depends on, say, the average of some input vector, you, as a function writer, will need to decide whether an `NA` in the input should cause the function to stop (perhaps testing with `anyNA()`) or whether the average should be computed with the missing values excluded (using `mean()` with `na.rm = TRUE` in this example).

- Another common input error arises from R's habit of converting a one-row or one-column matrix into a vector (see Section 3.2.1). Users might intend to pass a matrix to a function expecting one, using a call like `myfun(mymat[mymat$Price > 10,])` to select only those rows for which `Price` is greater than 10. If there is only one such row, though, R will silently convert that row into a vector. Code that relies on matrix attributes, such as trying to determine how many columns a matrix has using `dim()`, will fail.

- A third common error arises from the way that missing values propagate through computations. We very often use the `if()` function, but a call to `if(x)` produces an error if `x` is `NA`. When you observe this error, you will want to find the source of the missing value.

- Errors often arise when reading disk files (if they are not present) or writing them (if a folder does not exist or if permissions are not properly set). Check for these conditions with one of the file-handling functions such as `file.exists()`, to check whether a file is present, or `file.info()`, to see if a file is writeable.
- We commonly see a warning when a function expects a single result and gets a vector of length 2 or more. For example, in many cases, code will check the `class` of an object with code such as `if(class(obj) == "lm")` .... Since many objects have a vector of classes, this code will produce a warning (and examine only the first element of the class vector).
- An even more serious problem can occur when `sapply()` (Section 3.5) runs a function on a data frame or list that is expected to return a single value for each column in the data frame. We saw in Section 3.2.3 how a problem arises if the function in question can return results of different lengths.

5.6.3 Objects, Classes, and Methods

We showed an earlier example where calling `print()` on a data frame led to R calling another function, `print.data.frame()`. This is an example of a widely used programming approach in which the type of object passed to a function determines the action the function will take. In this example, `print()` is a "generic" function and `print.data.frame()` is a "method" that is applied to data frame objects. R has almost 200 different methods for the `print()` function; you can see them with the command `methods ("print")`. As in the `print.data.frame()` example, the names of methods are constructed from the generic function's name, a dot, and the object type. To give another example, we construct sequences of `POSIXt` objects using the `seq()` function (Section 3.6.6). R detects the class of the `POSIXt` object and runs the specific `seq.POSIXt()` function.

This approach, in which one function can have many methods, based on the class of the object passed to it, is part of "object-oriented programming," a widespread architecture of programming languages. R has two different ways to implement object-oriented programming. Neither is important enough to data cleaning to be part of this book, but you should be aware that many R functions are equipped to perform different duties based on different inputs. Sometimes, you will need to look up the specific function, rather than the generic one, in the help pages.

6

Getting Data into and out of R

Earlier chapters in this book have described what data in R looks like and how to manipulate it. In this chapter, we describe how to get data into R for analysis, and how to get updated data back out. Reading data into R is the first step in every data cleaning project, so it is in this chapter that the real work of data cleaning begins. But we start with a note on keeping track of your data's *provenance*, which is the word we use to describe the documentation of your data's history. You should know where you acquired every bit of your data, from what source, and on what date. A natural place to keep that information is in your scripts. Often, we have one or more scripts devoted to reading in the data, and these start with some description of the date, the source of the data, the commands to do the actual reading, and some notes on problems we encountered reading the data in.

Keeping track of the data's provenance is always important, but it is especially important if the underlying data is subject to change, perhaps because you extracted it from a database, a public site, or a web page under someone else's control. It is through this sort of documentation that you can make your research reproducible by others.

6.1 Reading Tabular ASCII Data into Data Frames

Most of the data we read – and write – in R comes to us in the form of rectangular or tabular data, that is, data arranged with observations in rows and measurements in columns. We expect that every row will have exactly the same number of items. Being able to get these data files into R cleanly is a critical part of data cleaning. Unfortunately, there are a lot of ways a file can be badly put together. In this section, we describe how to read tabular data files into R data frames and some approaches to try when things aren't working. Writing data from R to disk is generally straightforward and we discuss that briefly at the end

A Data Scientist's Guide to Acquiring, Cleaning, and Managing Data in R, First Edition.
Samuel E. Buttrey and Lyn R. Whitaker.
© 2018 John Wiley & Sons Ltd. Published 2018 by John Wiley & Sons Ltd.
Companion website: www.wiley.com/go/buttrey/datascientistsguide

of the section. In this section, we focus on ASCII text, and in the next section, we describe the minor complications brought about by UTF-8.

6.1.1 Files with Delimiters

Perhaps, the most common sort of file we read in is a delimited file in which each observation is represented by a single row. Within the line, the fields are separated by a delimiter, which will usually be a single character such as a comma, tab, semicolon, pipe character (|), or exclamation point. Sometimes, a space or spaces are used as the delimiter. The end of each line is marked with the end-of-line character (but, as we observe in Section 6.1.8, these can vary across platforms). The advantage of delimited files is that, being text, they are easy to move across systems and easy to inspect by eye (although of course fields will generally not line up). Unlike fields in fixed-width files, fields in delimited files need never be truncated nor made artificially too big. On the downside, like other text files, delimited files are not good at representing numeric data efficiently. Moreover, on occasion users will inadvertently insert the delimiter character into regular fields (we illustrate this later in the chapter).

The principal tool for reading in delimited files in R is the `read.table()` function, together with its offspring `read.csv()` and `read.delim()`. ("CSV" names the popular "Comma-Separated Values" file format.) These three functions are identical except for their default settings. All three of these produce data frames; if you need a matrix, the best approach is to construct a data frame and then convert it via `as.matrix()`. Two more functions, `read.csv2()` and `read.delim2()`, are also available; these are just like `read.csv()` and `read.delim()` except they expect the European-style comma for the decimal point and that `read.csv2()` uses the semi-colon as its delimiter.

The `read.table()` function and the others employ a host of arguments that allow most delimited files to be read in. These arguments are optional and have default values that are sometimes useful and sometimes not.

The most important of these arguments are as follows:

- `header`: a logical indicating whether the disk file has header labels in the first row. If so, set this to TRUE and those labels will be used as column headers (after being passed through the `make.names()` function to make them valid for that use).
- `sep`: the separator character. This might be a comma for a CSV, a tab (written `\t`) for a tab-separated file, a semi-colon, or something else.
- `quote`: a set of characters to be used to surround quotes, discussed as follows.
- `comment.char`: the character that is understood to introduce a comment line.

- `stringsAsFactors`: a logical that determines whether columns that appear to be characters are converted to factors or left as characters.
- `colClasses`: a vector that explicitly gives the class of each column.
- `na.strings`: a vector specifying the indicator(s) of missing values in the input data.

Other options control the number of lines skipped before the reading starts, the maximum number of rows to read, whether blank lines are omitted or included, and more, but the ones above are generally the arguments we worry about first. The choice of `sep` character can often be inferred from the name of the file (comma for files whose names end in CSV and tab for TSV, although this is not a requirement). When the separator is unknown, we either try the usual ones, use an external program to examine the first few lines of the file, or resort to the `scan()` function (discussed later in this section). The default value of `sep` is the empty string, `" "`, which indicates that any amount of white space (including tabs) serves as the delimiter. This is intended for text that has been formatted to line up nicely on the page (so that extra spaces or tabs have been added for readability). Setting `sep` to be the space character, `" "`, means that `read.table()` will split the line at every space (and never at a tab).

We have also found that the `quote`, `comment.char`, and `stringsAs-Factors` arguments, in particular, very often need to be set explicitly in data cleaning tasks. By default, the set of quote characters is set to be both `'` and `"` in `read.table()`, and to just `"` in the other functions. This means that a string inside quotation marks such as `"Ann Arbor, MI"` is treated as a single unit. This is a valid approach when the separator is a space, since otherwise that phrase would look as if it has been made up of three separate fields. The single quote mark would be useful in the corresponding British environment, where its use is more common. In our work, the single quote is found most often as an apostrophe, and if the single quote is part of the `quote` argument, the apostrophe in the phrase `Coeur d'Alene, Idaho` will be taken as starting a very long string that might not be ended until a later entry contains `Peter O'Toole` or `Martha's Vineyard`. We generally turn the interpretation of quotation marks off by passing `quote = ""`, or set the argument to recognize only the double quotation mark by passing `quote = "\""`.

Similarly, the comment character defaults to R's own comment character, the hash mark or pound sign (#). Lots of code has comments, but comments in data are rare. Much more often we see the pound sign as legitimate text in an expression such as `Giants are #1!` or `241 E. 58th St. #8A`. We generally turn comments off by passing `comment.char = ""`.

6.1.2 Column Classes

The `stringsAsFactors` argument is one of a set of arguments that aims to help R figure out what to do with the data that it reads in. We have encountered this name when constructing data frames with `data.frame()` and `cbind()` in Section 3.4. Its default `TRUE` value specifies that any column found to be character should be converted to a factor. This can cause problems in a couple of ways. First, it is often the case that numeric columns can have a small number of unexpected text items in them, particularly missing values codes that are different from the default `NA` that R expects. In this case, the `read.table()` function interprets these columns as character and then converts them to factors. Second, even for text data we generally want the raw text for purposes of data cleaning; we switch to factors only when we are ready to begin modeling. One way around this automatic conversion is to set `stringsAsFactors = FALSE`, and we almost always pass this argument when we are reading in data. The exceptions are when we know that the data is numeric (and pre-cleaned), and when we use `colClasses`, which we describe in the following paragraph. In fact, this issue arises so often that R has a built-in option to set the default behavior of `stringsAsFactors`. However, we rarely use this option because we want our scripts to be portable to other users who might not have set it, and for aesthetic reasons we hesitate to have our scripts set other users' options.

A more flexible approach is provided by the `colClasses` argument. This allows you to specify the column type for each of the columns at the time you read the table. Of course, this information is not always available – sometimes you have to read the data to figure out what is in it. Passing the `nrows` argument allows you to specify how many rows `read.table()` should read. So often we read just a few dozen lines and inspect the resulting data set to get an idea about what classes to expect.

The `colClasses` argument can be specified as a vector whose length is the number of columns in the input file, or as a named vector, in which case you can name specific columns, and R assigns classes to the rest. It does this by reading the entire file, so supplying column classes explicitly can often speed up the reading of a big file.

In addition to the basic types of `numeric`, `character`, and `logical`, you can also specify `Date` or `POSIXct`, and there is an approach by which you can convert the input into other classes as well (see the help for `read.table()`). The elements of `colClasses` are recycled in the usual way, so `col-Classes = "character"` converts all columns to characters – which is often a good place to start in a data cleaning problem where the data is poorly documented or of suspect quality. The `as.is` argument provides another way to keep columns from being converted.

As an example of where `colClasses` can be helpful, consider the case where a column consists of numbers that might have leading zeros, such as US five-digit ZIP codes. Without `colClasses`, such a column would automatically be converted to numeric, producing values whose leading zeros would be lost – so the ZIP code for Logan Airport in Boston would come out as the number 2128 instead of the expected 02128. The stringsAsFactors argument would have no effect here since R would see the column as numeric. In this example, we could replace the missing zeros using sprintf() as in Section 4.2.1, but a more direct approach is to specify "character" in the colClasses argument.

6.1.3 Common Pitfalls in Reading Tables

In this section, we describe common problems we encounter when reading text files into R and some ways you might address them. In any particular case, it is difficult to know which issue is causing the problem. After we describe some of these problems, we give an example of how we might go about diagnosing them with a small realistic data set that appears to have a deceptively simple problem.

Embedded Delimiters
We have mentioned that problems commonly arise when the table to be read includes # or quote characters. Another problem arises when the data has the separator character (say, a comma) included as part of some text. Data of the sort arises particularly often when the original source of the file is a spreadsheet. Textual comments in spreadsheets very often have commas (or tabs, which are introduced when the user enters a new-line character within a cell). It also happens that cities get recorded in a form like "Hempstead, Long Island" or "Westminster, Orange County." If those text fields are surrounded by quotation marks then R can interpret them correctly using quote="\"", but this is rarely seen in spreadsheet data. More often, embedded delimiters require some effort to correct, and in the following section we give an example.

Unknown Missing Value Indicator
Another set of problems arises when the "missing value" indicator is unknown. By default, R expects missing values to be indicated by NA, but the na. strings argument allows a set of values to be supplied. Any value in the input that matches an element of na.strings will be interpreted as a missing value – and blank fields will also be taken as missing, except in character or factor fields. For example, a spreadsheet from the Excel program can have values such as #NULL!, #N/A, or #VALUE!, so these would be good candidates for including in na.strings. If they are included, then columns that are otherwise numeric (or logical) will be correctly interpreted, whereas if they are not, then those columns will be interpreted as characters – and as we discussed earlier, character columns are treated as factors by default.

Empty or Nearly Empty Fields
Empty fields – those with nothing in them – generally do not cause problems, since they are brought in as NA values in numeric fields. As we noted

in Section 4.1.3, though, sometimes text data – particularly from spread-sheets – represents empty cells by strings with a single space (or, sometimes, a few spaces in a row). We sometimes think of these cells as "nearly empty." This problem is often hard to detect ahead of time, since empty and nearly empty cells of a spreadsheet look alike. So the first thing we do, when we read in a data frame, is to determine the number of numeric and character or factor columns (and logical, too, though these are rarer). For a data frame named `ourdf`, for example, we run the command `table(sapply(ourdf, function(x) class(x)))` and compare what we see to what we expect. In much of our work we expect 50–75% or more of the columns to be numeric, so if there are no, or only a few, numerics, we conclude that there are textual values – often, missing-value indicators or nearly empty values – in those numeric columns. If we know that a particular column (say, one called `NumID`) should be numeric but is being represented as character, we can tabulate the elements that R is unable to convert, with a command like `table(ourdf$NumID[is.na(as.numeric(ourdf$NumID))])`. This is often a good starting point for examining the set of missing value indicators in the data. These can then be included in the `na.strings` argument in another call to `read.table()` – or we can explicitly set them to NA ourselves.

Blank Lines

A less common problem occurs when the input file has blank rows. `Read.table()` will skip these by default, and this is often what we want. However, in some cases it is important that the lines from two different files correspond. In this case set `skip.blank.lines = FALSE` and blank lines will be included in the output. The entries in these lines will appear as NA in numeric columns and as the empty string `" "` in character ones.

Row Names

In Section 3.4, we noted that a data frame in R must have row and column names. When a data frame is produced by one of the `read.table()` functions, the default behavior is for R to create row names from the integers 1, 2, and so on, unless the header has one fewer field than the data rows, in which case R uses the first column's values as the row names. Remember that row names need to be unique; if yours are not, you can force R to supply integer row names by passing `row.names = NULL`.

You can also specify one of the columns to be used as row names explicitly, by passing its name or number with the `row.names` argument. (This argument can also be used with a vector of row names, but we rarely use that feature.) It can be useful to specify row names when they represent something important because the names can be used explicitly in subsetting statements.

6.1.4   An Example of When `read.table()` Fails

There are some data sets for which our initial attempts at using `read.table()` just will not work because of one or more of the problems we have described – or something else. Sometimes we correct these problems, when we find them, by modifying the original data directly and documenting that fact. More often, we can read the data into R by suitable choice of arguments to `read.table()`, and sometimes `read.table()` just cannot be used and we resort to the more primitive, but more flexible, function `scan()`, which we describe later in the chapter.

In this example, we show a small sample of the sort of text we are often supplied with and try to read it into R. The following text has been saved as a file named `addresses.csv` in our working directory.

```
ID,LastName,Address,City,State
001,O'Higgins,48 Grant Rd.,Des Moines,IA
011,Macina,401 1st Ave., Apt 13G,New York,NY
242,Roeder,71 Quebec Ave.,E. Thetford,VT
146,Stephens,1234 Smythe St., #5,Detroit,MI
241,Ishikawa,986 OceanView Dr.,Pacific Grove,CA
```

Because the file's name ends in `csv`, we will presume that the file uses commas as separators (although this is not always the case), and that the file includes a header row. In real life, it is a good idea to examine the file first, where possible, using a text editor or file viewer.

Using the lessons learned from the previous section, we know to specify the arguments `quote = ""`, `comment.char = ""`, and `stringsAsFactors=FALSE`. Our first effort produces this error:

```
> read.table ("addresses.csv", header = TRUE, sep = ",",
    quote = "", comment.char = "", stringsAsFactors = FALSE)
Error in scan(file = file, what = what, sep = sep, ...
  line 1 did not have 6 elements
```

This error is telling us that the longest line encountered contained six elements (fields), whereas at least one other – in this case, the header, line 1 – had fewer. Either the header or some of the data is lacking a field – or has too many. Notice that the error was issued by the `scan()` function, which is itself called by `read.table()`.

Using `read.table()`

Our next step in this process might be to examine the first row to make sure this is a header row and to determine the number of fields. When we add the `nrows = 1` argument to `read.table()`, and set `header` to `FALSE`, we extract the very first row in the file.

```
> read.table ("addresses.csv", header = FALSE, sep = ",",
    quote = "", comment.char = "", stringsAsFactors = FALSE,
    nrows = 1)
   V1       V2       V3     V4     V5
1 ID LastName Address City State
```

R has returned a data frame with one row. Since no row or column names were provided, R has added them (the 1 at the left and the V1 through V5 at the top). The header contains five fields, so we expect every row of the data to have five fields as well. We can determine the number of fields that R sees in each row with the count.fields() command. Since this command produces one number for every row in the file, we normally pass its output directly to table(), but here we show it explicitly.

```
> count.fields ("addresses.csv", sep = ",", quote = "",
                comment.char = "")
[1] 5 5 6 5 6 5
```

The fact that the second and fourth lines of the file (after the header) contain six fields and the others do not is now visible. We can suspect that those rows each contain an extra delimiter. Files with embedded delimiters are particularly painful to handle. We extract the first problematic line with read.table() by skipping the first two and reading only the third (using skip = 2 and nrows = 1). R returns a data frame with seven columns, as shown here.

```
>   read.table ("addresses.csv", header = FALSE, sep = ",",
    quote = "", comment.char = "", stringsAsFactors = FALSE,
    nrows = 1, skip = 2)
   V1      V2         V3        V4        V5 V6
1 11 Macina 401 1st Ave.  Apt 13G New York NY
```

We are prepared to conclude that the problem with the file is that some of the entries in the Address column contain embedded commas – but we would look at the other problem rows to be sure.

When there are delimiters embedded in fields, one quick way to get the data into R with read.table() is by passing the fill = TRUE argument. This is intended to produce a data frame with the largest number of columns necessary to hold any line. If it succeeds, and there are only a small number of defective lines, the final column of the new data frame will be almost empty. The rows where there are entries in the final column will help you figure out where the problems in the input data are arising. Here, we show the results of using the fill = TRUE argument, and assign the return value of read.table() to an object named add.

```
> (add <- read.table ("addresses.csv", header = TRUE,
                       sep = ",", quote = "", comment = "",
                       stringsAsFactors = FALSE, fill = TRUE))
```

```
              ID           LastName        Address     City State
001 O'Higgins        48 Grant Rd.     Des Moines      IA
011    Macina        401 1st Ave.        Apt 13G New York     NY
242    Roeder     71 Quebec Ave.    E. Thetford      VT
146  Stephens   1234 Smythe St.           #5 Detroit     MI
241  Ishikawa 986 OceanView Dr. Pacific Grove      CA
```

There are two things to notice here. First, R has produced row names from the ID column since the header had one fewer entry than the longest row. This also causes the column names to be shifted to the right. Had there been duplicate entries in that column, read.table() would have failed and we would have supplied row.names = NULL on our next effort. Second, the second and fourth rows' addresses have been broken at the extra delimiter. This causes those rows to extend over six columns, leaving them as the only ones with entries in the rightmost column.

If all the problematic lines appear to be broken in the same way, we would probably fix them directly in R. In this example, we would start by identifying the broken lines, paste columns 2 and 3 to complete the address, and then move columns 4 and 5 into positions 3 and 4. This code shows the steps we might take, and what the add data frame looks like at this point.

```
> fixers <- add$State != ""    # logical vector
> add[fixers, 2] <- paste (add[fixers,2], add[fixers,3])
> add[fixers, 3:4] <- add[fixers, 4:5]
> add
              ID              LastName        Address City State
001 O'Higgins           48 Grant Rd.     Des Moines      IA
011    Macina 401 1st Ave.  Apt 13G        New York      NY      NY
242    Roeder          71 Quebec Ave.    E. Thetford      VT
146  Stephens   1234 Smythe St.  #5           Detroit      MI      MI
241  Ishikawa       986 OceanView Dr. Pacific Grove      CA
```

All that remains is to adjust the column names, remove the rightmost column, and insert the current row names as a column (replacing them, perhaps, with integers). This code shows how this might be done.

```
# Save column names, then remove last column
> mycolnames <- colnames (add)
> add$State <- NULL
# Insert the ID column
> add <- data.frame (ID = rownames (add), add)
> colnames (add) <- mycolnames        # now assign column names
> rownames (add) <- NULL              # replace old row names
> rm (fixers, mycolnames)             # clean up!
```

It was convenient to save the column names before performing the other modifications and then to re-assign them at the end. We include this lengthy example because these are the sorts of problems we face almost every time we read text data into R. Note that in the last command we remove some temporary variables. Although we have not been showing this in our code, it is something we do regularly, to keep the workspace clean and reduce the risk of inadvertently re-using an existing object.

Using scan()

Sometimes, there are multiple problems with an input data set – highly variable numbers of fields, different separators used in different places, and so on. A good general-purpose data input tool is scan(), which with the sep = "\n" argument, reads entire lines into an R character vector. By default, scan() expects to encounter numbers, so in reading text we need to pass the what = character(), or, for short, the what = "" argument. Like read.table(), scan() has a host of arguments to let you handle all sorts of text files. This example shows the output of using scan() on our addresses.csv file.

```
> (addscan <- scan ("addresses.csv", what = "", sep = "\n",
                    quote = "", comment.char = ""))
Read 6 items
[1] "ID,LastName,Address,City,State"
[2] "001,O'Higgins,48 Grant Rd.,Des Moines,IA"
[3] "011,Macina,401 1st Ave., Apt 13G,New York,NY"
[4] "242,Roeder,71 Quebec Ave.,E. Thetford,VT"
[5] "146,Stephens,1234 Smythe St., #5,Detroit,MI"
[6] "241,Ishikawa,986 OceanView Dr.,Pacific Grove,CA"
```

We can fix addscan directly by replacing the third comma by another character – a semi-colon, say – in every row with six commas. This is less complicated that it might appear at first, and represents the sort of data cleaning we do regularly. We start by identifying the problem rows, either with count.fields() as before, or directly, using gregexpr() from Section 4.4.5.

```
> commas <- gregexpr (",", addscan)       # locate all commas
> length.5 <- lengths(commas) == 5        # identify long rows
> comma.be.gone <- sapply (commas[length.5],
                           function (x) x[3])
```

Each element of the commas list consists of a vector giving the locations of the commas within a line. In this last command, we have extracted the third element of each of these vectors. So comma.be.gone gives the location of the third comma on those lines with a total of five commas. Now we replace those commas by semicolons.

```
> substring (addscan[length.5], comma.be.gone,
             comma.be.gone) <- ";"
> addscan
[1] "ID,LastName,Address,City,State"
```

```
[2] "001,O'Higgins,48 Grant Rd.,Des Moines,IA"
[3] "011,Macina,401 1st Ave.; Apt 13G,New York,NY"
[4] "242,Roeder,71 Quebec Ave.,E. Thetford,VT"
[5] "146,Stephens,1234 Smythe St.; #5,Detroit,MI"
[6] "241,Ishikawa,986 OceanView Dr.,Pacific Grove,CA"
```

Now that addscan is exactly as we want it to be, we have at least three choices. First, we can write it back out to disk (using the write.table() function we describe later) in preparation for re-reading. This approach uses extra disk space, but it has the advantage of creating a clean data set for other users. Second, we can pass the addscan vector back to read.table() using the text argument, and it will be interpreted just as if the text had been read from a file. This example shows the output from that call.

```
> read.table (text = addscan, header = TRUE, sep = ",",
             quote = "", comment = "", stringsAsFactors = FALSE)
   ID  LastName            Address        City State
1   1 O'Higgins        48 Grant Rd.  Des Moines    IA
2  11    Macina 401 1st Ave.; Apt 13G   New York    NY
3 242    Roeder     71 Quebec Ave.  E. Thetford    VT
4 146  Stephens  1234 Smythe St.; #5     Detroit    MI
5 241  Ishikawa   986 OceanView Dr. Pacific Grove   CA
```

This approach is straightforward but may not be very efficient for very large character vectors. Notice also that the ID column has been interpreted as numeric, so that the leading zeros have been removed. We can correct this by passing the colClasses argument. In this case, since ID is the only column whose class needs to be specified explicitly, we would pass colClasses = c(ID = "character").

A final method of handling an object like addscan is to use strsplit() to create a list consisting of one character vector for each row, broken at its commas. We can then use do.call() and rbind() to combine the elements of the list, as described in Section 3.7.1. This approach is fast, and well suited to large data objects, although it produces a character matrix that needs to be converted into a data frame, with column names and classes that need to be set.

6.1.5   Other Uses of the scan() Function

As we have seen, the scan() function is the most general way to read data into R. In this section, we describe some other cases where its use might be necessary.

Headers, Page Numbers, and Other Superfluous Text

One case where scan() is necessary is when the data set being read in was formatted by some program that was expecting to produce printed material. Often data like that will contain page headers and footers, and these need to be detected and removed. When we encounter this, we generally use `scan()` with `sep = "\n"` to read the data in as lines, then use a regular expression (Section 4.4) to detect and remove the offending lines. For example, if a vector `old` returned from `scan()` contains lines that start with `Page:`, a command like `new <- old[!grepl("^Page:", old)]` will produce a new vector omitting those lines. In this case, you have to examine the original data to determine the format of the header and footer lines, and ensure that no "real" lines are deleted inadvertently. A similar problem can arise when the original program contains both data and also total and sub-total lines – these, too, will need to be detected and deleted.

Input Records on Multiple Lines
It also happens sometimes that the headers occupy several lines (as with other difficulties, this arises in data from spreadsheets). If only the headers, and not the data, wrap around lines, the natural way to handle this is to omit the headers using the `skip` argument; so `skip = 3`, for example, skips the first three rows of the file. Then the headers can be added back in after the data frame is created. When the individual records are broken across multiple lines, and the number of lines is the same for every record, it is possible to persuade `scan()` to read these data in pieces. This requires passing a list in the `what` argument – see the help for `scan()` for the details. In fact, though, we usually `scan()` the whole file in, as a series of lines, and then operate on the components. If every input record takes up three lines, say, then we know that lines of the first type are found in positions 1, 4, 7, and so on; we can generate this sequence with `seq(1, by = 3, to = n)` where n is the number of lines read. (Remember to account for the header if there is one.) Then lines of the second type are found at locations one greater than those of the first type, and so on. Having identified the lines that make up each type, we can then `paste()` the strings of different types into a character vector with one element per original observation. Finally, we can pass this vector to `read.table()` using the `text` argument as in the previous example.

All of this may seem like a lot of work, but, as we have claimed throughout the book, a huge proportion of our time as statisticians and data scientists is taken up with tasks like this. The more efficiently we can take care of data issues, the faster we can get to the modeling part.

6.1.6 Writing Delimited Files

The `write.table()` function acts to write a delimited file, just as `read.table()` reads one. (And, just as there are the `read.csv()` and `read.csv2()` analogs to `read.table()`, R also provides `write.csv()` and `write.csv2()`.) We normally pass `write.table()` a data frame, though a matrix can be written as well, and we generally supply the delimiter with the `sep` argument, since the default choice of a space is rarely a good one. A few other arguments are useful as well. First, the resulting entries from character and factor columns are quoted by default; we often turn this behavior off with quote = FALSE, depending on what the recipient of the output is expecting. Quoting becomes necessary, though, when character values might contain the delimiter, or when it is important to retain leading zeros in identifiers that look numeric (01, 02, etc.). Second, row names are written by default; we rarely want these, so we generally specify row.names = FALSE. In contrast, the default setting of the col.names argument, which is TRUE, usually is what we want. The exception is when we plan to do a number of writes to a single file. In that case, the first write will usually specify col.names = TRUE and append = FALSE, and subsequent ones will specify col.names = FALSE and append = TRUE.

6.1.7 Reading and Writing Fixed-Width Files

One alternative to the delimited file is the fixed-width file. In this approach, each field occupies the same positions on each line. For example, an account number might take up characters 1–9, the customer's last name characters 10–24, and so on. This sort of output was more common in the past because it is the preferred format of the COBOL language that is no longer widely used. Depending on the layout, it is possible for the fixed-width approach to use much less space than the delimited one. For example, a comma-separated file with a million rows and a thousand columns will have roughly a billion commas in it. (On the other hand, each record in our example will have 15 characters for a customer's last name, so the design will waste space for customers with names such as Lee, and truncate those with more than 15 characters.) Moreover, random access is possible in a fixed-width file; if the customer's last name starts in position 10, and each line has 351 characters, then the millionth customer's name must start at character 351,000,010. A program that needs that name can "seek" directly to the relevant character, whereas with a delimited file it would have to read a million lines of different lengths. Despite these advantages, fixed-width files seem to arise nowadays only from older systems.

The R function to read these files is read.fwf(). It has many of the same arguments as read.table(). The most important additional argument is widths, a vector of integers giving the lengths of the fields. In our example above, the first two elements of widths would be 9 and 15, those being the lengths of the account number and customer's name.

It is rare to have to write a fixed-width file – indeed, we have never had to. The gdata package (Warnes *et al.*, 2015) has a routine aptly named write.fwf() that appears to do this job. We have not tested it.

6.1.8 A Note on End-of-Line Characters

For historical reasons, Windows text files use two characters to denote the end of a line – carriage return (\r in R) and line feed (\n), whereas OS X and Linux use only the \n character (and older Apple computers used only \r). This can cause problems when passing text files between systems, but R is generally forgiving. The scan() function recognizes any of these line endings, and write.table() permits some flexibility in the eol ("end of line") argument. Mac and Linux users can also use gsub() to remove any \r characters. Although R is more forgiving than some other applications, you should be aware that text files' endings can differ from platform to platform.

6.2 Reading Large, Non-Tabular, or Non-ASCII Data

Most of the text data we get into R comes via scan() or read.table(). But there are at least two cases where we need more than these techniques alone can provide. First, some files – and we expect this to be ever more common in the future – are simply too big to fit into the main memory of the computer. We briefly discussed some ways around this limitation in Section 3.8. If the entire file is needed, then the techniques of that section may be necessary. Often, though, the file is huge but the subset of records that we need is not. In that case, we need the ability to filter the data set, without first reading it all into memory.

The second case involves files that are not in tabular formats suitable for read.table(). These might be text in a non-tabular format, such as the popular JSON and XML formats we discuss in this chapter; free-form text such as log files and other documents; or binary data such as images and sounds. For all of these cases, R provides the ability to perform basic file operations on disk files. By "basic file operations" we mean opening a file to get access to its contents, reading it bit by bit so that we can operate on the part that was read, writing results to the file (usually we will read from one file and write to another), seeking (i.e., resetting our current position in the file), and then closing the file. In fact, in most circumstances, we open two files, one for input and another for output. We read the input file sequentially (i.e., starting at the beginning and all the way through); when we encounter records of interest we write them, or something about them, to the output file; and then when the input file has been read we close both files. These basic file operations are most often performed on text files divided into discrete lines, but they also apply to files with binary or other data. In this section, we describe these basic file operations and how they might be used within R.

6.2.1 Opening and Closing Files

The first step in file handling is to open the file. We must first know whether the file contains text (which might be UTF-8) or whether the data is binary (as an image, video, or music file). This is not always easy to ascertain inside R, although the name of the file is often informative. Most often the file format is supplied to us by the client.

When we open a file in R, we are really creating a *connection*, which is a method of communication not only to and from files but also to and from other devices and processes. Files are very much the most common sort of connections we use, so in these sections we will focus on tools for handling files.

A file is opened with the `file()` function and its relatives. These related functions, such as `gzfile()`, provide the ability to open files in some of the popular zipped formats, like gzip. The help for the `file()` function shows the formats supported. (There is also an `open()` command, which is more suited to non-file connections.)

The `file` functions return a connection object that stores all the information that R needs to have about the connection, and we use this connection object in subsequent calls to the functions that will read from, write to, seek in, or close files. When we open a file, we pass an argument called `open` that describes whether the file is to be read from, written to, or appended to (`open = "r"`, `"w"` or `"a"`, respectively). If a + is added, the file is opened for both reading and writing (but `open = "w+"` truncates the file first), and if a b or t is added the file is explicitly opened in binary or text mode. So, for example, `open = "rb"` opens a binary file for reading, and `open = "a+b"` opens a binary file for reading and appending.

Once you have finished with a connection, you should close it with the `close()` function. This is a good practice even though R will close it for you when your session terminates.

6.2.2 Reading and Writing Lines

Once the connection object is available, we pass it to the reading and writing functions. The `readLines()` function reads text lines – that is, pieces of text terminated by the new-line character. We specify the number of lines to read with the n argument (n = -1 meaning to read all lines). Rather than read one line at a time, it feels as if it should be faster to read a large "chunk" of lines at once, process them, and then read another chunk. In reality, though, the situation is complicated by the way the operating system itself prepares "caches" of disk files in main memory. When programming, you have to balance the (possible) gain in speed of reading a chunk of lines at once with the simplicity of code to handle just one line at a time.

As an example, consider using `readLines()` to read lines from the `addresses.csv` file of the example from last section. (`readLines()` produces the same result as `scan()` with what = `" "` and sep = `"\n"`.) Operating on a file, `readLines()` opens the file, reads as many lines as requested with the n argument and then closes the file. The reading always begins at line 1. In this example, we read one line at a time from the `addresses.csv` file.

```
> readLines ("addresses.csv", n = 1)
[1] "ID,LastName,Address,City,State"
> readLines ("addresses.csv", n = 1)
[1] "ID,LastName,Address,City,State"
```

Here, the same line is returned from both calls because readLines () opens and closes the file each time. If you want to read the data in pieces, you will need to open a connection and pass the connection to readLines (). Operating on a connection, readLines () reads the number of lines requested and keeps track of its location in the file for future calls. Here, we read the first few lines of addresses.csv via a connection.

```
> con <- file ("addresses.csv", open = "r")
> readLines (con, n = 2)
[1] "ID,LastName,Address,City,State"
[2] "001,O'Higgins,48 Grant Rd.,Des Moines,IA"
> readLines (con, n = 2)
[1] "011,Macina,401 1st Ave., Apt 13G,New York,NY"
[2] "242,Roeder,71 Quebec Ave.,E. Thetford,VT"
> close (con)
```

The readLines () and scan () functions applied to a connection provide a natural way to read very large data files piece by piece.

Analogously to readLines (), writeLines () writes a vector of characters out to a file (adding in the new-line separator). Again, passing a file name causes the file to be opened, written, and closed – so in order to append data to a file, you will want to open a connection and pass the connection to write-Lines ().

Besides opening, closing, reading, and writing files, there are two other basic file operations to know about. When a file is opened for read or write, R maintains a "pointer" that describes the current location in the file. (Files opened for both read and write have two of these.) The seek () function with its default arguments returns the current location in the file (in terms of number of bytes from the start of the file). Passing the where argument lets you re-set the file pointer to a position of your choice. This is useful if you need to jump to a prespecified position. However, the help tells us that "use of seek on Windows is discouraged."

The final operation, flush (), can be used after a file output command to ensure that the write operation gets committed to disk right away. Without this operation, the output from the write operations may be cached – that is, saved up by the operating system for a convenient time. The flush () command will be useful when you are monitoring a program's output, or when it is important to perform a write right away to protect against a system crash.

6.2.3 Reading and Writing UTF-8 and Other Encodings

We described UTF-8 and other encodings in Section 4.5, and you have to expect that you will be called on to read some non-ASCII text soon and ever more frequently in the future. Many of the text-reading functions we describe in this chapter, such as read.table() and scan(), have two arguments in place to handle UTF-8-related chores. The fileEncoding argument lets you specify the encoding in the file that you are reading in, while the encoding argument specifies the encoding of the R object that contains the data read in. Remember, though, as we saw in Section 4.5.3, that UTF-8 inside a data frame will often be displayed with the <U+0000>-type notation.

When reading data line by line, it is best to ascertain in advance whether the file contains UTF-8. Then it can be opened by passing encoding = "UTF-8" to the file() command, and read using readLines(), again with encoding = "UTF-8". There is no cost to passing these options to a file containing simple ASCII text, since ASCII is a subset of UTF-8. However, if the file was created with latin1 or another different encoding, certain characters will be handled incorrectly with the UTF-8 options.

Writing UTF-8 is best accomplished by first creating a file connection with the file() function with open = "w" and encoding = "UTF-8". Then text can be written to the connection using writeLines() with the use-Bytes = TRUE argument. (We have not always had success using write.table() with UTF-8 data.) By default the useBytes argument is FALSE, which tells R to convert encoded strings back to the native encoding before writing. For non-UTF-8 locales, particularly in Windows, this conversion can lead to unexpected results. Be aware that operating systems and locales treat UTF-8 differently – in some cases, inconsistently.

6.2.4 The Null Character

The "null" is the character whose hexadecimal value is 00, sometimes denoted in R by 0x00 using R's hexadecimal notation (so this is not the same as R's NULL value). Null characters should generally not be found in regular text and in fact are not permitted in R. However, the null is used as an end-of-string marker in the C language, and you have to expect to encounter some text with nulls in it. Moreover, we occasionally encounter text files with nulls embedded in them, for whatever reason. By default, scan() and read.table() stop reading when a null character is encountered and resume with the next field. Setting the skipNul argument to TRUE allows scan() and read.table() to skip over nulls. For delimited data, this is generally a safe choice, although you will not see any warning that nulls were detected and skipped. If there are "intentional" nulls in the text, and you need to detect and keep them, you will need to read the file as binary data using readBin(), which we discuss as follows.

6.2.5 Binary Data

The readBin() function reads binary data. We rarely use this to read actual binary data like images because data like that is rarely part of a data cleaning exercise. However, sometimes the data is so messy that this is the one of the few approaches that seems to work (see our next example). It is also one way to read text data with embedded nulls if you want to preserve all the characters in the original text. This arises when a fixed-width file has embedded nulls.

The readBin() function requires that you specify the number of bytes to be read, since it does not recognize end-of-line characters. The return value of readBin() is a vector whose class is raw – and indeed it looks on the screen like a stream of hexadecimal bytes. There are only a couple of things we can do with raw data in R (unless we have some custom plan for it). We can write it back out, using writeBin(), or we can convert it into data in one of the R formats. If we know that the raw data represents text, we can convert it with rawToChar() – unless there are embedded nulls. If our vector myvec is raw, then nulls can be replaced with a command like myvec[myvec == 0x00] <- as.raw(0x20). This will replace all the nulls by the character whose value is hexadecimal 0x20 – the space. So if necessary we might read in such a file in chunks of arbitrary size, convert the nulls to spaces, then write the data back out as binary or convert to text. If all has gone well, the resulting file should then be able to be read by read.fwf() or readLines().

To set up the next example we construct a character vector representing some entries in a fixed-width file. We embed a null in one of the entries and then write the resulting vector to a disk file called nully.txt.

Each entry has 16 characters, counting the new-line appended for convenience. The strings contain a 3-character id (e.g., 001), a 10-character name (Jenkins, including three trailing spaces), and a 2-character state.

```
> thg <- c("001Jenkins    MI\n", "0020'FlahertyIA\n",
            "003Lee        HI\n")
```

Now we replace the apostrophe in the second string with a null character. Since nulls are illegal in R, some extra steps are required to make this modification. We convert the string to a raw vector named second.bytes using the charToRaw() function. This produces the hexadecimal values 30 30 32 representing "002" and so on. We then replace the fifth element of second.bytes with the null character, indicated by as.raw(0x00).

```
> (second.bytes <- charToRaw (thg[2]))
 [1] 30 30 32 4f 27 46 6c 61 68 65 72 74 79 49 41 0a
```

```
> second.bytes[5] <- as.raw (0x00)
> second.bytes
 [1] 30 30 32 4f 00 46 6c 61 68 65 72 74 79 49 41 0a
 > rawToChar (second.bytes)
Error in rawToChar(second.bytes) :
  embedded nul in string: '002O\0FlahertyIA\n'
```

The final command shows that after the modification, this vector cannot be converted back to character because it has the embedded null.

Now let us write that vector to a disk file. In order to write the sec-ond.bytes item we will need to use writeBin (), so we will use that for the other strings as well. In this code, we write the three strings individually to a connection opened for binary writing.

```
> con <- file ("nully.txt", "wb")
> writeBin (charToRaw (thg[1]), con)
> writeBin (second.bytes, con)
> writeBin (charToRaw (thg[3]), con)
> close (con)
```

The nully.txt file is now complete; it consists of three text lines of which the second has an embedded null. When we read that into R, read.fwf () omits the part of the second line following the null character and emits a warning, as we show here.

```
> read.fwf ("nully.txt", c(3, 10, 2))
  V1          V2   V3
1  1 Jenkins       MI
2  2            O <NA>
3  3 Lee           HI
Warning message:
In readLines(file, n = thisblock) :
  line 2 appears to contain an embedded nul
```

Despite indications in the help file, read.fwf () does not respect the skip-Nul argument. When we use scan (), we have two unappetizing choices. If skipNul is FALSE, scan () will stop reading the second line after the null just as read.fwf () does. But if skipNul is TRUE, scan () will produce only 14 characters for the second line – and the fields will no longer line up. The following example shows the output from scan () when applied to this file.

```
> scan ("nully.txt", what="", sep="\n", skipNul = TRUE)
Read 3 items
[1] "001Jenkins   MI"
[2] "002OFlahertyIA"
[3] "003Lee       HI"
```

The removal of the null has led to the second string being one character too short. For example, its "state" field does not line up with the others'.

The best way around this may be by reading the binary data directly using `readBin()`. Here, we show how that might be done, exploiting the fact that each line is known to contain 16 characters. We open the file for binary reading by passing the `open = "rb"` argument to the `file()` function, read all 48 characters, and convert null characters to space (the character with hex value 0x20).

```
> con <- file ("nully.txt", "rb")
> lns <- readBin (con, what="raw", n = 48)
> lns[lns == as.raw (0x00)] <- as.raw (0x20)
> rawToChar (lns)
[1] "001Jenkins   MI\n002O FlahertyIA\n003Lee        HI\n"
> (lns <- strsplit (rawToChar (lns), "\n") [[1]])
[1] "001Jenkins   MI"
[2] "002O FlahertyIA"
[3] "003Lee        HI"
```

The final command splits the string at the new-line values to produce a vector of three equal-length strings. Given the starting and ending locations of the fields, we can then produce a matrix by breaking the strings into their component pieces. This example shows how that might be done.

```
> start <- c(1, 4, 14)
> end <- c(3, 13, 15)
> sapply (1:3,
          function (i) substring (lns, start[i], end[i]))
     [,1] [,2]        [,3]
[1,] "001" "Jenkins  " "MI"
[2,] "002" "O Flaherty" "IA"
[3,] "003" "Lee       " "HI"
```

This example is complicated, but handling data with embedded nulls or other problematic characters is a difficult problem that really does arise in practice. Sometimes, reading the data as binary is the only road available.

6.2.6 Reading Problem Files in Action

In this section, we show a function we wrote to handle a real-life problem reading text data. We were given a series of large XML files. We discuss XML in Section 6.5.3, but for this purpose think of XML as text. For unknown reasons, these files contained embedded null characters, and also a small number of "control" characters (non-ASCII characters with hexadecimal values $\geq$ 80). In general, XML may contain UTF-8 and other non-ASCII characters, but never nulls – and these control characters were known to be erroneous.

Each one of these files took up around 600 MB and consisted of one text line with no end-of-line character anywhere. Regular text tools run into problems handling lines of this size, as does R. Using `scan()` or `readLines()`,

R would try to read one of these files into memory as a character vector with one (enormous) entry. Officially, a character string in R can contain just about 2 GB, but we had no success in reading this object into R in order to break it into manageable pieces.

Instead our approach was to read each file as raw data in pieces. When we converted the pieces to character, we discovered that the XML files contained tags such as <ROW> and </ROW>, which supplied a natural place into which to insert new-line characters to break the text into lines. It was also during this investigation that we discovered the embedded null and control characters. We wrote a small function to read the entire file bit by bit, remove the offending null and control characters, add the new-lines at the appropriate places, and write the resulting bits back out. The output from this function was a text file that could be read handily, one line at a time, in groups of lines, or using an XML reading function of the sort we describe in Section 6.5.3.

We give the details of this function in three pieces. In the first piece of the function, we open the input file as binary and the output file as text. The on.exit() functions (Section 5.1.3) ensure that the files are properly closed even if the function aborts; without the add = TRUE argument the expression in the second call would replace the action specified in the first. The chunk argument describes the number of characters we will read at one time.

```
function (xml.in, xml.out, chunk = 10000)
{
# Open input file as read only, binary
fi <- file (xml.in, open = "rb")
# Open output file for write only, text
fo <- file (xml.out, open = "wt")
on.exit (close (fi))
on.exit (close (fo), add = TRUE)
```

In the second piece of the function, we read chunk characters as raw data. The while(1) starts an infinite loop that is ended when the function encounters break. If no data is read, the input file has been used up (we might say "exhausted"). If fewer than chunk characters are read, we have reached the end of the file – but we still have to process the final chunk. We find the unwanted characters – the null, whose hexadecimal value is 0x00, and the non-ASCII, whose values are 0x80 and above – and replace them by spaces.

```
while (1) {                          # loop until "break"
# Read text. If none is returned, the file is empty.
    txt.raw <- readBin (fi, "raw", n = chunk) # the maximum
    if (length (txt.raw) == 0) break
# Replace those are 0x00 or >= 0x80 with 0x20 (space)
    txt.raw[txt.raw == as.raw (0x00) |
            txt.raw >= as.raw (0x80)]  <- as.raw (0x20)
    txt <- rawToChar (txt.raw)
```

At the end of this last operation, txt contains the character values from the input, except with spaces where nulls and other non-ASCII characters used to be. In the rest of the function, we add the new-line characters after every instance of </ROW> (using the gsub() function from Section 4.4.6) and write the text out. We cannot use writeLines() because we do not want to insert a new-line character at the end of the 10,000-character chunk. Instead, we use the writeChar() function. By default, this adds a null character after its end-of-string character, but when we set eos = NULL the string is written out with no terminator. (We could alternatively have opened the file to write binary and used writeBin() to write the raw data. Writing text data with writeBin() produces a null character in the output.) Finally, we check to see whether the number of characters read is less than the size of chunk. If so, we must have exhausted the input file, and we break, relying on on.exit() to close the files. (We use number of characters read, rather than written, because that number does not count the number of new-line characters inserted.)

```
# Replace </ROW> with </ROW>\n wherever the former appears
    txt <- gsub ("</ROW>", "</ROW>\n", txt)
# Write output. If txt is short, input is exhausted; quit.
    writeChar (txt, fo, eos=NULL)
    if (nchar (txt.raw) < chunk) break
} # end "while"
}
```

This example demonstrates the sorts of tasks that we, as data scientists, are called on to perform in order to read data as part of a data cleaning exercise. As a data scientist, you will need to be prepared to handle this sort of messy data.

6.3   Reading Data From Relational Databases

A lot of data is stored in *relational databases*. A database has two parts: first, a set of tables of data together with rules that describe their content and keys that link the tables together. The second part is software to access the data in customized ways. The software is often called a "relational database management system," and the acronyms RDBMS or just DBMS are often used. Popular examples of these programs include Access and SQL Server, from the Microsoft Corporation; Oracle and the open-source MySQL, from the Oracle Corporation; and the open-source PostgreSQL and SQLite. All of these use something called the "Structured Query Language," or SQL, a (mostly) standardized language designed specifically for interacting with database management systems. In this section, we discuss how to connect to a database and extract its data into R for cleaning and management.

Remember that database programs are specifically designed and engineered to hold and manipulate large amounts of data. So it is almost always a good idea to let the database do the work of filtering and merging data sets, rather than reading all the data into R and operating on it there. Of course, when the data tables in question are small, it doesn't matter much one way or the other where the work is done. But where the data is large, we recommend using the database as much as possible – which means learning at least a little SQL.

6.3.1 Connecting to the Database Server

The first step in using a database is connecting to it. With some exceptions discussed in what follows, a database system will run as a "server" in a process – that is, a running program – located either on your computer, or on another computer on your network. Some person or organization will need to be in charge of that program (starting it, stopping it, updating the data and permissions, etc.). That person (the database administrator) will know the name of the machine on which the server is running, and any user/password information you will need to access data in the system. In order to connect your R session to the database server, you will need a *driver*, which is a piece of software that lets the operating system connect to the database. In some cases, drivers will already be present on your computer, but in others, you will need to acquire and install one yourself. Your database administrator will be able to tell you what driver to use and how to install it. The first time you connect to the database you will provide a "data source name," or DSN, that will be used to refer to the database on subsequent occasions.

Open Database Connectivity

The Open Database Connectivity (ODBC) protocol is an effort to make different database software appear the same to clients like R. Just about all databases support ODBC, and the R package RODBC (Ripley and Lapsley, 2015) provides an interface to ODBC-compliant databases. (Some databases, such as the well-known Oracle one, support additional, specific packages that may be more efficient than RODBC.) If you have a DSN named "source" in place, for example, the command odbcConnect ("source") will make the connection; additional arguments let you specify a username (argument uid) and password (pwd) if required. Once the connection is made, the function returns an object (a "handle") that holds the details about the connection. This handle is then passed to all the other functions that communicate with the database. In this example, we show how we might connect to a database via ODBC, then use the sqlTables () command to list the names of all the tables in the database.

```
han <- odbcConnect (dsn = "source", uid = "us", pwd = "abc")
sqlTables (han) # list all table names
```

Generally, the functions whose names start with odbc are the lower-level ones, and the ones whose names start with sql are easier to use with data frames.

Once you know the names of the tables in the database, the `sqlColumns()` function will return some information about the columns in a specific table, such as their names and types.

While the connection is open, SQL commands (see the following sections) can be issued directly through the `sqlQuery()` function. Once the connection han is no longer needed, it can be closed with either the `close(han)` or the `odbcClose(han)` commands.

6.3.2 Introduction to SQL

All relational databases use SQL to access and manage data. SQL is a big subject, and there are many books and web sites devoted to teaching it. Inevitably, perhaps, different databases can have slight differences in the SQL and data types they support. In this section, we describe the basic SQL commands that you might need to extract data from databases into R. These commands will normally be passed to the database through one of the ODBC functions, such as `sqlQuery()`, as a character string – see the following few examples. SQL commands are not case-sensitive; table and column names might be, depending on the database. Here, we follow one common convention, where we put SQL keywords in upper-case letters and table and column names in lower-case.

The SELECT Command
The most important SQL command is SELECT, which is the command used to create a data frame in R from a table in the database. Suppose that we know, from our earlier call to `sqlTables()`, that a particular table is called `accounts`. Then the SQL command `SELECT * FROM accounts` will return the entire table. We would normally specify this query as a character string passed as an argument to `sqlQuery()`. This example shows how we can acquire an entire table, presuming that the handle han created above is still valid.

```
acc <- sqlQuery (han, "SELECT * FROM accounts")
```

Here, the asterisk asks for all columns, so after this operation completes, the new data frame `acc` will have all the data from the database table `accounts`. Often we will want only a subset of rows and columns. We can use the `sqlColumns()` function to learn the names of the columns in the table; we can then supply the desired names explicitly in the SELECT statement. The SELECT command has many other possible additions that control the selection of subsets of rows. For example, the next command will return only the three named columns, and only the rows for which accyear was ≥ 2016.

```
recent <- sqlQuery (han, "SELECT accno, accyear, accamt
                    FROM accounts WHERE accyear >= 2016",
                    stringsAsFactors = FALSE)
```

The `sqlQuery()` function supports a `stringsAsFactors` argument but not the `colClasses` one. In addition to returning the data itself, the database can perform simple arithmetic operations. For example, `nn <- sqlQuery (han, "SELECT COUNT(*) FROM accounts")` gives the number of rows in the table. Other operators compute maxima or minima, combine columns arithmetically, compute logarithms, aggregate data into groups, and so on.

Joining Tables

Besides extracting a table, or part of a table, the most important thing a database can do for us is to match up two tables, according to the value of a column in each one, and return the results of the match. In SQL, we call this a "join"; in R, we call it a "merge," based on the `merge()` function that does the same thing for data frames (see Section 3.7.2). So, for example, suppose that in our database table `accounts` has a column called `accno` and table `payment` has a column called `acct`. Suppose each of these two columns contains account numbers in the same format. We want to produce a new table with all the columns of `accounts` and all the columns of `payment`, and all the rows for which the two account numbers match. This command shows how SQL can be used to join the two tables.

```
matchers <- sqlQuery (han, "SELECT * FROM accounts, payment
    WHERE accounts.accno = payment.acct")
```

The database is in charge of sorting the tables to make the account numbers line up. Typically, we expect the result of this command to have as many rows as there are account numbers that are common to the two tables. (This can be different, though, if there are duplicated account numbers.) This so-called "inner join" is just one way to join tables. The "left join" produces a new table with one row for each entry in `accounts` (again, if there are no duplicates in the index used to do the join). Entries in `accounts` with no match in `payment` are returned, but of course there are missing values for those rows' entries in the columns from `payment`. This command shows how to produce a left join between the tables in this example.

```
matchers <- sqlQuery (han, "SELECT * FROM accounts
        LEFT JOIN payment ON accounts.accno = payment.acct")
```

"Right" and "outer" joins (Section 3.7.2) are constructed similarly.

Getting Results in Pieces

The `sqlQuery()` command actually performs two tasks. First, it sends the query to the database, and then it fetches the results. For really big tables, it makes sense to separate these tasks; the first query starts the retrieval process, and then subsequent calls retrieve rows chunk by chunk. When we want a single table, the `sqlFetch()` command will get the first batch, with the number of rows given by the max argument; subsequent calls should be made to `sqlFetchMore()`, again using the max argument. When executing a more complicated query, a call to `sqlQuery()` with max can be followed by a call to `sqlGetResults()`. (The argument `rows_at_time` is an instruction to the database, which does not affect the number of rows returned.)

Other SQL Commands

There are many other SQL commands, but most of them (e.g., INSERT, UPDATE, DELETE, and CREATE TABLE) are intended for data management and will normally be used by the database administrator rather than by the users of data. There are two more SQL commands other than SELECT that every data handler should know. One is CREATE TEMPORARY TABLE, which, as its name suggests, creates a temporary table that will be deleted when the SQL connection is closed. (Whether you have permission to create such a table is decided by the database administrator.) In a recent project, for example, we needed to extract rows for a particular set of keys from a number of large tables. It was convenient to create a temporary table and insert those keys into it (which we did via the `sqlSave()` function). We could then use `sqlQuery()` to construct an inner join that returned only the rows corresponding to keys in the temporary table. In this way, we allowed the database, rather than R, to be the data manager.

The second command worth noting is EXPLAIN. This command does not perform any action; instead, it causes the database to describe what steps it would have taken, had the EXPLAIN not been specified. This can be useful when designing a query against a very large database, or one that will return a very big result set. If there are two different approaches, EXPLAIN might give information as to which is more efficient. Different databases approach this in different ways, returning different information, and indeed some do not support EXPLAIN at all, so consult your database's documentation if you want to use this feature.

Serverless Databases

Microsoft Access and SQLite are two "serverless" databases. With these products, the entire database, together with details of table layouts and so on, is stored in one large file. Clients such as R treat the file as a database, acting as their own server. This makes these two databases particularly well suited to smaller applications. For connections to Access, you can either set the Access file up as a DSN, or use the Access-specific functions like `odbcConnectAccess()` in the RODBC package to connect to the file. The RSQLite package (Wickham *et al.*, 2014) connects R to SQLite databases; it looks much like the RODBC package, but the function names are slightly different. In either case, SQL commands can then be used to extract data.

Our extended exercise in Chapter 8 uses the RSQLite package, so here we present a few of the functions you will need to communicate with RSQLite from R. These functions include the following:

- dbConnect() initializes an RSQLite connection. We would normally start a session with a command like han <- dbConnect (SQLite(), dbname = <fname>), where <fname> is the name of the file containing the data. This command creates a handle named han, which will be passed to the other SQLite functions.
- dbListTables() lists the tables in the database. In our example, the command dbListTables(han) would produce a character vector with the names of the SQLite tables.
- dbListFields() lists the fields (columns) in a table.
- dbGetQuery() executes a query and captures the returned data, analogously to sqlQuery() in the RODBC package.
- dbSendQuery() and dbFetch() create a query and then receive data from it. These are similar in use to sqlQuery() followed by sqlGetResults(), except that dbSendQuery() returns no data at all; it only prepares the database to return data in subsequent calls to dbFetch().

Other (NoSQL) Databases

Recent years have seen the growth of the so-called "NoSQL" databases. Sometimes, these actually support SQL-type commands; their "NoSQL" nature comes from the way transactions are handled within the database. Others have a different model for storing and extracting data. For example, the well-known MongoDB system uses a version of JSON (see Section 6.5.3). Most of these databases have the ability to connect from R, but you will need to find the right package for each one.

We can only barely scratch the surface of SQL, and interacting with databases, here. If you are going to use databases regularly, it will definitely be worth your while learning more. Remember that data-management tasks such as subsetting and merging will almost always be more efficient in the database than in R.

6.4 Handling Large Numbers of Input Files

R provides a set of tools that allow us to interact with the computer's operating system. These allow us to perform tasks such as creating and removing directories and listing files that match patterns, and these tasks typically form part of any data cleaning project. It is particularly important to be able to handle files and directories automatically when there are hundreds or thousands of them. For example, we sometimes receive data in the form of a set of directories, each filled with zipped files. We want to avoid unzipping these files manually, and instead use R to unzip them all at once.

There are at least two ways to have R interact with the operating system. First, R has a set of built-in commands that perform file- and directory-related tasks. These include `list.files()`, which allows you to list only the files whose names match a regular expression (Section 4.4), `unzip()` for unzipping zip files, and a set of functions whose names start with `file` – among them, `file.copy()`, `file.remove()`, and `file.rename()`.

The second way to interact with the operating system is by calling system utilities directly through the `system()` function. This method may allow more flexibility, but will normally be less general, since the set of utilities available will be different between operating systems. Using this approach will make your efforts more difficult to reproduce.

Besides manipulating existing files, R also provides tools for downloading, particularly the `download.file()` function. We talk more about acquiring data from the Internet in Section 6.5.3. The ability to download and then access a file entirely within R contributes to the reproducibility of your code and solutions.

Example

As an example, consider a data set consisting of a directory containing 12 sub-directories of our working directory. Suppose that the sub-directories have names such as `2016.Jan` and `2016.Feb`. For this example, each sub-directory contains a few hundred comma-separated values files, each file individually zipped. Each file has the same named columns in the same order. The total size of all the files is not enough to overwhelm R, so the goal is to read all of the files into one R data frame, with the resulting data frame containing all of the original columns, plus two more columns giving the month and year associated with each row.

This is only an example. In practice, the files might be huge or in an odd format. They might have been prepared with another tool like gzip or tar. As a data scientist, you have to expect to receive data in whatever way the supplier can imagine.

In this example, we would use `unz()` to open each of the zip files. To do this, we need to know not only the name of the zip file but also the original file's name. If the name or names of the file or files inside a zip file are unknown, they can be retrieved via the `unzip()` function with the `list = TRUE` argument; but in this example, we will presume that the zip file's name is the same as the original name, except that the ending `.csv` has been replaced by `.zip`.

Suppose that the first file in the `2016.Jan` directory is called `Alameda.zip`. We can open and read that file with code like this:

```
fi <- unz ("2016.Jan/Alameda.zip", "Alameda.csv", "r")
out <- read.delim (fi)
```

Notice that the `read.delim()` functions and the other `read.table()` offspring can read from the connection directly. If the file was too big to read all at once, we might use `scan()` – interestingly, `readLines()` is not available for connections from `unz()`. We chose `read.delim()` here because it sets the separator character to the tab, the quote argument to the double-quote only, and `header` to `TRUE`. Of course, we may have to experiment to find the proper settings of these arguments.

Now that we can read one file, we need to establish the loop to read them all. Finding the names of all the zip files in any subdirectory below this one is straightforward using the `list.files()` command. We can restrict the directories to search by supplying a vector of sub-directory names, which might be the output from the `list.dirs()` command, but here we will assume that the only sub-directories present are the relevant ones. We need the full names of the files in order to open them, but we want only the file name, not the path part, in order to reconstruct the original file name. So we call `list.files()` twice. In the first call, we extract only the file names. Then a call to `sub()` will produce the name of the unzipped file by replacing the ending `zip` of the file name with `csv`. This code shows how this might be done.

```
zips <- list.files (pattern = "\\.zip$",
                    recursive = TRUE, full.names = FALSE)
csvs <- sub ("\\.zip$", "\\.csv", zips)
```

Here, of course, `"\\.zip$"` is a regular expression that restricts attention to files whose names end with `.zip`.

Now we need to know the year and month associated with each directory. We can find this in the vector of full names, which we produce by calling `list.files()` a second time with the `full.names = TRUE` argument. Then the year appears in characters 3–6 (because each file name starts with the working directory, `./`), and the month in characters 8–10. In a more complicated situation, we might need a regular expression or another approach to find these values. In this example, our code might look like this.

```
fullzips <- list.files (pattern = "\\.zip$",
                        recursive = TRUE, full.names = TRUE)
year <- substring (fullzips, 3, 6)
mon <- substring (fullzips, 8, 10)
```

At the end of this operation, we can construct a loop that sequentially reads each file, adds a column with month and year, and appends it to a data frame. This example shows what that code might look like.

```
result <- NULL # empty object
for (i in 1:length (zips)) {
    fi <- unz (fullzips[i], csvs[i], "r")
    out <- data.frame (Year = year[i], Month = month[i],
```

```
                    read.delim (fi, stringsAsFactors = FALSE))
     result <- rbind (result, out)
}
```

In this example, we used repeated calls to `rbind()` to construct the result. This is an inefficient operation, since R needs to adjust the size of the data frame on every iteration of the loop. However, it is easy in implementation, and we only need to run this code once. A more efficient approach might be to create the data frame ahead of time (if we knew or could estimate the total number of rows needed) or to read the files separately and join them at the end.

6.5 Other Formats

A number of newer formats for storing data are becoming increasingly commonly used. Handling this data often requires the use of packages that are not included in base R. In this section we describe some of these formats and the tools used to read and write them – but, as always, keep in mind that packages tend to evolve faster than R itself does.

6.5.1 Using the Clipboard

The "clipboard" is a mechanism for moving text data between programs. In Windows, R sees the clipboard as a file named "clipboard" (so this is a bad name for a regular disk file). There is also a larger version called "clipboard-128." As we mention below, the clipboard is particularly helpful for bringing in data from spreadsheets like Excel: you can simply highlight a rectangular area in Excel and copy to the clipboard; then in R, `read.table("clipboard", sep = "\t")` will bring the data in. All of the usual arguments to `read.table()`, particularly `header` and `stringsAsFactors`, will need to be set in the usual way. Conversely, we can put an R data frame into a spreadsheet by running a command like `write.table(mydf, "clipboard", sep = "\t")` in R, then switching to the clipboard and using that program's "paste" command.

The procedure is somewhat different across Windows, Mac, and Linux, however, and it does require the user to use the copy and paste commands. So an approach that uses the clipboard might be difficult for other users to reproduce. Still, the clipboard is a good way to get quick and easy access to data from other programs. In Mac, the two commands above would look like `read.table(pipe("pbpaste"), sep = "\t")` and `write.table(mydf, pipe("pbcopy"), sep = "\t")`. Linux is more variable, but the help for the `file()` function gives some suggestions.

In using the clipboard to copy text in from other programs, you need to be aware that some word-processing software may, depending on the settings, automatically convert certain characters into others that "look nicer." (This doesn't appear to be a problem with spreadsheet programs.) Specifically, if you type into Microsoft Word `"She said it wasn't so -- and I believed her"`, that program will convert the quotation marks to the curved so-called "smart quotes" (like the ones seen surrounding "smart quotes"). Similarly, the apostrophe will be curved and the two hyphens will be converted into a dash. None of those characters are ASCII, and this text is not a valid R string, because R does not recognize the quotation marks – so if you try to paste this text directly into an R session, you will see an error. If the text is surrounded with ordinary R-style quotation marks, then you will have a valid R string. You can replace these non-ASCII characters using `gsub()` – for example, `gsub("[^[:print:]]", "", a)` removes all the so-called "non-printable" characters from a, leaving only letters, numbers, and spaces. An alternative is to copy the text from the word processor to the clipboard and `scan()` it into R from there, but the way clipboards handle non-ASCII text is subject to change.

Be aware that many applications use the clipboard. If you copy text from the a spreadsheet to the clipboard, but then copy anything else, your clipboard contents will be changed. This includes copying text in an R script window, as, for example, when you highlight the text of a command and right-click to execute that command.

6.5.2 Reading Data from Spreadsheets

In our work, we very often need to read data in from spreadsheets, and by a very large margin the most commonly used spreadsheet is Microsoft Excel. Excel uses at least two file formats, an older one identified by names that end in .xls and a newer one identified by names ending in .xlsx. Different packages handle these formats: the gdata package has a `read.xls()` function, while xlsx (Dragulescu, 2014) provides a `read.xlsx()` function.

But an Excel "workbook" can contain many spreadsheets, and need not be rectangular as a data frame must be. While it is possible to specify a specific sheet of a workbook, we have found that if there are just a few moderate-sized data sets, it is often fastest to copy them to the clipboard and read them into Excel from there. Another common approach is to use Excel to write the spreadsheet as a tab- or comma-separated file.

Copying from the clipboard has at least two obvious disadvantages: first, it makes it harder for another user to reproduce your work, since they need to open the Excel workbook. This supposes that the user has Excel, or at least one of the open-source spreadsheet programs that can read the Excel formats (and often older formats or very complicated, macro-laden spreadsheets can cause problems with these other tools). Then the user has to find the proper sheet, and copy the proper cells to the clipboard – and this leads to the second problem, because, as we mentioned earlier, the Windows and Mac/Linux implementations of clipboard are not the same. To make your work reproducible you should give instructions as to how to read your data that work on any machine. Alternatively, you might use the spreadsheet program to save the worksheet in a text format, like a tab-delimited one. That way other users will be able to read the data directly into R.

Another issue that has caused trouble in the past when reading data from Excel spreadsheets via the clipboard is that confusion can arise if the rows have different lengths. When reading from a file, the `fill = TRUE` argument to `read.table()` will add blank fields on the ends of lines, but this has not always been successful when reading from the clipboard. As a quick manual adjustment, you can add a new column out at the right edge of the spreadsheet containing all zeros, say, and then read the data in.

If you are confronted with a large number of spreadsheets, you will find it necessary to use one of the packages like `xlsx` to automate the reading process. The decision about whether to use a package to read an Excel file or to read it through the clipboard depends on the number of sheets needed, their size and complexity, and the sorts of documentation that are going to be required. We usually read our Excel sheets in via the clipboard – but we acknowledge the difficulties that come with that.

One aspect of Excel that can cause confusion is its convention regarding dates. Dates can be displayed in many user-selectable formats, but internally a date is represented by the number of days since December 30, 1899, so that March 1, 1900 is day 61. (There is no support for dates before January 1, 1900, and in an additional complication, day 60 is understood by Excel to have been February 29, 1900 – even though 1900 was not a leap year.) Times are indicated by fractional days, so 61.75 represents 6:00 p.m. on March 1, 1900. Often when you read in an Excel column using one of the `read.table()` functions, your output will contain text-format dates that can be handled in the usual way, assuming you know the display format. (This is another example where you want to remember to set `stringsAsFactors` to `FALSE`.) If you read in an Excel column (say, `df$indate`) with numeric dates, they can be converted to `Date` objects with a command such as `as.Date(df$indate, origin = "1899/12/30")`. If you need times of day as well, recall from Section 3.6.2 that `Date` objects have their non-integer time parts truncated under some circumstances. So the safest plan is to use Excel to export the dates and times in a text format. Alternatively, you might convert the numeric days to seconds, by multiplying by 86,400, and then converting the resulting values into a vector of one of the POSIX time classes, with a command like `as.POSIXct(86400 * df$indate, origin = "1899/12/30", tz = "UTC")`. In this example, we selected the UTC time zone explicitly since otherwise R would have chosen the local time zone.

6.5.3 Reading Data from the Web

A lot of data is now stored on the World Wide Web. Some of this is stored statically, that is, in files on a server somewhere. This will often be HTML data, like tables in ordinary web pages. However, a lot of data is not stored in a page; rather, it is held in a database and returned dynamically, in response to requests. For example, think of a web page that displays next week's flights between San Francisco and New York. This page is generated dynamically in response to your input parameters, and might be different if generated a few hours from now. Moreover, some services return responses in a more complicated format like XML or JSON. In this section, we talk about how to read files in common web-based formats; then we look briefly at retrieving dynamic data from web servers.

Copying Tables from the Web via the Clipboard

HTML, the "hyper-text markup language," is the format for displaying most web pages. So a lot of data in the world is embedded in HTML, usually inside tables. The HTML code for a simple 2 × 2 table might look like this example.

```
<html>
<table><tr><th>Name</th><th>Amount</th></tr>
<tr><td>Dylan</td><td>116.34</td></tr>
<tr><td>Garcia</td><td>953.21</td></tr>
</table></html>
```

HTML is made up of "tags," like `<html>` and `<td>`, that often come in pairs – so, for example, a row of a table starts with `<tr>` and ends with `</tr>`.

Tables in web pages are often easy to copy to the clipboard. We can simply highlight them with the mouse and use the usual copy command (control-C in Windows, command-C on Mac). Then `read.table("clipboard")` with the default value of the `sep` argument will very often produce acceptable results. You may want to set other options, such as `header` and `stringsAsFactors` as well.

Reading Web Pages in HTML

If we need to acquire a large number of web pages, an automatic procedure is necessary. One simple way to acquire a web page, if the address is known, is through the `getURI()` function of the `RCurl` package (Temple Lang, 2015a). For example, the command `groucho <- getURI("https://en.wikipedia.org/wiki/Groucho_Marx")` will retrieve the Wikipedia page on Groucho Marx, in HTML, and save it as a character vector of length 1. (The task of converting from HTML to text is not, alas, a trivial one. We give one approach after we discuss XML as follows.) More often, we want to extract data that has been formatted in an HTML table. Our usual tool for ingesting HTML tables is the `readHTMLTable()` function from the XML package

Temple Lang (2015b). It returns a list, with one entry for each table on the web page. For some web pages, this function works flawlessly. However, a lot of web pages are designed more for display than for serious data storage. Formats can change over time and the HTML used does not always adhere strictly to standards. Even when tables are returned cleanly, it is often true that the first row contains the headers, and the columns have all been made into factors.

Although the output from `readHTMLTable()` may require additional processing, using that function is almost always a better solution than writing a custom function to look through the HTML tags, maybe using regular expressions. If you will need to read substantial amounts of HTML as part of your project, we recommend downloading the HTML pages to your local machine, perhaps using `download.file()` to make a copy on disk, or `getURI()` to read the text into R. That way, if the developers of the web change the format or data, your code will continue to work on your local copy.

XML

XML, despite standing for "eXtensible Markup Language," is not so much a language as a method of defining strict rules for document layouts. An XML document will normally be expressed as a nested list in R. The XML package handles the reading and writing of XML documents, and in fact reads XML in two distinct ways. The `xmlTreeParse()` function reads in a file (or, with the `asText` argument, takes in some text that is already in R) and produces a tree-like object of class `XMLDocument`. This acts like an R list, so if you know the exact names of the fields of interest, you can extract them. As an example, consider this simple XML file:

```
<?xml version="1.0" encoding="UTF-8"?>
<Fields>
<Client><Name>Dylan</Name><Amt>116.34</Amt></Client>
<Client><Name>Garcia</Name><Amt>953.21</Amt></Client>
</Fields>
```

If we write this into a file called `example1.xml`, we can read that file into an `XMLDocument`. The `XMLDocument` object is a long and complicated list. With enough information, we can extract the value of the first `Amt` field directly, as in this example.

```
> xx <- xmlTreeParse (file = "example1.xml")
> xmlValue(xx$doc$children[["Fields"]][[1]][["Amt"]])
[1] "116.34"
```

The `xmlValue()` function converts the list element, which is an object of class `xmlNode`, into text. But clearly this approach is difficult for large or deeply nested documents. A better approach to handling XML is to read the file into R using the `xmlParse()` function, which produces an object of class `XMLInternalDocument`. We cannot extract elements from these documents using the list-type notation above, but documents of this sort can be searched with the xpathSApply() function using syntax derived from the XPath language intended for this purpose. A description of XPath is beyond the scope of this book, but lots of documentation and examples are available on the Internet. Here, we show the use of the simplest XPath command, the // command that performs a basic search. Notice that we search for Amt without needing to know the names of its parent nodes.

```
> yy <- xmlParse (file = "example1.xml")
> xpathSApply (yy, "//Amt")
[[1]]
<Amt>116.34</Amt>

[[2]]
<Amt>953.21</Amt>
```

The output of xpathSApply() here is a list of objects of class xmlNode. In the following example, we use the ordinary sapply() function to have xmlValue() operate on each of the xmlNodes, finally producing a vector of (character) amounts.

```
> sapply (xpathSApply (yy, "//Amt"), xmlValue)
[1] "116.34" "953.21"
```

The xpathSApply() function is also useful for converting HTML text retrieved from a URL into readable text. For example, recall that in the last section we saw how we might retrieve the Wikipedia entry for Groucho Marx using the getURI() function. Recall that the entry was saved in a character vector of length 1 named groucho. Then, analogously to the xmlTreeParse() function, the XML package provides a function htmlTreeParse(). When used with the useInternalNodes = TRUE argument, this function produces an object of class HTMLInternalDocument. This class is a particular sort of XMLInternalDocument. Therefore, the xpathSApply() function can be used as before. In this example, from Luis (2011), we search for the HTML "new paragraph" tag, <p>, and apply the xmlValue() command to extract the value from each paragraph found into a list. We then use unlist() to produce a vector. The following commands show how the text might be extracted from the HTML. The output is a character vector with one entry for each paragraph in the original HTML document.

```
> grou.tree <- htmlTreeParse (groucho,  useInternal = TRUE)
> unlist (xpathSApply (grou.tree, "//p",  xmlValue))
 [1] "Julius Henry Marx (October 2, 1890 - August 19, ...
 [2] "He made 13 feature films with his siblings the ...
 [3] "His distinctive appearance, carried over from ...
  :  :  :
```

XML handles Unicode in a natural way and elements of an XML document can be expected to be encoded in UTF-8.

JSON

JSON, the "JavaScript Object Notation," is another text-based format for containing list-like data. For example, Twitter messages are often stored in JSON, one message per JSON object. A JSON object is enclosed in braces and essentially consists of series of pairs like "name" : value, separated by commas. The "value" part of the object can be a value or another series of "name" : value pairs. JSON also supports an "array" object, analogous to an R vector. So a JSON object can be directly represented by an (possibly nested) R list.

The rjson (Couture-Beil, 2014), RJSONIO (Temple Lang, 2014), and jsonlite (Ooms, 2014) packages read and write JSON objects and make the underlying JSON essentially transparent to the user. Often you will be presented with a file containing a whole set of JSON messages, one per line. If the file is small, it might be easiest to read the entire file into R using scan() with sep = "\n" and what = "", and then apply one of conversion functions like fromJSON() to each of the messages. In this example, we show what some of the data from the previous XML file might look like as text after its JSON representation is read into an R object named zz.

```
> zz
[1] "{\"Name\":\"Dylan\",\"Amt\":\"116.34\"}"
[2] "{\"Name\":\"Garcia\",\"Amt\":\"953.21\"}"
```

Now we can use sapply() to have the fromJSON() function (we used the one from the RJSONIO package) operate on each line.

```
> sapply (zz, fromJSON, USE.NAMES = FALSE)
        [,1]      [,2]
Name  "Dylan"   "Garcia"
Amt   "116.34"  "953.21"
```

The USE.NAMES = FALSE argument prevents the converter from constructing unwieldy column names.

If the file is too big to import into R directly, it can be opened and read one line at a time, as discussed in Section 6.2 earlier in this chapter.

Like XML, JSON is able to handle Unicode in a native way, so you should expect to see UTF-8 in the data you acquire.

Reading Data Via a REST API

REST, which stands for "representational state transfer," is the most straightforward of the ways to send data from a web server to a client like R. (Another popular approach, SOAP, will not be discussed here.) Data suppliers will often permit clients to establish REST connections to retrieve data by means of specially formatted requests. The description of those requests is often published in an API, "applications programmer interface." For example, Google Maps publishes an API that describes how to extract map data from its database, and Bing Translate has a different API describing how to use that tool to translate text from one language to another. If you want to use a commercial API, be sure you understand the terms of use.

In many cases, developers have created R packages to make using the API as straightforward as possible. In these examples, there are the RgoogleMaps package (Loecher and Ropkins, 2015) for Google Maps and the translateR package (Lucas and Tingley, 2014) for Bing Translate.

Each API will have its own rules, particularly regarding authentication. If no package exists, but you can see the web page, you can often emulate the actions of a user by creating your own request. This can be sent to the server as a "get" or "post" request via the getForm() and postForm() functions in the RCurl package, or with the GET() function in the httr package (Wickham, 2015). In either case, you will need to know the name-value pairs that the server expects. Often these can be deduced by reading the underlying HTML in your browser, or by examining the requests sent to the server when you click manually (since for "get" requests that information appears in your browser's URL line).

As an example, at the time of this writing, the US Census Bureau maintained an API that lets you look at certain values associated with international trade. This API, for which documentation is available at the URL www.census.gov/data/developers/data-sets/ international-trade.html, expects a "get" request to be sent to the location //api.census.gov/data /timeseries/intltrade/ exports, with arguments get giving the fields to be retrieved and YEAR and MONTH specifying the year and month of interest. This command shows the sending of the request with the result being stored in an object called cens. In this example, we request the year-to-date value of exports ("ALL_VAL_YR") for each of the "end-use codes" ("E_ENDUSE") and their descriptions ("E_ENDUSE_LDESC") for April of 2016.

```
> url <-  paste0 ("https://api.census.gov/data/timeseries/",
                  "intltrade/exports/enduse")
# For GET(), enclose API arguments via "query" as a list
> cens <- GET (url, query = list (
              get = "E_ENDUSE,E_ENDUSE_LDESC,ALL_VAL_YR",
              YEAR = "2016", MONTH = "04"))
```

The cens object is an object belonging to a special class called "response." Operating on this object with the content() function produces a list that be reshaped into a matrix via do.call() and rbind(). This example shows that call and a small part of the result.

```
> do.call (rbind, content (cens)) [1:4,]
     [,1]          [,2]
[1,] "E_ENDUSE"    "E_ENDUSE_LDESC"
[2,] ""            "TOTAL EXPORTS FOR ALL END-USE CODES"
[3,] "0"           "FOODS, FEEDS, AND BEVERAGES"
[4,] "00000"       "WHEAT"
     [,3]          [,4]    [,5]
[1,] "ALL_VAL_YR"    "YEAR"  "MONTH"
[2,] "465400958493"  "2016"  "04"
[3,] "38996430386"   "2016"  "04"
[4,] "1606226019"    "2016"  "04"
```

The resulting matrix will often need some cleaning before it can be converted into a data frame, particularly with regard to column headers. In this well-behaved example, all of the components of the list produced by content () had the same length. In general, that might not be true. Here, we could extract every month for every year by passing suitable values of YEAR and MONTH parameters. As elsewhere, it might be a good idea to save the data to disk so that its provenance is assured if the provider were to change the interface or modify the data. REST APIs almost always deliver their data as JSON, XML, or HTML.

Streaming Data

Sometimes, we need to capture streaming data, like feeds from sensors or from a supplier like the Twitter platform. We have not encountered the need for this in our own data cleaning problems, but at least in some cases the connection is straightforward. We can open a "socket," which is a communications endpoint, once we are given an IP address for the server and a "port number," an integer that specifies the address of the socket. The socketConnection () function establishes the connection. You will probably want to specify blocking = TRUE so that subsequent reads do not complete until something is actually read.

6.5.4   Reading Data from Other Statistical Packages

In days gone by, a statistician would often need to read data saved in a format specific to another statistical package, such as SAS, SPSS, or Minitab. The recommended package foreign (R Core Team, 2015) provides interfaces to these and some other formats. Again, though, formats evolve and very often it will be safest and maybe even easiest to receive data as tab-delimited text or in another text format. In any case, our experience has been that the need to import data from other statistical packages is very much less than it used to be.

6.6   Reading and Writing R Data Directly

R's own format for saving objects is a binary one, which is only readable by R itself. It is often useful to save objects in R format as an archive, a backup, or so that they can be passed to another user or machine because the format of R data files is the same across all computers and operating systems. The primary functions for saving and loading R objects are saveRDS() and readRDS(), for individual objects, and save() and load(), for groups of objects.

The saveRDS() function (the letters RDS evoke "R data serialization") takes an object and produces a disk file with all of that object's data and attributes. Saving a data frame to a spreadsheet-type text file can lose some information, and in any case saveRDS() works on any R object. Each call to saveRDS() applies to exactly one R object. So, for example, saveRDS (myobj, "newfile") produces a disk file named "newfile" with a binary representation of the R object myobj. The complementary action is performed by readRDS(): in this case, readRDS("newfile") returns the object just as it was saved. Note that readRDS() does not replace the existing myobj; instead, it simply returns the object. You can save it with a command like newobj <- readRDS("newfile"), which will create a new object newobj that is identical to the original myobj.

You can save a whole set of objects with the save() function. The output of save() is one big file with all the referenced objects stored in it. The save() functions let you specify the objects as objects, so, for example, save(myframe, myresults, myfunction, file = "output") saves three objects into a file called "output". But, perhaps more conveniently, it also lets you specify objects by name using the list argument. Alternatively, that last command could have been written save(list = c ("myframe", "myresults", "myfunction"), file = "output"). In this case, the second command requires slightly more typing, but the savings are clear when it comes time to save every object whose name starts with projectA, with a command like save(list = ls(pattern= "^projectA"), file = "output"). Here, of course, the caret sign (^) is part of a regular expression (Section 4.4) that extracts from ls() only objects whose names start with projectA. To save all the objects in your workspace, you can use the save.image() command. This is a useful way to move your entire workspace over to a different machine, for example, and this command is called when you quit R and ask to "save the workspace." The save.image() function creates or updates a file named .RData by default.

The load() function serves as the complement to save(), restoring all the objects stored on disk by save(). It will over-write any existing object with the same name as one being restored, so load() can be dangerous. A useful alternative is `attach()`, which allows you to add an R data file to the search path, that is, the set of places that R will look for objects. In this way, a set of objects can be made read-only. This is particularly useful for large, static data sets that need not be loaded into your working directory.

6.7   Chapter Summary and Critical Data Handling Tools

This chapter discusses getting data into R. Most often this will come in the form of text files arranged in a tabular format, with one observation per row and one measurement per column. Section 6.1 discusses different methods of reading these files, primarily through the `read.table()` function and its offspring. These functions will be able to handle a great many of these types of files. You will need to know whether the file is delimited or fixed-width. In the former case, you will need to know the delimiter, whether there are headers, whether we expect quotation marks, and other attributes of the file. For fixed-width files, we need to know the widths of each of the fields.

However we acquire a text file, we will probably want to set `stringsAs-Factors = FALSE` so that character data are not converted into factors. We may need to look for missing value indicators or other anomalies and re-read the data. Indeed, reading data into R is very often an iterative process, requiring us to refine our approach on each step until the data is exactly what we expect.

Some data cannot be read with `read.table()` because it is too broken, too big, or not tabular. Data is sometimes "broken" by having extra delimiters embedded, and we give an example of how to handle a file broken in this way. We usually approach broken files using `scan()` or, if necessary, `readBin()`.

Section 6.2 discusses approaches for very large or non-tabular data. We can open a file and read it piece by piece, processing the pieces one at a time until the file is exhausted. This is the usual approach for log files, JSON or XML (formats we describe later in the chapter), or any sort of text that is non-tabular. Binary files can be read in this way as well, though this is rarely needed. One time this need does arise is when, for whatever reason, the source file includes embedded null characters.

This section includes some code that we used in a real-life example where some (purportedly) text files both lacked new-line characters and also included embedded null and control characters. The example describes some prepro-cessing steps we had to take in order to make the data readable.

In Section 6.3, we describe how R can connect to a relational database in order to extract data. In order to interact with a database you will need to know at least a little of the SQL. This language works with all major databases and provides a framework for extracting and merging tables and subsets of tables.

Section 6.4 describes another common problem in data cleaning – how to handle large numbers of directories and files. We give an example of the sort of task we are called on to perform. Handling problems of this sort requires more than just understanding how to read and process individual files. It is also necessary to know how to navigate the operating system, and to understand the R tools that make it possible to perform file-system tasks such as listing the files in a directory and managing zipped files.

We spend some time on acquiring data in other formats in Section 6.5. Most of the non-text data we get is in the form of spreadsheets, so it is important to know how to access the data inside these files. Often the clipboard provides a simple way of transferring the data from a spreadsheet, though this is not very automatic. The clipboard is also a reasonable way to grab one or two tables from a web page in order to read them into R. We also show how to read a table from a web page directly, via the `readHTMLTable()` function in the XML package. We can also read the HTML text of a web page – but then we are faced with the problem of extracting the important information from among the HTML tags.

Data scientists need to be familiar with XML and JSON, two text-based formats that are in increasingly common use. Add-on packages provide the ability to read data in these formats into R objects. These are the common formats for data returned from the Web via a REST query, and we give an example of such a query.

Finally, we discuss how R stores its own objects. R's internal format is binary and not human-readable, but there is no better format for passing R data between different machines.

7

Data Handling in Practice

In our experience, a data cleaning project arises out of a modeling or data exploration problem. We are given some data (or perhaps a description of data that the project sponsor plans to eventually provide) and, usually, a problem to be solved. There is no fixed method for undertaking a data cleaning project, but we think of the process as having four parts: acquiring and reading the data, actually cleaning the data, combining the data (when it comes from multiple sources), and preparing the data for analysis. (We sometimes use "data cleaning" in both a broad sense and also as the name of a specific set of tasks. Here, we are using "data handling" as the umbrella term for these four tasks.) Of course, the "cleaning" part is never really finished, and often the most important cleaning tasks are discovered as data sets are combined, or even as the modeling proceeds. In this chapter, we describe the tasks associated with each of the four parts of data cleaning. Then, we emphasize the importance of reproducibility and documentation and give a detailed example at the end.

7.1 Acquiring and Reading Data

Acquiring data is, of course, the act of actually taking delivery of the data. Very often the final data, the data that will be used for building models, will come not in one big file but from a number of sources and in varying formats. So it is important for the data cleaner to be prepared to read in text, spreadsheet data, XML, JSON, and to handle non-standard formats as well. The exercise in Chapter 8 includes examples of all of these data types.

Acquiring data turns out to be more difficult than you might expect. Data providers are sometimes reluctant to release data, fearing the loss of proprietary or sensitive information. Some providers try to be helpful by providing summarized data, or by taking it on themselves to delete or fill in records with missing values. Sometimes, the data sets are so big that just moving them can be a challenge. We have used e-mail attachments, DVDs, secure file transfer,

A Data Scientist's Guide to Acquiring, Cleaning, and Managing Data in R, First Edition.
Samuel E. Buttrey and Lyn R. Whitaker.
© 2018 John Wiley & Sons Ltd. Published 2018 by John Wiley & Sons Ltd.
Companion website: www.wiley.com/go/buttrey/datascientistsguide

downloads from cloud-based servers, and even hard drives sent through the mail for transfer. Our advice is to get as much data as possible, at as detailed a level as possible. It is disruptive to your project to realize after you receive the data from your first request that an important file is missing; the person sending you the data may be less inclined to focus on your second or third request. Of course, another issue is that often we don't know what's in the data until we receive it, and only then can we evaluate whether we have what we need – and, often, once we receive some data we understand enough about the problem to determine what data we should have asked for in the first place.

Once we have taken possession of the data, the next step is almost always to read the data into an R data frame using the techniques of Chapter 6. The initial cleaning process begins here, since it is at this point that you will start to identify missing value indicators, determine column classes and get an idea of the size and complexity of the data. This is also a good point to ensure that your column names are meaningful and tractable. For instance, we recently got a data set of credit bureau data in which the nearly 200 columns had unwieldy names like "Number Open Installment Trades with Credit Limit <5000 with bal >0 and reported within 6 months." Our first task was to change all the names to ones that would be more manageable in R. This was time-consuming, tedious, difficult to automate – and necessary.

Another important element you will usually want in any data cleaning project is a *key* field, an indicator that uniquely identifies each observation. For a piece of equipment, this might be a serial number; for a person from the United States, it might be a Social Security Number (although these are sensitive, we generally ask our providers to construct and provide a different, unique identifier). In many cases, one individual may have multiple records – in a medical example, each person may have many visits to a doctor, for example. We might then construct our own key, combining social Security Number with date. It is particularly important to have a key field when combining data from different sources; we talk more about this in Section 7.3.3.

7.2   Cleaning Data

The actual steps in data cleaning will depend on the data, and what we expect to find in each column. Of course, before anything is changed we want to see what the data looks like. In general, whenever we receive a data set, we tabulate the keys, looking for duplicates. If there are duplicate keys, we try to see if entire records are duplicated, and, if there are, we may delete the duplicates and record this fact. But if there are duplicate keys that go with distinct records, we have to evaluate whether this describes real observations, errors, or another condition.

We look at every column's type (character, numeric, etc.), and count the number of missing values in every column. Even when there are thousands of columns, it is useful to tabulate the column classes and to draw a histogram of, or get summary statistics on, the numbers of missing values. Often a set of columns will have the same number of missing values, and you will then find that they are all missing on the very same observations. Frequently, this will arise because those observations all failed to match some specific data source when the data frame was being constructed. You then have to decide whether to keep those columns, remove them, or maybe create a new logical column describing whether each observation was, or was not, missing those columns.

For numeric columns, we very often want to see the mean value (among non-missing items) and, usually, the range. The range helps us spot anomalies – negative numbers where they are unexpected, or 999 codes used as missing values – quickly. For columns that are supposed to be integer or character, we will often want to know the number of unique values; if this is very different from what we expect, we would investigate further. For example, a column measuring "number of home mortgages" will most commonly have the values 0 or 1. If such a column had hundreds of distinct values we might want to investigate. Conversely, a column named "Salesperson ID" might be expected to have hundreds of values. In that case if there were only a few, we would want to understand why. For categorical or integer variables with only a few values, we will tabulate them, looking for unusual values. If we encounter a column with values "A," "B," "Other," and "other," for example, we will almost certainly consider combining those last two values. As with numeric columns, it is helpful to look at maxima and minima of date fields. We tabulate dates by month or quarter, looking for anomalous conditions like months with no observations.

Once we have identified missing or clearly erroneous data, we face a decision. If the data came recently from a specific provider, we might return to that provider, point out the issues, and hope for corrected data. More often, we will have to act on our own and take steps to keep those values from disrupting our analysis. For example, suppose we have a data set giving information about soldiers. If a field giving a particular soldier's age contains the value 999, and we expect to need the age in our analysis, we might make a note of the soldier's identification or other key value, then delete that record and continue. Deletion should be a rare tactic. If, say, 30% of soldiers had the 999 code, we might need to do something else. We might replace the erroneous value with a valid one using an "imputation" method, or we might mark the 999 values as NA. Alternatively, if we do not anticipate using the age in modeling or other efforts, we might let the value stay as it is – but the fact that there are some soldiers whose age is equal to 999 is still important information about the quality of the data. You will want to report data quality issues to the data provider and project sponsor.

Each data frame will need to be examined on its own, but the cleaning process also needs to consider the collective set of data frames that go into the project.

For example, one data frame might indicate sex by a code like M or F and maybe a missing or unknown code, say, Z. A second data frame might have a column that gives TRUE for females and FALSE for males. Either of these schemes is adequate on its own, but if the data frames need to be combined, we will need to select a scheme from one data frame and impose it on the other.

Moreover, if two data sets provide the same information – sex, in this example – for the same observations, it is generally a good idea to see how often they agree, as a measure of data quality. In the case of sex, we expect to see almost no disagreements – people do change sex, but rarely, and disagreements are probably more likely to be due to transcription or other errors. More often, in our experience, we will see two sources agreeing almost all the time when both are present, but one source reporting many more missing values than the other. This can give us information about the overall data quality of the sources. Inevitably, experience and outside knowledge will help you spot anomalies. As an example, we were given a data set of car loans in which the cars were about 70% used and 30% new. When the same company sent us an update, the new file described cars that were about 30% used and 70% new. Neither is unreasonable taken alone, but when we saw both files we were certain an error had been made – and we were right.

7.3 Combining Data

We discussed combining data frames in Section 3.7. In that section, we focused on the mechanics of using R to combine data frames. As we described there, data frames can be joined three ways: by row (stacking vertically), by column (combining horizontally), or using a key (which we call merging). This section looks at some of the practical considerations we encounter when combining data frames in real data cleaning problems.

7.3.1 Combining by Row

As we noted earlier, most data cleaning projects involve data from a number of sources. These might be different sets of similar observations that should be combined row-wise. For example, we might get identically formatted tables from each of several laboratories that should be combined, one table on top of the next, into the final data set. Suppose we wanted to combine data sets named NYC, ATL, and PHX, representing input from our labs in New York, Atlanta, and Phoenix. First we will need to ensure that the data sets have exactly the same column names – often names will differ in case, or in the use of dots as separators. Second, columns with the same name should have the same class – character, numeric, logical, or date. Third, we usually want the set of values in categorical variables to match. If one data set's column Success has values Yes and No, say, and the other uses TRUE and FALSE, we will want to modify one to match the other. Fourth, we examine the key fields to ensure that they will be unique in the new, combined data set. If not, we might construct a new key that adds NYC, ATL, or PHX onto the front or rear of the existing key. Even if the keys are unique, we normally append a new column to each table, giving its source, just to be unambiguous.

We combine data sets like these with R's rbind() command , which we introduced in Section 3.7.1. This function will respond properly if columns with the same names appear in different orders in the two data sets. However, it will not complain if categorical columns do not have the same sets of values. So when we combine data sets in this row-wise manner, we often use code like that in the following examples to ensure that they do have the same values. We start by ensuring that all three data frames have the same number of columns, and that their names match. We sort the names because the columns might be in different orders in the different data frames.

```
# Values at right show expected output from each command
length (unique (c (ncol (NYC), ncol (ATL), ncol (PHX)))) # 1
all (sort (names (NYC)) == all (sort (names (ATL)))   # TRUE
all (sort (names (NYC)) == all (sort (names (PHX)))   # TRUE
```

We now check that the column classes match one another. Here we use the slightly different technique of calling all.equal() on the two vectors rather than all() on the comparison. The all.equal() approach will be necessary when comparing lists.

```
all.equal (sapply (NYC, class),
           sapply (ATL, class) [names (NYC)]) # TRUE
all.equal (sapply (NYC, class),
           sapply (PHX, class) [names (NYC)]) # TRUE
```

The class() function returns a vector of length 2 or more, rather than a single entry, for some columns (like, e.g., columns of POSIX date objects). In that case, we can replace sapply(NYC, class) by sapply(NYC, function(x) class(x) [1]).

In the next step, we identify the sets of categorical or factor variables, and extract from each one its unique values. In the following code, we explicitly convert any factor variables to character for the purpose of comparing their unique values.

```
cats <- names (NYC) [sapply (NYC, class) == "character" ||
                sapply (NYC, class) == "factor"]
levs.nyc <- lapply (NYC[,cats],
           function (x) unique (sort (as.character (x))))
levs.atl <- lapply (ATL[,cats],
           function (x) unique (sort (as.character (x))))
levs.phx <- lapply (PHX[,cats],
```

```
                function (x) unique (sort (as.character (x))))
all.equal (levs.nyc, levs.atl) &&
        all.equal (levs.nyc, levs.phx) # TRUE
```

The `levs` objects are lists of levels, which we sorted alphabetically (since `unique()` does not sort). The `all.equal()` functions produce logical values, which we combine with the `&&` operator. If the result is TRUE, we know that all three data frames' sets of character or factor variables have exactly the same sets of values.

The final step in this operation is to create a column identifying each data frame's source and then to combine the three data frames, as we show here.

```
NYC$Source <- "NYC"
ATL$Source <- "ATL"
PHX$Source <- "PHX"
big <- rbind (NYC, ATL, PHX, stringsAsFactors = FALSE)
```

Notice the use of the `stringsAsFactors = FALSE` argument in the call to `rbind()`. As we said in Section 4.6.5, `rbind()` behaves more gracefully with factors, or mixtures of factors and characters, than some other R functions. Still, we recommend using the `stringsAsFactors = FALSE` argument during the data cleaning process. We generally want to create factors only at the end of the cleaning process (see Section 7.5).

7.3.2 Combining by Column

Two data frames with the same number of rows can be combined "horizontally" using the `data.frame()` function. This straightforward operation produces a result whose number of columns is simply the sum of the numbers of columns in the components. However, the joining is done naïvely. If the components are data frames A and B, the first row of A is joined to the first row of B, the second to the second, and so on. The `data.frame()` function ensures that the column names in the result are distinct, so some of the column names in the second data frame may be changed. The `cbind()` function does not de-conflict column names, so we recommend using `data.frame()` for this job. The row names in the result come from the first data frame that has (non-default) ones.

7.3.3 Merging by Key

A more sophisticated operation is needed when two data sets have information about the same observations but possibly in different orders. In this case, the data needs to be "merged," that is, combined into one wide data set. We do this by joining the tables according to their key values; in R, we use the `merge()` function (see Section 3.7.2). In its simplest form, `merge()` takes two data sets and returns a new one with the values from each key combined into one row. If keys are unique, and every key appears in both data sets, this operation is straightforward. The behavior when the keys are duplicated is slightly tricky; we make sure that our keys are always unique. We may also need to decide what to do about records that appear in one table but not both. The merge() function accepts arguments that control this behavior.

Two facts about merge() are worth remembering. First, the return from the merge() function is, by default, sorted according to the key, so the order of the rows may have changed compared to the ordering in the source tables. A second, more important point has to do with what happens when the two source tables have columns with the same name. If both of the original tables contain a column named State, for example, the output will contain two columns State.x and State.y. The term State is now not enough to name a column unambiguously, so code that worked on the State column in either of the two original data sets will fail on the merged one. Moreover, if the merged data is now merged again with a third input, that third input will contribute a column just called State (since that name is now not a duplicate). If you intend to keep both of a pair of like-named columns after a merge, we recommend changing their names in a controlled way, ahead of time.

7.4   Transactional Data

One type of data that is worth further mention here is *transactional data*. In contrast to tabular data, in which we might expect one row per key, transactional data sets often have many rows for each key, with each row representing a single transaction. Think of a log of clicks at a website, for example, identified by user; each user may contribute dozens of clicks in a single session. Or think of a data set of bank transactions identified by the customer's account number. If the interest is in individual transactions, then the data set is well on its way to being useful. However, if the interest is in account numbers, we may want to summarize all the transactions for a particular customer so as to produce a data set with one row per account rather than one row per customer.

In the rest of this section, we illustrate working with transactional data by reference to a real-life problem we encountered recently. This example is lengthy, but it serves to show some of the techniques that will be useful when handling this and other sorts of data.

7.4.1   Example of Transactional Data

We were given a large data set regarding a particular survey taken by soldiers that was intended to elicit the soldier's emotional state. The key field was an identifier that was unique to each soldier. This survey was administered approximately every year, so most soldiers appear multiple times in this data set. The actual survey data set had several million rows, and each row contained the answer to perhaps 150 questions, but for this demonstration we will show a sample survey data set with only one question (to which is answer is an integer on the scale of 1–5). Our sample survey data frame `survey` has seven rows, as shown here. Like the original, our sample data is sorted by `Date` within `ID`.

```
> survey
  ID       Date Response
1 AA 2012-09-26        3
2 AA 2014-01-16        4
3 CC 2013-03-13        3
4 CC 2014-04-30        5
5 CC 2015-03-31        4
6 DD 2013-06-03        2
7 EE 2013-12-02        4
```

We would consider this to be tabular data if our interest were primarily in each survey response. If our interest were primarily in each soldier, we would consider this to be transactional data. We have already seen some ways to summarize data like this. For example, we might compute the average `Response` for each `ID` using the `tapply()` function, with code like `with(survey, tapply(Response, ID, mean))`. More generally, we might be interested in building a data set with one row per soldier, where each row has the earliest date taken, perhaps, the average response, the number of responses, and so on.

One useful tool for transforming transactional data into a tabular form is the `rle()` function from Section 2.6.5. Since the records are sorted by ID, the `rle()` function, applied to the IDs, computes the "runs" of ID values. It returns a list with two elements named `lengths` and `values`. The `values` component is a vector of distinct soldier IDs (one entry for each ID for which there is at least one survey), and the `lengths` component gives the number of times that ID appeared in each run. That number is, of course, an integer giving the number of surveys taken by each soldier. This code shows the list produced as output of the call to `rle()`. Despite the special print format, the elements of this object can be accessed in the same way as elements of an ordinary list.

```
> (rle.out <- rle (survey$ID))
Run Length Encoding
  lengths: int [1:4] 2 3 1 1
  values : chr [1:4] "AA" "CC" "DD" "EE"
```

This output is useful for many tasks that need to be performed on transactional data. For example, since `lengths` gives the lengths of the runs for each ID, we can identify the ending points of the runs for each soldier with `end <- cumsum(rle.out$lengths)`. Then the starting point can be computed with `start <- c(1, end[-length(end)] + 1)` – here we start the first run at 1 and start the last one after the second-to-last endpoint. With these starting and ending points in hand, we can answer even difficult and complicated questions about the contents of the records within each run. For example, suppose we wanted to identify soldiers who had an increase of exactly 1 between one value of the Response and the next. Assuming that records are sorted by Date within ID, we can construct a function diff1 that extracts the set of records associated with a particular index of start and end and determines whether any of the differences are equal to 1. Then we can apply that function to each pair of corresponding start and end values, as shown in the following code.

```
> diff1 <- function (i) {
      recs <- survey[start[i]:end[i],]
      if (any (diff (recs$Response) == 1)) TRUE else FALSE
}
> sapply (1:length (start), diff1)
[1]   TRUE FALSE FALSE FALSE
```

The output shows us that AA is the only soldier with an increase in Response of exactly 1 from one survey to the next. In this example, we could also have used tapply (), which has the additional advantage of not relying on global variables (as our diff1 relies on start and end and survey). However, tapply () cannot be applied to a data frame. If we needed all the information for each soldier, another alternative is to combine split () with lapply (), but that approach seems to be slower and more memory-intensive.

7.4.2 Combining Tabular and Transactional Data

We continue this example by reference to the real-life problem that inspired it. We were actually given two large data sets. One contained the surveys we described earlier. The second listed soldiers who had undergone deployment overseas, giving an ID and the starting and ending dates of the deployment. Many soldiers had more than one deployment. When read into R, the actual deployment data frame had some hundreds of thousands of rows, but for this example we use five deployments. This code shows what the five sample deployments look like, as stored in an R data frame called deploy.

```
> deploy
   ID     Start        End
1  AA  2014-05-05  2014-11-08
2  BB  2012-10-15  2013-07-19
3  CC  2013-08-16  2014-04-03
4  CC  2015-11-01  2015-05-17
5  EE  2013-02-20  2013-05-18
```

Like the surveys, this data set has been sorted to be in ascending order of ID. Our ultimate goal was to identify soldiers who had taken the survey both before and after deployment, to see whether deployments might be associated with changes in emotional state. To do that, we wanted to create a data set with one row per deployment. Each row of this final data will indicate the latest survey for each soldier, among those that preceded the deployment start date, and the earliest survey among those that follow the deployment end date. In this way, we would have the surveys that most closely bracketed the deployment. Soldiers might appear twice in the data set, possibly bracketed by different pairs of surveys. In fact it would, in theory, be possible for two deployments by the same soldier to be bracketed by the same pair of surveys, but we judged this to be unlikely and not damaging to the analysis. In this example, the deployment data set is already tabular (since we are interested in deployments, not individual soldiers), and the survey data set is transactional. A natural first step is to look for missing values, especially in responses and dates.

Once we were satisfied with the quality of the data, we decided to create, as an intermediate product, a data set with one row per deployment, each row containing the dates of all the surveys for that soldier. Of course, different soldiers take the survey different numbers of times, so we found the maximum number of survey taken by any soldier with a command like `max(rle.out$lengths)`. We might have used `max(table(survey $ID))`, although we would expect that to take much longer.

In this case, the maximum number of surveys taken is three, by soldier CC. So we created a character matrix with three columns. We used characters because Date objects in a matrix get converted to numeric. This character matrix was called `datemat`. This code shows how the `datemat` matrix might be constructed. Notice that, for the moment, this matrix is constructed without an ID.

```
> deploy.unique.ID <- unique (deploy$ID)
> datemat <- matrix ("", nrow = length (deploy.unique.ID),
                ncol = max (rle.out$lengths))
```

In order to fill `datemat`, we use the `rle()` function from the example above and the idea of a matrix subscript from Section 3.2.5. However, we need to exclude soldiers who took the survey who are not in the set of deployers. In this code, we remove those entries from the survey data frame, producing `surv.short`, and then re-run `rle()`.

```
> surv.short <- survey[is.element (survey$ID, deploy$ID),]
> rle.out <- rle (surv.short$ID)
```

We can now create a two-column matrix subscript, to be used to enter dates into the `datemat` matrix. Each row of the matrix subscript, as you recall, gives a row and column number of an entry to be filled. The column numbers are the values from 1 to 3 giving the column of `datemat` where the date of the survey will be recorded. For example, the first soldier, AA, took two surveys, so we will fill columns 1 and 2 of that soldier's row. We will want to generate a vector like `1:2` for that soldier. The second soldier took three surveys, so we will fill all three columns, using a vector like 1 : 3, and so on. We can compute a list with the relevant vectors using sapply(), as we show in the following code. Then unlist() extracts a vector of values from the list.

```
> surv.lens <- sapply (rle.out$length, function (i) 1:i)
> (col.surveys <- unlist (surv.lens))
[1] 1 2 1 2 3 1
```

The col.surveys vector gives the columns into which the dates need to be placed. The IDs that go along with each of these entries are precisely the entries in surv.short$ID. However, rather than the text IDs, we want the (numeric) row number of datemat, which we can get using the match() function to match the IDs from the surveys to the set of unique deployment IDs. This code shows how we construct the vector giving the row of datemat desired for each survey.

```
> (row.surveys <- match (surv.short$ID, deploy.unique.ID))
[1] 1 1 3 3 3 4
> (mat.subset <- cbind (row.surveys, col.surveys))
     row.surveys col.surveys
[1,]           1           1
[2,]           1           2
[3,]           3           1
[4,]           3           2
[5,]           3           3
[6,]           4           1
```

We can now see that this matrix can be correctly used as a subscript. (We can also see why datemat has no extraneous columns like ID; we want to refer to the first date column as column number 1.) The date of the first survey should be entered into the first row and first column of datemat; the second survey was taken by the same soldier, so its date, too, should go into the first row, but this one should go into the second column; and so on.

The final steps are these. First, we use the matrix subscript to fill the datemat matrix with the survey dates. We make these character explicitly. Then we create a data frame consisting of the unique IDs from the deployment file, together with the dates from the datemat matrix. We merge the original deploy data to this new data frame by ID, creating a data set with one row per deployment (the merge() command, you will recall, takes care of the fact that some soldiers deploy more than once). These commands show the construction of the final combined data set, which we call dd.

```
> datemat [mat.subset] <- as.character (surv.short$Date)
> date.df <- data.frame (ID = deploy.unique.ID, datemat,
          stringsAsFactors = FALSE)
```

```
> (dd <- merge (deploy, date.df, by = "ID"))
   ID     Start        End           X1          X2         X3
1 AA 2014-05-05 2014-11-08 2012-09-26 2014-01-16
2 BB 2012-10-15 2013-07-19
3 CC 2013-08-16 2014-04-03 2013-03-13 2014-04-30 2015-03-31
4 CC 2015-11-01 2015-05-17 2013-03-13 2014-04-30 2015-03-31
5 EE 2013-02-20 2013-05-18 2013-12-02
```

With this data set in hand, we can now determine which deployments are bracketed by surveys. We need to be aware that the Start and End columns are Date objects, whereas the survey dates in the three rightmost columns are character. We also need to be aware that some entries in those last three columns are empty. For each row we extract the largest date "to the left of" (i.e., smaller than) the non-entry survey dates, using - Inf when none is found. Then extract the smallest date to the right, using Inf if none is found. This code defines a function bracket () that performs this computation and shows the effect of it operating on each of the rows of dd. The result is named brack.

```
> bracket <- function (i) {
    dat <- dd[i,]                          # extract ith row
    dts <- dat[,4:6]                       # grab dates and...
    dts <- dts[dts != ""]                  # omit empties
    left <- max (-Inf, dts[dts < as.character (dat$Start)])
    right <- min (Inf, dts[dts > as.character (dat$End)])
    c(left, right)
}
> (brack <- sapply (1:nrow (dd), bracket))
        [,1]          [,2]     [,3]              [,4]                [,5]
[1,] "2014-01-16" "-Inf" "2013-03-13" "2015-03-31"      "-Inf"
[2,] "Inf"        "Inf"  "2014-04-30" "Inf"        "2013-12-02"
```

As we noted in Section 5.1.2, bracket () is a function that relies on variables in the workspace (in this case, dd). We usually avoid this reliance, but this function provides a convenient way to operate on the rows of dd, and we will only use this function once.

The result in brack gives one column per row of dd. Only the third row of dd – the first deployment of soldier CC – is bracketed by surveys. Now we simplify the dd data set by combining its ID with the transpose of the brack matrix. Having identified the "bracketing" survey dates, we now want to extract the responses for those surveys. The natural way to do this is to identify every survey by a unique key consisting of the soldier's ID and the date. We construct these keys both in the new dd data set, and also in the original survey data set. Then match () can be used to bring in the responses from the two bracketing surveys. This final piece of code shows how this is accomplished. Notice that the columns from brack are now named X1 and X2.

```
> dd <- data.frame (ID = dd$ID, t (brack),
                    stringsAsFactors = TRUE)
> left.key <- paste0 (dd$ID, ".", dd$X1)
```

```
> right.key <- paste0 (dd$ID, ".", dd$X2)
# Add key, then use match
> survey$key <- paste0 (survey$ID, ".", survey$Date)
> dd$ResponseLeft <-
          survey$Response[match (left.key, survey$key)]
> dd$ResponseRight <-
          survey$Response[match (right.key, survey$key)]
> dd
  ID          X1          X2 ResponseLeft ResponseRight
1 AA 2014-01-16         Inf            4            NA
2 BB       -Inf         Inf           NA            NA
3 CC 2013-03-13  2014-04-30            3             5
4 CC 2015-03-31         Inf            4            NA
5 EE       -Inf  2013-12-02           NA             4
```

Obviously, the bracketed deployments are the ones with both responses present. If we were writing a script to identify these deployments, we would take a minute here to remove the temporary variables we created – left.key, right.key, and so on.

7.5   Preparing Data

We draw a distinction between the "cleaning" step, where we detect and adjust anomalies, and the "preparation" step (although these two certainly overlap). In the preparation step, we create new columns for the purpose of making modeling easier or more revealing, without affecting the existing columns. One such action is binning, where we create a new character vector with a small set of levels (such as "small," "medium," and "large") from a numeric vector. As another example, it is common in regression problems to transform a numeric variable by taking its logarithm. We might combine categorical variables, converting a three-level Race factor and a two-level Sex factor into a single six-level factor, and so on. All of these steps are intended for modeling, not data cleaning, and the specific steps will depend on the models being used.

Another common action is creating a new, small set of categorical levels from an existing, much larger set. It is helpful to have a cross-reference table that connects one set to the other. For example, given a set of US states, we might want to create a new column of the corresponding census regions (Northwest, Midwest, South, and West – we use this example in Chapter 8 as well). Suppose that we have a data set dat with a column named State already in it. We can use the cross-reference data frame state.tbl from the cleaningBook package. This data frame has State in one column and Region in another. Then the match() function allows us to add a Region column to dat with a command like dat$Region <- state.tbl$Region[match (dat$State, state.tbl$State)].

In this example, we can also use merge() to join the dat and state.tbl data frames. We are most accustomed to using match() for tasks that involve a column or two because we often do not need all the columns from the second data set to be added to the first. The important difference between match() and merge() arises in the case of duplicate keys. The match() finds only one match (the first one) if there is one, whereas merge() returns all of the records with the matching key.

Here, the match() function produces a vector the same length as dat$State, each entry of which gives the number of the element of state.tbl$State matched by that element of dat$State. Then we look up the values of state.tbl$Region that correspond to those matches to find the regions. (Elements in dat that do not match the cross-reference table will produce NA in the output.) This use of a cross-reference table is very common and makes code to create the new columns easy to read and repeatable – but make sure that the cross-reference table does not have duplicated keys.

Although it is technically a modification of an existing column, we include in the data preparation step the act of changing the class of one column to another class. The most common of these transformations arises when converting a character vector to a factor (Section 4.6) using the factor() or as.factor() functions, since we generally avoid factors when we first read in the data. Eventually, factors may be needed for modeling efforts. When converting a character vector into a factor, remember that you can control the ordering of the factor levels (which otherwise defaults to alphabetical). The "baseline" level of a factor is the first one, and it is often useful to select the baseline carefully, as the most common or least interesting level, perhaps.

Changing the class of one or two columns in a data frame is straightforward. Changing the class of many things requires some care. In particular, it is generally a bad idea to use apply() or sapply() for this task on a data frame because these functions return a matrix (in which all of the entries must be of the same class). The lapply() function can be used, though it produces a list that then needs to be manipulated. An inelegant but easy alternative is a simple for() loop.

7.6 Documentation and Reproducibility

There are at least two sorts of documentation in a data cleaning process: the documentation provided to you with the data and the documentation you generate as you go through the steps. The first of these is often called a "data dictionary." This should contain a manifest of all the files delivered, with the names of each column and the possible values. This is a good place to record the source of the data and the dates on which each piece of it was received. The more detailed a data dictionary is, the easier we can expect the data cleaning tasks to be. However, data dictionaries are often incomplete – for example, it is common to find levels or missing value indicators in the data that are not listed in the dictionary. In some cases, the dictionary is just wrong; this might happen when you are provided an outdated version, for example. All you can do in this case is to try to communicate with the data provider and make some educated guesses. We talk about the role of judgment in the next section.

The second sort of documentation in a data cleaning effort is the documentation that you generate to describe what you did. At a very minimum, you should produce your R scripts and any custom functions that you wrote as part of the effort – and, like all scripts and functions, these should be laid out in a clear way, with enough comments that a new user can figure out what you did.

More often we produce a real write-up, just for the data handling effort, laying out all of the steps that we took in text, rather than just as R comments. It is particularly important to list actions that resulted in observations being deleted, with reasons and counts. In fact, most of our reports include a flowchart describing the number of observations at each step in the data cleaning process. Figure 7.1 shows an example of such a chart. In this example, observations came from two sources, as shown in the upper corners. A small number of observations are deleted because they lack payment information;

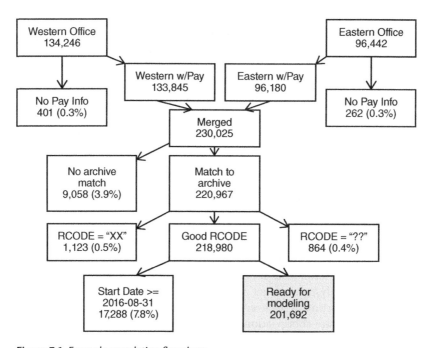

Figure 7.1 Example population flowchart.

then the two remaining sets of observations are merged into one data set of 230,025 observations. In subsequent cleaning steps, we lose observations that fail to match back to a particular archive, that have unexpected values of a field called RCODE, and whose start dates are too recent. The rectangle in the bottom right gives the number of observations that have survived the different cleaning steps.

We also recommend that you create, as one of your products, a master table with every key and the disposition of the record for that key (in our example, "no payment information," "illegal RCODE," etc.). That way you and the sponsor can quickly identify the outcome associated with every record.

Perhaps the most important goal of the documentation that you produce is to make the data handling process "reproducible." That is, any R user should be able to take your data, and your scripts and functions, run through the data handling process from beginning to end and produce exactly the same output that you did. Sometimes, this will be impossible – if, for example, you are acquiring data from a database that gets updated frequently. But usually you want to think of this as a requirement. In fact, it may be worth moving your data, scripts, and functions to a new directory (or even a new machine, perhaps with a different operating system) and re-running your handling process there, to ensure that you aren't, for example, relying on variables in your R environment that won't be present in the new directory.

Notice that the ordering of the steps will affect the numbers in the flowchart. Suppose that some of the rows were both missing payment information and also had illegal RCODEs. Then the counts associated with those two exclusions will depend on the order in which they are applied. In this case, we would expect the final count to be the same regardless of the order of the operations (although the master table may change). However, in other cases, particularly those involving judgment (next section), we have to expect that two different data cleaners will end up with two slightly different data sets, depending on the choices they make.

7.7 The Role of Judgment

The data scientist is confronted with data and with rules for preparing it, and yet inevitably is called on to exercise his or her judgment during the cleaning process. As an artificial example, imagine a data set called indat that included city names and two-letter state abbreviations. As part of the data cleaning process you, as the analyst, construct a table of the length (i.e., nchar()) of the abbreviations, expecting to see every entry with the value 2. However, you find that a number of state abbreviations in fact have four characters each, so you tabulate the set of state abbreviations with four characters. So far, your code might look like this:

```
table (nchar (indat$State))

   2    4
9203   84
table (indat$State[nchar (indat$State) == 4])
CITY
  84
```

Something seems to have gone wrong here. You tabulate the values in the CITY field for the 84 records whose State field has the CITY value, and you see this:

```
table (indat$City[nchar (indat$State) == 4])
NEW YORK
     84
```

At this point, the issue seems clear: these 84 records presumably should have been recorded as "city = 'New York', state = 'NY' " but instead were recorded as "city = 'New York', state = 'City'." Having identified the issue, though, some steps remain. Are the data suppliers aware of this anomaly? They will need to be informed, maybe right away if fresh data is required, but maybe, for comparatively unimportant problems, in the final project documentation. Does this error suggest that other fields in those same records are less reliable? Is it acceptable to change the state for these 84 records to NY? Are there other entries correctly labeled "city = 'New York,' state = 'NY' " (or "city = 'New York City,' state = 'NY' "), and, if so, do these differ from the mislabeled ones, perhaps in terms of date?

Issues like this arise in almost every data cleaning problem. The analyst has the responsibility of alerting the data provider as to problems, but she must also forge ahead. The most important rule is that *everything must be documented*. Documentation will appear in the code, but it must also be in the human-readable materials returned to the client. We are always wary of making changes to our customers' data, and yet we very often end up doing just that – informing the customer of what changes were made, why, and how many records were affected.

One more place where the analyst's judgment can be required is in missing value handling. Some missing values appear to have arisen more or less at random; the rest of the record and entries for that field in other records are generally not missing. Missing values like these can often be incorporated into the modeling process.

Other records might have almost all missing entries. Since these carry almost no information, they will often need to be discarded. On the other hand, fields for these observations that are present might be informative about some items of interest. For example, if a set of records, missing most fields, contains age and sex information, those values might be useful when assessing the population of customers, even if they are not useful for modeling outcomes. So, at each stage, it is important to report the number of observations used for any particular graph, table, or statistic.

Often values marked as missing actually indicate something. For example, one field might carry information about whether a customer has ever declared bankruptcy. Suppose that such a field has only two unique values: Y and the missing value NA, and suppose that only a few percent are marked Y. It might be reasonable to judge that NA was recorded for customers with no bankruptcy, change those to N, and proceed (documenting this change, of course, and reporting it). Now suppose that this field had three distinct values: Y making up, say, 2% of the values, N making up 94%, and NA accounting for the remaining 4% of values. Here, the way forward is not as clear.

Judgment arises when combining the levels of categorical values. For example, one field might record whether an applicant rents a home, owns it, lives with parents, or has some other housing situation; imagine that the documentation specifies that these choices will be represented with values R, O, P, and X, respectively. Suppose that when you tabulate that field, you find about 60% R values, 20% O values, 10% P values, and 3% X values; but you also find 4% r, in lower-case, and 3% missing values. Even though r is not listed as a possible choice, it seems reasonable to assign them to the R group, with corresponding documentation to be included in the final report. On the other hand, if instead of r the value had been J, we might have made a different choice. And what about the missing values? Since R is the most common group, it will under some circumstances make sense to insert an R into those records. Alternatively, since missing value is "other than R, O, or P," we might move those items with missing values into the X group – or we might create a new label called Missing. The path to take has to depend on the frequency of anomalous entries, the frequencies of the existing entries (as, here, where R is the most common), and the ultimate goals of the analysis, and these call for the analyst's judgment in consultation with the data providers.

7.8   Data Cleaning in Action

In this section, we demonstrate some of our approaches on some data inspired by a real problem we investigated. This data concerns somewhat more than 100 homes in the eastern part of the United States. It comes in the form of three CSV files, which you can find in the cleaningBook package. Each property is described by its size (in number of bedrooms and number of bathrooms), the state in which it is located, and its area (in square feet). This information is held in two separate files, named BedBath1.csv and BedBath2.csv. The electrical usage, measured at a meter, for each property has been recorded over six consecutive calendar quarters. This information is held in a third file, EnergyUsage.csv, which should include all the homes in the first two files.

Homes are identified by a serial number, which consists of one of the letters
A, H, or P, followed by three digits and then a "trailer" made up of three more
digits; trailers are one of 001 through 009.

The ultimate goal of the effort was to model the changes in electrical usage
across time, particularly in specific subsets of houses that are similar in terms
of their size and location. The goal of the data cleaning portion is simply to
combine the three data sets into one that is suitable for the modeling effort. In
the following sections, we handle each file one at a time.

7.8.1 Reading and Cleaning `BedBath1.csv`

Reading

Since the `BedBath1` file has a name ending in `.csv`, it seems reasonable to
presume that it is comma-separated. We might start using `scan()` to extract
and examine a few rows of the file, but very often we wade right in with the
hope that the first call will produce the desired result. In this case, we start with
a call to `read.csv()` and then show a few rows. Recall that this function calls
`read.table()` with `quote= "\""` and `comment.char = ""` as well
as `sep = ","`.

```
> bb1 <- read.csv ("BedBath1.csv", stringsAsFactors = FALSE)
> bb1[1:4,]
                            SerText   Bed   Bath SqFt State
Prop # P477005 and land           3      3  1580   PA
H644009 as identifier             3  2 1/2  1490   CT
House Num H260008                  2      1   910   CT
Property A834009      house and land   2 1 1/2   980   CT
```

We have learned a few things here. First, it appears that we have encountered an
embedded comma problem – the fourth row has one more entry than the others. As a result, the text from the first column has been made into row names. If
any row had had too many commas, `read.csv()` would have failed. Second,
the numbers for `Bath` must be text because they include entries like 2 1/2.
We may want to convert that number to 2.5. Third, the property identifier is
enclosed inside some text, and not in a consistent location from row to row.
We will need to extract the ID from the surrounding text.

The first thing to handle is the embedded comma. Let us double-check by
extracting the first few rows of text using `scan()` to ensure that that is, in fact,
the issue. This code shows how we might do that.

```
> bb1 <- scan ("BedBath1.csv", sep = "\n", what = "")
Read 77 items
> bb1[1:5]
[1] "SerText,Bed,Bath,SqFt,State"
[2] "Prop # P477005 and land,3,3,1580,PA"
```

```
[3]  "H644009 as identifier,3,2 1/2,1490,CT"
[4]  "House Num H260008,2,1,910,CT"
[5]  "Property A834009, house and land,2,1 1/2,980,CT"
```

There really is a comma after the property ID, and before the word "house," in the fifth line. In the next step, we use count.fields() to see how frequently there is one extra comma and to examine what rows with extra commas look like.

```
> table (count.fields ("BedBath1.csv", sep = ",",
                       comment.char = ""))

 5  6
66 11
> bb1[6 == count.fields ("BedBath1.csv", sep = ",",
                         comment.char = "")]
 [1] "Property A834009, house and land,2,1 1/2,980,CT"
 [2] "Property P589004, house and land,3,3,1560,NY"
 [3] "Property P450001, house and land,3,2,1400,PA"
      :  :  :
 [8] "Property A303001, house and land,3,2,c. 1460,PA"
      :  :  :
```

All 11 of the lines with 6 fields include the "house and land" notation. So we will just remove the first comma from each of those 11 lines. Notice also that in the eighth line the square footage value, c. 1460, is not numeric. We will need to address this shortly. First, though, we remove the first comma in each of the over-long lines using sub(). Then we can pass the result as the text argument to read.csv() to produce a data frame.

```
> comm <- (6 == count.fields ("BedBath1.csv", sep = ",",
          comment.char = ""))
> bb1[comm] <- sub (",", "", bb1[comm])
> bb1 <- read.csv (text = bb1, stringsAsFactors = FALSE)
> bb1[1:4,]
                        SerText Bed  Bath SqFt State
1            Prop # P477005 and land   3     3 1580    PA
2            H644009 as identifier   3 2 1/2 1490    CT
3               House Num H260008   2     1  910    CT
4  Property A834009 house and land   2 1 1/2  980    CT
```

In the first command, we located the rows with six fields (i.e., five commas). In the second, we removed those commas. After the call to read.csv() in the third line, we can see that the fields appear to line up, at least in the first few rows. We move on to the cleaning step.

Cleaning

Now we examine the classes of the columns using a call to sapply().

```
> sapply (bb1, class)
     SerText          Bed         Bath          SqFt         State
 "character"    "integer"  "character"  "character"  "character"
```

This final command shows that the `Bed` field has been recognized as `integer`, which suggests that the fields are properly lined up. It also confirms our previous observation that the `Bath` and `SqFt` columns will need to be cleaned in order to make them numeric.

Now let us extract the ID from the `SerText` field. Since we know that the ID consists of an A, H, or P followed by six digits, we can extract the ID with a regular expression, as shown in the next code segment.

```
> (bb1$ID <- regmatches (bb1$SerText,
              regexpr ("[AHP][[:digit:]]{6}", bb1$SerText)))
 [1] "P477005" "H644009" "H260008" "A834009"   ...
> table (is.na (bb1$ID))
FALSE
   76
> table (nchar (bb1$ID))
 7
76
```

The second command, of course, shows us that no `ID`s are missing, and the third, that every `ID` has seven characters. We might look further into the `ID` values by ensuring that they all really do start with A, H, or P, that they all end with a three-digit number of the form 00x, and so on.

As to the `Bath` column, we can use `sub()` to replace every instance of `1/2` with `.5`. Notice how the text to be replaced includes the space that separates the two parts of, for example, `2 1/2`. After that substitution, we should be able to convert the column to numeric. We will create a new variable with the numeric version of `Bath` first, to ensure that the conversion went successfully. This code shows how we can compare the original `Bath` with the newly constructed version.

```
> bath <- as.numeric (sub (" 1/2", ".5", bb1$Bath))
> table (bath, bb1$Bath, useNA = "ifany")
bath   1 1 1/2  2 2 1/2  3
   1   5      0  0     0  0
   1.5 0     18  0     0  0
   2   0      0 18     0  0
   2.5 0      0  0    20  0
   3   0      0  0     0 15
```

We can tell that this conversion has succeeded by examining the table, and we can see that there are no missing values in the `bb1$Bath` column. As a result, we can replace the `Bath` column in the data set with the `bath` variable just constructed, as we do here.

```
> bb1$Bath <- bath
```

The final preparatory step for this data involves addressing the non-numeric entries in the SqFt column. The non-numeric entries, of course, would be turned into NA by as.numeric(). The following command shows how we can use this fact to show the set of non-numeric SqFt entries.

```
> bb1[is.na (as.numeric (bb1$SqFt)),"SqFt"]
 [1] "~ 1510"        "c. 970"         "~ 1460"
 [4] "c. 1470"       "c. 920"         "approx. 1510"
 [7] "~ 1580"        "c. 1460"        "~ 1600"
[10] "~ 1560"        "approx. 1440"  "~ 1460"
[13] "approx. 1450"
Warning message:
In '[.data.frame'(bb1, is.na(as.numeric(bb1$SqFt)), "SqFt"):
  NAs introduced by coercion
```

In another example, there might have been too many to view, but here we can see that the non-numeric entries come in three types: those that start c., those that start ~, and those that start approx. The next step requires some judgment. We will elect to remove the qualifiers and report the square footage using the integer given; but we would certainly report this choice.

One way to extract the numeric part is, as before, with a regular expression. In the first command, as shown below, we search for a sequence of digits, and then use regmatches() to extract that sequence. This produces a character vector we name sqft. Then, we extract the values of sqft, which correspond to non-numeric entries in the original bb1$SqFt vector. We display the first, second, and the sixth elements of that subset to ensure that each different sort of "approximate" notation is corrected properly.

```
> sqft <- regmatches (bb1$SqFt,
                  regexpr ("([[:digit:]]+)", bb1$SqFt))
> sqft[is.na (as.numeric (bb1$SqFt))][c(1, 2, 6)]
[1] "1510" "970"  "1510" # warning message suppressed
```

Now that sqft appears to contain the correct value for every row, we can convert it into a numeric vector and assign the result to the SqFt column of bb1. This code shows that operation, together with the first few rows of the modified data frame.

```
> bb1$SqFt <- as.numeric (sqft)
> bb1[1:3,]
                     SerText Bed Bath SqFt State      ID
1 Prop # P477005 and land    3  3.0  1580     PA P477005
2    H644009 as identifier    3  2.5  1490     CT H644009
3       House Num H260008    2  1.0   910     CT H260008
```

Our data cleaning for this file is nearly complete. The SerText column is redundant but not otherwise bothersome. However, a few checks remain.

First, we examine the classes of the column to ensure they are as we expect – character for the first and last two, numeric for the others. Second, we look for duplicated rows and duplicated ID values. We could use any(duplicated()) here, but we are in the habit of using table(). That way, if there are duplicates, we know how many are there.

```
> sapply (bb1, class)
     SerText          Bed         Bath         SqFt        State
 "character"    "integer"    "numeric"    "numeric"  "character"
          ID
 "character"
> table (duplicated (bb1))     # duplicated rows?
FALSE
   76
> table (duplicated (bb1$ID)) # duplicated IDs?
FALSE   TRUE
   75      1
```

Apparently there is a duplicated ID. Let us determine its value and then extract the rows for that ID.

```
> bb1$ID[duplicated (bb1$ID)]
[1] "P888009"
> bb1[bb1$ID == "P888009",]
                  SerText Bed Bath SqFt State       ID
23    Property ID P888009   2  1.5  920    PA P888009
49 P888009 as identifier   2  1.5  920    PA P888009
```

The good news is that these two rows are identical except for the original SerText. It is almost certainly safe to delete one of the two. Still, the fact of the duplication might reveal something about the process by which the data has been collected, stored, or transmitted, and it should be reported. The following commands show how we might delete one of these two rows as well as the SerText column. We examine the dimensionality, mostly for our awareness. Finally, we tabulate the State column, again just for our general awareness.

```
> bb1 <- bb1[-23,]          # using row number from above
> bb1[bb1$ID == "P888009",]  # double-check!
                  SerText Bed Bath SqFt State       ID
49 P888009 as identifier   2  1.5  920    PA P888009
> bb1$SerText <- NULL        # delete columns
> dim (bb1)
[1] 75  5
> table (bb1$State, useNA = "ifany")
CT NY PA
28 17 30
```

Deleting row 23 is a quick operation, but it is slightly dangerous, in that if it were inadvertently repeated a different row would be (wrongly) removed. It might be safer to use a command like

```
> bb1 <- bb1[-(which (bb1$ID == "P888009")[2]),]
```

Here, if there is a second row with the given ID, it will be removed. If not, the value of which(bb1$ID == "P888009")[2] will be NA, and the attempt to compute bb1[-NA,] will produce an error.

As a final cleaning step for this data frame we might examine our summary statistics for our numeric columns (Bed and SqFt), looking for missing and anomalous values – but in this case, it may make sense to wait until the final data set has been constructed.

7.8.2 Reading and Cleaning BedBath2.csv

Reading

We continue the data cleaning exercise by reading the BedBath2.csv file. As before, it is not implausible that everything will be well formatted, so we call read.csv() and examine the first few lines.

```
> bb2 <- read.csv ("BedBath2.csv", stringsAsFactors = FALSE)
> bb2[1:3,]
[1] "P957001\t3\t2\tNew York\t1440"
[2] "H429005\t2\t1.5\tNew Jersey\t950"
[3] "P226003\t2\t1.5\tNew York\t930"
```

Apparently this file, despite having a name that ends in .csv, is in fact tab-separated. Naturally we try again, adding sep = "\t" to read.csv() as shown here. (We might just as well have used read.table() or read.delim().) We also examine the dimension of the resulting data frame and the classes of its columns.

```
> bb2 <- read.csv ("BedBath2.csv", sep = "\t",
                   stringsAsFactors = FALSE)
> bb2[1:3,]
   PropId Bed Bath      State Size
1 P957001   3  2.0   New York 1440
2 H429005   2  1.5 New Jersey  950
3 P226003   2  1.5   New York  930
> dim (bb2)
[1] 40  5
```

The data frame appears to have been constructed successfully.

Cleaning

A natural first step in the cleaning process, as with bb1, is to examine the classes of the columns. This code shows how we can do that.

```
> sapply (bb2, class)
    PropId         Bed          Bath        State         Size
"character"   "integer"   "numeric"  "character"  "integer"
```

We see a few things here. First, the IDs, called `PropId` here, seem to be whole (at least, in the first few rows). We might use `table(nchar(bb2$PropId))` to examine them further. The `Bath` and `Size` columns are properly numeric, as well. The `State` entries are full names rather than two-letter postal codes, but this is easily handled. The data appears to have been read in properly. Let us look for duplicate keys, both within this data set and between the two.

```
> table (duplicated (bb2))
FALSE
   40
> table (duplicated (bb2$PropId))
FALSE
   40
> length (intersect (bb1$ID, bb2$PropId))
[1] 0
```

Our 40 `PropId` values are distinct, and they do not overlap with any of the `ID` values in `bb1`. In order to join the two bb data sets, we will need to convert the two-letter state codes into state names, or vice versa. Let us tabulate the `bb2` state codes.

```
> table (bb2$State, useNA = "ifany")
Connecticut   New Jersey    New York
        10           15          15
```

It seems reasonable to convert these state names to their corresponding two-letter codes. We could construct an ad hoc cross-reference table for this purpose, but we can just as easily construct a table of state names and codes from the built-in R objects `state.name` and `state.abb`. The following code shows how we can build this cross-reference table.

```
> state.xref <- data.frame (Name = state.name,
                Abbr = state.abb, stringsAsFactors = FALSE)
> state.xref[1:3,] # check
      Name Abbr
1 Alabama   AL
2  Alaska   AK
3 Arizona   AZ
```

Now we use `match()` to extract the row numbers of `state.xref` where the entries of `bb2$State` are found. Extracting the `Abbr` entries for those row numbers produces the desired two-letter codes. We call that vector of codes `state.2` and cross-tabulate it with the original `State` values as a check.

```
> state.2 <- state.xref$Abbr[match (bb2$State,
                                    state.xref$Name)]
> table (state.2, bb2$State, useNA = "ifany")
state.2 Connecticut New Jersey New York
     CT          10          0        0
     NJ           0         15        0
     NY           0          0       15
```

Since that has worked, we can now replace the `State` values with the `state.2` vector. The following command completes the data cleaning for `BedBath2.csv`.

```
> bb2$State <- state.2
```

It may be worth noting, particularly for readers accustomed to SQL, that we could have "joined" the `bb2` and `xref` tables with `merge()`, as in this example.

```
> merge (bb2, state.xref, by.x = "State", by.y = "Name",
         all.x = TRUE)
```

This command produces one row for every entry in `bb2`, since `all.x = TRUE`. The `State` column of `bb2` is matched with the `Name` column of `state.xref`.

7.8.3   Combining the `BedBath` Data Frames

We can now stack the two `bb` data frames vertically; they have the same columns, of the same type, with the same values. We need only to ensure that the column names match. To do that, we can rename the `PropId` and `Size` columns of `bb2` to `ID` and `SqFt`, so as to match `bb1` (or, of course, vice versa). We need not re-order the columns; the `rbind()` function for data frames will take care of that. This code shows the renaming, and the call to `rbind()` that produces the final `BedBath` data set.

```
> names (bb2)[names (bb2) == "PropId"] <- "ID"
> names (bb2)[names (bb2) == "Size"] <- "SqFt"
> bedbath <- rbind (bb1, bb2, stringsAsFactors = FALSE)
```

Notice that to identify the first column to rename we use `[names (bb2) == "PropId"]` rather than `[1]`. The `ID` column is column number 1, but perhaps in another iteration it might end up in a different position. Relying on the name, rather than the number, is safer.

Once we have the combined data set, we should examine it. It is always a good idea to check for missing values, to count the number of unique entries, construct a few more tables, and compute summary statistics. The following commands show a few of the computations that might perform in this example.

```
> sapply (bedbath, function (x) sum (is.na (x)))
   Bed  Bath  SqFt State    ID
    0     0     0     0     0
```

```
> sapply (bedbath, function (x) length (unique (x)))
  Bed  Bath  SqFt State    ID
    3     5    35     4   115
> with (bedbath, table (Bed, Bath), useNA = "ifany")
   Bath
Bed  1 1.5  2 2.5  3
  2  7 25   0  0 0
  3  0  0  31 21 23
  4  0  0   0  8 0
> summary (bedbath$SqFt)
   Min. 1st Qu.  Median    Mean 3rd Qu.    Max.
    860     985    1450    1334    1495    1690
```

The first command shows that this data set has no missing values. The second shows, first, that the ID numbers are unique, as intended, and that there are only 35 distinct values of SqFt. These values were rounded, so this is not implausible. The cross-tabulation of Bed and Bath is also plausible, with bigger houses having both more bedrooms and more bathrooms. Finally, the summary () of the SqFt column shows no obvious anomalies.

7.8.4 Reading and Cleaning EnergyUsage.csv

Reading
Now we read in the data set with the energy usage data. We start with read.csv() as before.

```
> kwh <- read.csv ("EnergyUsage.csv",
                   stringsAsFactors = FALSE)
> kwh[1:3,]
    Serial X2016.Q1  X2016.Q2  X2016.Q3 X2016.Q4
1 A594-005 2271.074  2245.196  2767.31  3713.24
2 P957-001 3565.268  3255.392  2880.485 3446.105
3 H625-003  2919.32 2334.8498 2821.3652    #N/A

    X2017.Q1  X2017.Q2
1 3647.2811 3499.3139
2   3440.72   3485.93
3      #N/A      #N/A
> sapply (kwh, class)
      Serial     X2016.Q1     X2016.Q2     X2016.Q3
 "character"  "character"  "character"  "character"
    X2016.Q4     X2017.Q1     X2017.Q2
 "character"  "character"  "character"
```

The file appears to be comma-delimited, but the "energy usage" columns are all of mode character. For at least the last few, this must be, at least in part, due to the #N/A missing value code. Recall that R produces valid column names when it reads data in. In this case, it has added the letter X to the front of column names like 2016.Q1; we will continue to use those modified names.

Let us read the data again, specifying that value as the missing value string. We also observe that the Serial field looks as if it contains the ID, but with a hyphen.

```
> kwh <- read.csv ("EnergyUsage.csv", na.strings = "#N/A",
        stringsAsFactors = FALSE)
> kwh[1:3,]
    Serial X2016.Q1 X2016.Q2 X2016.Q3 X2016.Q4
1 A594-005 2271.074 2245.196 2767.310 3713.240
2 P957-001 3565.268 3255.392 2880.485 3446.105
3 H625-003 2919.320 2334.850 2821.365       NA

  X2017.Q1 X2017.Q2
1 3647.281 3499.314
2 3440.720 3485.930
3       NA       NA
```

The data has been properly read in. Some missing values remain, and we will keep our eye on them to see, if, for example, they arise more frequently in some time periods or locations than in others.

Cleaning

We start by examining the classes just as before.

```
> sapply (kwh, class)
      Serial     X2016.Q1     X2016.Q2     X2016.Q3
 "character"    "numeric"    "numeric"    "numeric"
    X2016.Q4     X2017.Q1     X2017.Q2
   "numeric"    "numeric"    "numeric"
```

Since the columns all have the expected class, we turn our concern to the Serial field. We will need to remove the hyphen to get these values to match up with bedbath. This code uses sub() to perform that task.

```
> kwh$Serial <- sub ("-", "", kwh$Serial)
> kwh$Serial[1:4]                                    # check
[1] "A594005" "P957001" "H625003" "P462004"
```

That conversion seems to have succeeded, although as before we might look more deeply. Let us now look for duplicate rows, duplicate keys, and duplicate values within columns.

```
> table (duplicated (kwh))              # duplicate rows?
FALSE
  116
> table (duplicated (kwh$Serial))       # duplicate keys?
```

```
FALSE   TRUE
  115      1
> sapply (kwh,
       function (x) length (unique (x))) # duplicate values?
Serial X2016.Q1 X2016.Q2 X2016.Q3 X2016.Q4 X2017.Q1 X2017.Q2
   115       112       108       104       103        94        95
```

Let us start with the item with the duplicate value of `Serial`. As we did before, we will extract both the rows for this `Serial` value.

```
> kwh$Serial[duplicated (kwh$Serial)]
[1] "P888009"
> kwh[kwh$Serial == "P888009",]
     Serial X2016.Q1 X2016.Q2 X2016.Q3 X2016.Q4
16 P888009       NA       NA 2797.175 3700.685
88 P888009 2244.566 2526.494 2797.175 3628.685

   X2017.Q1 X2017.Q2
16       NA 3608.844
88 4310.686 3608.844
```

First, we note that the duplicated key is the same one that was duplicated in the bed and bath data. Second, the two rows for this key are not identical, as they were there. Our inclination is to drop the first of these two rows, reasoning that they are equal when not missing, except in one place. Again, this is a judgment we make pending communication with the data provider. In this next piece of code we remove row 16, identified as the first of the duplicates.

```
> kwh <- kwh[-(which (kwh$Serial == "P888009")[1],]
```

The issue of duplicates within columns is subtler. Each of the numeric columns has at least a few duplicate values, and this is probably not surprising. We might expect a few matches just by coincidence. However, there may be a trend toward more duplication as we move to the right of the data set. In the next line, we use the `table (table ())` approach to examine the frequency of common values. If common values are just coincidence, then most likely we would see sets of pairs, each with a common value, rather than a group of four or five entries with the very same value.

```
> table (table (kwh$X2017.Q2))
 1  6
93  1
```

There is, in fact, a set of six observations with the very same value in the `X2017.Q2` column. This seems unexpected. In this code, we display those six observations.

```
> which (6 == table (kwh$X2017.Q2))
4847.51
     50
```

```
> kwh[!is.na (kwh$X2017.Q2) & kwh$X2017.Q2 == 4847.51,]
      Serial X2016.Q1 X2016.Q2 X2016.Q3 X2016.Q4
31   P308007 4059.905 3875.015  3034.91  3990.26
44   H958007 3771.095 5358.575  3034.91  3990.26
48   H419006 5360.750 1078.055       NA       NA
60   H619001 3570.185 2400.890  3034.91  3990.26
112  A542003 2126.240 2951.270  3034.91  3990.26
116  A436004 1181.540 2951.270  3034.91  3990.26

      X2017.Q1 X2017.Q2
31      4512.2  4847.51
44      4512.2  4847.51
48      4512.2  4847.51
60      4512.2  4847.51
112     4512.2  4847.51
116     4512.2  4847.51
```

The value 50 returned from the which() command just indicates that the entry of interest happened to be the 50th entry in the table. We are more interested in the duplicated value, which is 4847.51. We can see that a number of properties have the same value not just for the X2017.Q2 column but for others as well.

Once again the analyst needs to come to some judgment as to how to proceed. In the real-life case from which this example was derived, we were able to communicate with the data provider and learn that these readings were estimated on occasions when meters could not be read, the estimation deriving from an average of a set of properties. We continued constructing the data, documenting our findings.

7.8.5 Merging the BedBath and EnergyUsage Data Frames

The two data sets are nearly ready to merge. They have keys in the same format and issues with the data have been resolved. All that remains is to ensure that the two sets of keys do, in fact, refer to the same properties. In this code, we tabulate the number of keys in bedbath that appear in kwh, and vice versa.

```
> table (is.element (bedbath$ID, kwh$Serial))
TRUE
 115
> table (is.element (kwh$Serial, bedbath$ID))
TRUE
 115
```

Where there are no duplicates, we need not do this in both directions – but we recommend it anyway. Since all the keys match, we can now merge the two data sets by the Serial and ID keys. This code shows how we construct the final data set for this example.

```
> properties <- merge (kwh, bedbath, by.x = "Serial",
                       by.y = "ID")
> properties[1:4,] # Check
   Serial X2016.Q1 X2016.Q2 X2016.Q3 X2016.Q4 X2017.Q1
1 A195008 4226.522 3961.223 4117.505 4683.680       NA
2 A255003 3558.008 3512.932 3645.375 4182.305 5108.536
3 A294008 3897.872 3352.718 2073.440 3013.130 3644.720
4 A301008 3327.296 3365.249 2997.545 5168.420 4151.660

  X2017.Q2 Bed Bath SqFt State
1 7022.795   2  1.0  950    NY
2 5695.186   3  2.5 1460    CT
3 3590.420   3  2.5 1510    NY
4 3080.435   3  2.0 1430    NJ
```

Our `properties` data set is complete and appears to be clean, although it still has missing values. Moreover, we have not examined the usage numbers very carefully. These following commands give examples of the sorts of analyses we might perform to examine these numbers. We start by creating a vector `Xcols` to identify the columns of usage – that is, the ones whose names start with X.

```
> Xcols <- grep ("X", names (properties), value = TRUE)
> sapply (properties[,Xcols], function (x) sum (is.na (x)))
X2016.Q1 X2016.Q2 X2016.Q3 X2016.Q4 X2017.Q1 X2017.Q2
       4        6        5        7       15       16
> sapply (properties[,Xcols], range, na.rm = T)
        X2016.Q1 X2016.Q2  X2016.Q3 X2016.Q4 X2017.Q1 X2017.Q2
[1,]     976.010   881.09  680.1299  680.690 1138.697 2123.470
[2,]    5847.704 10267.73 5448.1001 8484.425 9307.250 8421.106
```

The number of NA values increases slightly with increasing quarter, ending up at about 10% of the rows. In the second command, we compute the range of each column. The maxima of the usage values increase, but none are negative or otherwise obviously anomalous.

We might also compute other summary statistics, like, for example, typical usage by state. For one quarter's usage, this is easy to compute using the `tapply()` function, as we demonstrate in the first command as follows. The second command shows how this might be computed simultaneously for every quarter.

```
> tapply (properties$X2016.Q1, properties$State, mean,
          na.rm = TRUE)
      CT       NJ       NY       PA
3123.335 3321.658 3416.334 3237.445
> sapply (properties[,Xcols], function (qtr) {
      tapply (qtr, properties$State, mean, na.rm=TRUE)})
```

```
    X2016.Q1 X2016.Q2 X2016.Q3 X2016.Q4 X2017.Q1 X2017.Q2
CT 3123.335 2776.943 2871.059 4005.165 4461.140 4918.352
NJ 3321.658 2953.894 2892.502 3922.922 4445.038 4556.398
NY 3416.334 3120.687 3056.265 4043.530 4602.037 5085.058
PA 3237.445 3092.234 3239.677 3996.064 4669.660 4829.615
```

This last command loops over the columns whose names appear in Xcols, calling tapply() for each one. The results are assembled into a matrix automatically. We might plot this matrix; we might plot usage by square footage for each state or quarter; we might examine the distributions of values by quarter, perhaps with boxplots; and so on. After some investigation like this, we can now begin the modeling process. This would be the stage at which to convert the State column into a factor variable.

We note here that our final product consisted of one row per property. To strictly conform with the notion of "tidy" data from Chapter 1, in which each usage observation occupies one row, one more transformation is necessary. We know that the final data set will have $115 \times 6 = 690$ rows. The usage entries will come from the Xcols columns. We can extract these using the stack() function, which both produces the vector of 690 usage entries, and also includes a second, factor vector identifying the source of the usage by name. This code shows how we might do this.

```
> stack.output <- stack (properties, Xcols)
> stack.output
        values        ind
1     4226.522 X2016.Q1
2     3558.008 X2016.Q1
3     3897.872 X2016.Q1
  :    :    :
115 3825.980 X2016.Q1
116 3961.223 X2016.Q2
  :    :    :
```

We can see the transition from values that originated in the X2016.Q1 column to ones from the X2016.Q2 column after the 115th row. Now we replicate the remaining columns six times, and attach the result to the stack.output object.

```
> usages <- data.frame (
          properties[rep (1:nrow(properties), 6),c(1, 8:11)],
          stack.output)
> usages[1:3,] # check
   Serial Bed Bath SqFt State    values        ind
1 A195008   2  1.0  950    NY 4226.522 X2016.Q1
2 A255003   3  2.5 1460    CT 3558.008 X2016.Q1
3 A294008   3  2.5 1510    NY 3897.872 X2016.Q1
```

After this operation, our new `usages` data set is 690 × 7. If we need to add columns giving the year or the quarter, we can use a command like `usages$Year <- substring (usages$ind, 2, 5)`.

7.9 Chapter Summary and Critical Data Handling Tools

This chapter describes some of the practical steps we need to take in a real data cleaning problem. These include acquiring the data, cleaning the data, combining cleaned data sets from different sources, and, finally, undertaking any necessary data preparation steps. All four of these steps require detailed documentation, both to describe the steps you took and to make them reproducible.

The documentation you produce should also describe steps where you exercised judgment. This might involve deleting records with mostly missing values, or replacing a small number of missing values with another value. You might document anomalies on which you took no action at all – for example, if you observe that all the loans in a data set had dates whose days of the week were Monday or Wednesday, that might seem peculiar but not impossible, depending on the business practices of the data provider. Of course, the more you know about the organization, the data, and the way it is gathered and processed, the better your judgment can be.

Some data is transactional, meaning that it can reflect multiple observations for each item of interest. We demonstrate some approaches for handling this sort of data. While the demonstration requires a certain amount of explanation, the script to actually perform the tasks requires only a few dozen lines of code.

The final section of the chapter goes through an example of cleaning some fairly small data sets. This example demonstrated a number of the challenges that face us in our day-to-day business of handling data: embedded delimiters, inconsistent key conventions, missing or duplicate values, and so on.

There are, inevitably, many more ways that data can need cleaning that the example did not touch upon. It did not, for example, involve data from non-delimited formats such as Excel, JSON, or XML, or importing data from a relational database. It did not require us to write a specialized function, nor did it require the handling of dates or times. Many of these complications are taken up in the extended exercise in the following chapter, but you should be aware that data you get will very often involve a combination of input types and require a number of approaches.

8

Extended Exercise

In this chapter, we set up a guided data cleaning task, from beginning to end. This data (including the company and personal names and addresses) is entirely fabricated and is intended only to demonstrate some of the concepts in this book – but every quirk you see in this data is based on actual data we encountered doing real projects. Unlike the smaller examples in earlier chapters, these data sets are large enough so that you cannot spot all of their anomalies by eye. However, you will be able to open and examine these outside of R – unlike some of the data sets we deal with in real life.

This exercise requires time and focus to complete. You will get the most benefit from this book if you read the chapter all the way through and try to perform all the tasks in the exercise. Part of the exercise is figuring out exactly what needs to be done at each step and in which order. We have included some "pseudocode" – high-level descriptions of the algorithms we used to perform the tasks – and some hints in Appendix A. However, we recommend you only use that when you find yourself stuck. The actual code we used to do the cleaning is available in the `cleaningBook` package. Again, you will receive the most benefit when you try to solve the problem in it entirely before looking at our code – and you may find a different, or better, way of getting the job done.

8.1 Introduction to the Problem

This data comes from a hypothetical client company called Hardy Business Loans, which lends money to small businesses. Sometimes, the borrower is the business itself; other times, the borrower is one (or more) of the business's principal owners or partners. The loans are for small- to medium-sized pieces of equipment: for a restaurant, this might be a pizza oven or espresso maker; for a trucking business, it might be a truck or a copying machine; for a gardening business, it might be a backhoe. Hardy Business Loans has acquired portfolios of loans from two different companies, "Beachside Lenders" and "Wilson and

A Data Scientist's Guide to Acquiring, Cleaning, and Managing Data in R, First Edition.
Samuel E. Buttrey and Lyn R. Whitaker.
© 2018 John Wiley & Sons Ltd. Published 2018 by John Wiley & Sons Ltd.
Companion website: www.wiley.com/go/buttrey/datascientistsguide

Sons," and inevitably the data for these two different portfolios has different layouts and fields.

Each portfolio consists of applications and loans, each identified by a key (although application keys are different from loan keys). Every loan should have a corresponding application, but some applications do not lead to loans – they are said to be "unbooked," whereas those that are made into loans are "booked." An application might end up unbooked because the lender declined the application, or because the borrower found the money elsewhere, or perhaps for other reasons.

At the time the application is made, the lender consults several other companies that provide information about the creditworthiness of the borrower. In real life, these would include various credit reporting agencies, which supply information about the credit habits and experience of individuals, and also corresponding repositories of similar information for businesses. Our "agency" data is modeled on the sorts of data made available from these reporting agencies.

In many cases, the reporting agencies supply many columns containing "low-level" data for each customer, and also a single "agency score." Low-level data might include, for example, the number of times a customer was 30 days late on a credit card bill, the number of department store charge cards he or she has, whether he or she ever declared bankruptcy, and dozens of similar items. The agency score is a single number intended to rate the customers' overall creditworthiness that combines all the low-level information using an algorithm that is typically proprietary. Since Hardy acquires data from several agencies, each borrower might have several agency scores. Lenders like Hardy use the scores, but they might want access to the low-level data as well. For example, a used-car dealer might want to build a custom score that focuses specifically on borrowers' past record with car-loan payments. In our case, the list of variables we need in the output includes a few of these low-level variables and also all of the agency scores.

8.1.1 The Goal

The goal of the data cleaning exercise is to produce tabular data with one row per loan and with all the necessary columns of descriptive data. (The set of columns to be retained will be discussed shortly.) We will also need to report on observations that were omitted and the reason, whether it was too much missing data, no matching records in agency data, or something else. We may need to show the distribution of loans by region of the country and by calendar quarter, through tables, graphs, and perhaps by other variables as well.

Our output will be in two data frames (or, if you prefer, one big data frame with records of two types). The first data set comes from the booked loans. For these loans, we will need to construct the "response variable" for later modeling efforts. This is the measurement that describes the outcome of the loan.

In other applications this might be a number, but in this case it will be one of the levels "Good" or "Bad." (We give the definitions of those terms used in the material that follows.) So each row of this part of the output will contain one of those values as a response, a number of measurements on different variables (the "predictors"), and perhaps one or more keys that allow the final data to be linked to the components from which it was built.

The modeling step – which is not part of this exercise – will use the predictor variables to predict the response variable. If the responses in the booked loans can be predicted accurately, Hardy Business Loans could use that model as a screening tool by which to evaluate the risk of new loans or of its portfolio.

In addition to the predictors and the response for booked records, we must also construct a similar data set using the records from unbooked applications. By applying the model to the set of unbooked applications, Hardy can learn about the rates at which it is turning away potentially successful borrowers. Of course, these unbooked records do not have response variables. But it may be possible to estimate how unbooked applications would have fared, based on the statistical model from the booked ones. So we need to prepare the unbooked applicants and the loans in a common way.

8.1.2 Modeling Considerations

The data sets that we produce at the end of this exercise are a beginning, not an end. We can expect to make further changes as the modeling proceeds. These are the steps we called "preparing data" in Section 7.5. For example, we might choose to transform a numeric variable by, say, taking its logarithm. Categorical variables may need to be re-grouped, or numeric ones binned. We might exclude more records as we determine their data to be unreliable. The processes of cleaning, preparing, and modeling are iterative ones.

Another consideration is that we might want to divide the data into pieces, one piece (the "training set") for building models and a second piece (the "test set") for evaluating them. This division might be performed at random, with, say, 30% of the entire data set retained as a test set, but we might also sample using a more complicated scheme if, say, we wanted the training set to have a higher proportion of Wilson and Sons loans, or newer loans, than the data as a whole. In any case, this important consideration is not part of our exercise.

8.1.3 Examples of Things to Check

To the extent possible you should check every column against the data dictionary. We have intentionally (and, probably, unintentionally) introduced anomalous entries into the data to mirror the sorts of problems we encounter in practice. Follow the steps mentioned in Section 7.2 in looking for duplicates and ensuring that the set of column classes is as expected. Look at the maxima and minima of numeric and date columns, and tabulate the categorical ones.

Examining each column in isolation is a good start, but it is also worthwhile to compare pairs of columns. Of course, there are a lot of pairs and often they cannot all be checked. But it may be worthwhile to build two-way tables of important categorical variables, keeping an eye out for unexpected results like months with almost no observations.

In practice, you will often find that some predictor variables are available from more than one source. When two offerings of the same variable are available, you might consult the data provider to see if they are considered to be equally reliable. As we said in Section 7.2, it is useful to compute the proportion of times that the two agree – often, we find that two versions of a variable (call them "A" and "B") have the same values when both are present, but that A is missing much more often than B. In that case we will use B, possibly augmenting its own missing entries by values taken from A. When A and B disagree on other than missingness, we exercise our judgment in deciding how to move forward. In this exercise, we do not expect that sort of overlap in variables to occur – but it does happen in practice.

8.2   The Data

The data for this exercise needs to be constructed by combining inputs from seven sources. The sections following this one describe each of these sources in detail, and give layouts or sample data. The seven sources are as follows:

- the two loan and application portfolios, one from Beachside and one from Wilson, giving information about the borrower and the product to be purchased with the loan;
- the scores database, giving scores for the borrowers from four agencies, including a score called "KSC" or "KScore";
- the co-borrower scores, giving agency scores for co-signers of those loans that have them;
- a set of updated KScores, which may supersede the KScore in the borrowers' data;
- a set of loans to be excluded from the final data set; and
- the payment matrix, showing payment information for up to 48 prior billing periods.

Figure 8.1 shows a diagram of one process that can be used to construct the final data. The loan and application portfolios (two left items, top row) contain the information about borrowers and loans. The layouts of these tables are described in Section 8.4. These tables include low-level predictors; these will then be joined to the scores database (Section 8.5), shown in the top center-right of the figure, which contains the agency scores for the loans and

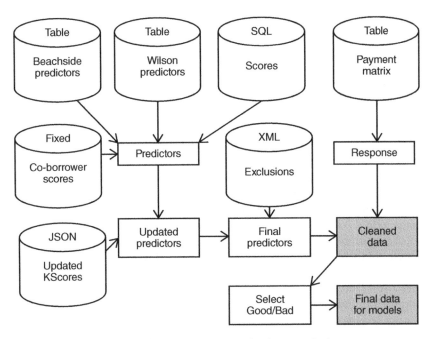

Figure 8.1 Schematic of the data cleaning process for the example data.

applications in the two portfolios. Some loans have co-borrowers; those scores are supplied in the co-borrowers data (Section 8.6), shown at center left in the figure.

There are then two modifications that need to be imposed on the data. First, a set of updated KScores (bottom left of figure) is available; loans and applications appearing in that data set may have to have their KScore values updated (see Section 8.7). In addition, a small number of loans and applications should be excluded from the modeling effort, based on some exclusion data (middle right of picture). We apply this exclusion as the last step in generating the predictors, because the excluded records need to be updated anyway, for a later effort, which is not part of this exercise. The payment matrix (Section 8.9), shown at top right, is used to generate the response variable for the modeling process. The algorithm described in that section can be used to determine whether the performance of a loan was "Good," "Bad," or "Indeterminate." The final data set will include only those loans whose performance was "Good" or "Bad." The final set of predictors is joined with the response (for the booked records that have one) to produce the cleaned data (gray box, mid-lower right). Finally, we exclude unbooked records or those whose response was "Indeterminate" to produce the subset of records that will be used in the initial modeling effort (bottom right of figure).

8.3   Five Important Fields

There are five fields that are vital to this exercise, which are as follows:

Application Number: A 10-digit number identifying the application. Every application has a unique application number, and application numbers should be distinct between the two portfolios.

Loan Number: A field identifying the loan for booked applications. In the Wilson portfolio, the loan number is supposed to consist of a six-digit customer identification, followed by a three-digit "instance" number. The instance number starts at 001 and increases when a previous customer receives a second or third loan. In some cases, though, the instance is missing. In that case 001 can be used. The Beachside portfolio identifies loans by a six-digit number with no instance. It is possible for the same six-digit number to be used in both portfolios, purely by happenstance, which, combined with the fact that some Wilson loans do not have instance numbers, means that six-digit loan numbers are not necessarily unique.

Application Date: The date on which the application was completed. For the purposes of evaluating unbooked loans in the modeling process, we must restrict ourselves to using only information that was available by this date. So if a particular unbooked application is dated November 30, 2016, we will ignore scores, co-borrower information, and updated KScores recorded after that date.

Loan Date: The date on which a loan is "booked" (made official). For booked loans, scores and other updated information recorded after this date should be ignored.

Active Date: We will use the term "active date" to identify the application date for unbooked applications and the loan date for booked loans. This date is important because it marks the date on which a decision is made, and agency scores, for example, that are recorded after the active date will need to be ignored. Unlike the other important fields, active date has to be inferred.

8.4   Loan and Application Portfolios

The two portfolios acquired by Hardy Business Loans come from two sources: Beachside Lenders and Wilson and Sons. Both sets of data provide low-level reporting agency data recorded at or before the active date for both unbooked applications and loans.

The data for Beachside Lenders appears as an Excel workbook named `Beach.xlsx` in the newer `.xlsx` format. Data for the Wilson portfolio comes in an Excel workbook named `wilson.xls` in the older `.xls` format. The Wilson data can contain multiple loans for one borrower (although each has a separate application number). We might treat these multiple loans as if they are independent (although they are not), or we might keep only the most recent ones (although in that case we presumably lose some information), or we might try combining multiple loans for the same borrower. In any case, the number of multiple borrowers is so small that it will almost certainly make no difference. For this example, we will keep all of the loans as if they are independent.

Most of the variables that we need to extract or, in some cases, construct, for the modeling effort are given in Table 8.1 and are laid out in the following three sections. The table lists the desired columns both by the Beachside names and by their Wilson names, which are, inevitably, different. The two layouts in the following sections, and Table 8.1, serve as the data dictionary (Section 7.6) for the loan and application portfolios. In theory, you would hope that the data dictionary would give a complete and accurate description of the data. In our example, though – just as in real life – you may find slight discrepancies between what the dictionary says the data should look like, and what is actually in the data. Finding these discrepancies and adjusting for them – and documenting them – is part of the exercise!

8.4.1 Layout of the Beachside Lenders Data

The Beachside portfolio contains information about 23 attributes of 8621 loan applications. Those 23 columns are described here. A number of columns, such as the Dbl and KAK columns in the final entry on the list, contain information that is never used. This is a common occurrence.

- APP_NO, APP_DT, LOAN_NO, LOAN_DT: Application number and application date for every entry; loan number and loan date for booked loans
- STAT: The status of the application (Booked, Decline, TUD; see below)
- CUST_NM, CUST_ADD1, CUST_CT, CUST_ST, CUST_ZIP: Name, address, city, state, and ZIP code of customer
- TOT_COST, LOAN_AMT: Total cost of equipment and amount of loan
- GCORP, Local: Used to construct "credit risk" (see section 8.4.3)
- TIB: Time in business, in years
- ASSET_NEW: T if the equipment was to be purchased new, F if purchased used
- BUS_TYPE, ASSET_TYPE, Dbl, KAK, Folds, JL, 2BC, MM ? : Unused.

The STAT column describes the status of the loan. For booked loans, this will be "Booked." For unbooked applications, this can be either "Decline," meaning that the lender declined to make the loan, or "TUD," which indicates that the borrower "Turned Us Down." This happens either because a borrower finds more favorable terms elsewhere, or changes her mind about whether the purchase is necessary (or goes out of business or another unusual event takes place).

8.4.2 Layout of the Wilson and Sons Data

The Wilson data has 10,587 rows and 23 columns. Most of these columns carry the same information as in the Beachside portfolio, though with different names. The Wilson columns are shown here.

- `Appl Number, Appl Date, Loan Number, Loan Date`: Application number and date for every entry; loan number with instance and loan date for booked loans
- `Application Status`: Application status, like the STAT column from Beachside. Values are Approved (booked), Declined, Incomplete (equivalent to "TUD" in Beachside)
- `Customer Name, City, State, Zip`: Identification of customer
- `Total Cost, Net Loan Amount`: The cost of the equipment and the size of the loan
- `GC Indicator, Local Cred`: Used to construct "credit risk"
- `Business Start Date`: Date on which business began operating
- `New/Used Indicator`: Indicates whether the equipment being purchased is "New" or "Used"
- `Customer Type, Equipment Class, CVR Indicator, Reclass Indicator, Minimum GM, 2nd Gen PP, GS Indicator`: Unused.

8.4.3 Combining the Two Portfolios

Table 8.1 shows the columns required for the modeling effort that can be found in, or derived from, the two portfolios or the additional data. In a real example, we might keep dozens, scores, or even hundreds of columns, some formed by transforming or combining others. For each column in the final data set, we give the corresponding columns in the two loan portfolios: "derived" denotes columns that need to be constructed, using details that follow the table. Just as in real life, we will need to combine columns with different names and values that nonetheless represent the same underlying measurement.

The Time in Business field measures the amount of time that the borrower has been in business – in other words, its age (in years). In the Beachside case, this is given directly, in years, by the TIB column. In the case of Wilson, we will need to deduce this from the date that the business was reported to have started, given by the Business Start Date column. The age is the time between the business start date and the active date (i.e., the Loan Date for booked loans, the Application Date for unbooked ones).

The Region column represents the census region associated with each state. Table 8.2 gives a table showing which state (by abbreviation) is assigned to which region. This information is also available in the `cleaningBook` package in a more convenient form, as a 50-row data frame called `state.tbl`. Observations from locations not in any region (such as Canada or Puerto Rico) should be given the value "Other" for the Region field.

Table 8.1 Columns required for predictive model

Name	Beachside	Wilson	Notes
App Number	`APP_NO`	`Appl Number`	Application number
App Date	`APP_DT`	`Appl Date`	Application date
Loan Number	`LOAN_NO`	`Loan Number`	Loan number (if booked)
Loan Date	`LOAN_DT`	`Loan Date`	Loan date (if booked)
AppStat	`STAT`	`Application Status`	Booked, declined, or TUD
Time in Business	`TIB`	Derived	Time in business
State	`CUST_ST`	`Customer State`	Customer state/province
Region	Derived	Derived	Customer region (see notes)
Cost	`TOT_COST`	`Total Cost`	Total equipment cost
Loan Amount	`LOAN_AMT`	`Net Loan Amount`	Loan amount
Down	Derived	Derived	Down payment (numeric)
New/Used	`ASSET_NEW`	`New / Used Indicator`	New/used indicator: `T` ("new") or `F` in Beachside, `New` or `Used` for Wilson
CredRisk	Derived	Derived	Credit risk (see notes)
Source	Derived	Derived	Beachside or Wilson
Co-borrower	Derived	Derived	(see notes)

Table 8.2 State abbreviations by census region

Region	State
Midwest	IL, IN, IA, KS, MI, MN, MO, NE, ND, OH, SD, WI
Northeast	CT, ME, MA, NH, NJ, NY, PA, RI, VT
South	AL, AR, DC, DE, FL, GA, KY, LA, MD, MS, NC, OK, SC, TN, TX, VA, WV
West	AK, AZ, CA, CO, HI, ID, MT, NV, NM, OR, UT, WA, WY

The loan amount is usually smaller than the equipment cost, since most customers will make a down payment or trade in an older piece of equipment. The Down column is computed as Cost − Loan Amount; this may be useful in a predictive model since companies that can make large down payments may be healthier – or, alternatively, a large down payment may leave them short on cash.

The CredRisk credit rating is derived from two other columns present in the portfolio files. First, the GCORP or GC variable gives the borrower a letter grade from A (the highest score) to D. Second, the Local score gives a number from 1 (the highest) to 3. We will need to create a new credit risk predictor by combining those two indicators into a single column with values A1, A2, A3, B1, and so on – except that C3 and all the D ratings should be combined into a single level called X.

The co-borrower indicator shows whether an applicant has a co-borrower. This is determined by the existence of co-borrower scores in the data of Section 8.6. Application numbers for which co-borrowers appear in that data should be given a co-borrower value of TRUE, and all others should be given the value FALSE.

8.5   Scores

Each customer may have been assigned scores by the different agencies. Primary borrowers' scores are stored in an SQLite repository called scores.sqlite, accessible via SQL (see Section 6.3). Agencies report scores fairly frequently, and customers' scores can change from time to time. For each customer, we want the score that was the most recent at the time of the active date. Scores that are recorded after the active date are not to be used in our modeling efforts. However, the active date is not part of the scores database; it comes from the loan and application portfolios. In our example, each customer can have scores from up to four agencies. These scores have the names "Rayburn," "KScore," "J&G," and "NorthEast." Valid values for scores are 200–899, so values outside this range should be ignored.

In the database, customers are identified by an eight-digit customer number, which is not the same as an application or loan number. The database contains a table named CScore containing this customer number, the agency scores, and the month associated with the scores. Each customer may have many records, one for each reporting month, so this table does not have a unique key (although one could be created by combining the customer number and month). A second table, CusApp, links customer numbers to application numbers. The following section shows the layouts of these tables.

8.5.1   Scores Layout

The four agency scores are supplied in the scores database as an SQLite repository. The repository contains two tables. The layouts are shown in Tables 8.3 and 8.4. In the "format" columns, each 9 corresponds to a digit, and YYYYMM, of course, corresponds to a four-digit year and two-digit month. The CScore table holds the scores. Each set of four scores corresponds to a single month, given in the ScoreMonth field.

Table 8.3 `CScore` table

Name	Format	Description
Customer	99999999	Customer number
RAY	999	Three-digit Rayburn score
JNG	999	Three-digit J&G score
KSC	999	Three-digit KScore
NE	999	Three-digit NorthEast score
ScoreMonth	YYYYMM	Month associated with scores

Table 8.4 `CusApp` table

Name	Format	Description
Customer	99999999	Eight-digit customer number
Appl	9999999999	Ten-digit application number

The `CusApp` table cross-references the customer number to the application number.

8.6 Co-borrower Scores

Some personal borrowers specify co-borrowers, who are other individuals who co-sign for the loan, thereby promising to pay the lender if the original borrower defaults. Borrowers with co-borrowers might be expected to be more likely to pay the loan back, on average, depending, perhaps on the creditworthiness of the co-borrower. Co-borrowers have their own agency scores; that information (for both of the portfolios) is stored in the text file called `CoBorrScores.txt`. This file consists of a series of transactional records, each co-borrower being represented by between three and a few dozen records. Records come in different types, the different types being indicated by the three-letter sequence starting in position 9. The first record for each co-borrower is the master record with three-letter sequence `J01`. This `J01` record contains the application number associated with that co-borrower, in character positions 20–29. Any other characters in the `J01` line can be ignored.

All the records for a single co-borrower will be on separate lines following the `J01` record. These other records can be of several types; for our purposes, we are interested only in records of type `ERS`, which give co-borrower scores.

Records with types other than J01 or ERS should be ignored. Each ERS record reports a score type (with Rayburn, KScore, J&G, and NorthEast being abbreviated by RAY, KSC, JNG, and NTH, respectively), the score value, and a score date in format MM/DD/YYYY (and followed by other information not needed for this exercise). For each co-borrower we want the latest value of each score that precedes the active date, except that, as before, only scores in the range 200–899 should be used. The following section shows examples of the records in the co-borrower file for a particular co-borrower.

8.6.1 Co-borrower Score Examples

Co-borrowers can have different numbers of records; the only way to tell that we have seen all the records for a particular individual is by observing that the next record has type J01 (except for the very last co-borrower in the file). As with the scores database, we want to extract from the co-borrower file the agency scores immediately before the active date, and, again, the active date is not found in the file. Here are some example records from the CoBorrScores.txt file; assume that these are the only records for this co-borrower.

```
SuppDat J01 AppNum 3385219170 Source 2151 Seq 661 Modl N ...
SuppDat BBR Check 2 Center 21 Audit F ...
SuppDat ERS NTH 720 10/31/2016 Mod N Report1 YNY
SuppDat ERS JNG 692 12/12/2016 Mod Y Report1 YYY
SuppDat ERS NTH 999 12/31/2016 Mod N Report1 NNY
SuppDat FOE OfcCode 22X OfcState NY OfcReg 22 OfcHold N...
SuppDat ERS RAY 999 10/31/2016 Mod Y Report1 NNN
SuppDat ERS NTH 717 11/30/2016 Mod N Report1 YNY
```

In this example, we see scores for application number 3385219170. The second and sixth lines have codes BBR and FOE; these lines should be ignored. The JNG score has the single entry 692, and that pair of score and date should be retained. The RAY score is given as 999, so no Rayburn score is retained for this co-borrower. There are three reports of a score of type NTH; of these, the most recent has value 999 and should be ignored. So two (score, date) pairs need to be returned for the NTH score for this co-borrower. Therefore, this co-borrower should be associated with a total of three pairs of scores and dates. The actual NTH score entered into the final database will depend on the active date for this application. If the active date is October 30, 2016 or earlier, none of the three NTH rows in the example apply, and no NTH score will be used. If the active date is between October 31, 2016 and November 29, 2016, the third row of the example (the first of the NTH rows) applies, and the NTH score for this co-borrower should be reported as 720. Finally, if the active date of the application is November 30, 2016 or later, the last row of the example applies and the NTH score should be reported as 717.

8.7 Updated KScores

The scores database includes a column called KSC, which reports KScores, one of the agency scores to be used in the modeling. Many of these KScores are missing in the original scores database. However, in the time since that database was assembled, the lenders have acquired a new set of KScores from the vendor of KScores, and they want to insert those scores into the predictor data frame. These scores are delivered as JSON records in one file named KScore.update.json. (Technically, a file with a set of valid JSON records is not itself valid JSON, but there you have it.) This file is small enough that it can be read into memory all at once, though if it were not we could certainly read one line at a time in the style of the examples in Section 6.2. Updated KScores refer to primary borrowers only, not to co-borrowers. Not every customer will have an updated KScore, and some updates will refer to customers not in our analysis. The appid field in a JSON record will introduce an application number, but those application numbers have been treated as numeric, with leading zeros inadvertently removed. JSON records with fields called KScore will be relevant, as long as the score is between 200 and 899. Each record will contain a field called record-date; scores whose values of record-date are more recent than the active date of the application in question should also be ignored. If there is more than one update for a particular account, we should use the more recent among those whose record-date value precede the active date for this account. The KScore.update.json file may contain other fields, too, including values of other scores, but those scores, too, should be ignored. Only the KScore and its corresponding date and application number are of interest for this portion of the data preparation.

8.7.1 Updated KScores Layout

The values of KSC retrieved from the scores database described in the previous section need to be updated for those applications that appear in the KScore.update.json file. This file consists of a set of entries ("messages") in JSON format. Messages that do not include a field named KScore are not of interest. From those that do, we will extract the application identifier (appid, with leading zeros truncated), the score itself (KScore, represented as a string) and the date associated with the score (record-date, in MM-DD-YYYY format).

Example messages might look like this:

```
{"appid":"442480", "Rayburn":"721", "NorthEast":"999",
        "record-date":"09-20-2016"}
{"appid":"621877", "KScore":"999", "J&G":"744",
        "record-date":"03-31-2016"}
{"appid":"3826", "Rayburn":"699", "KScore":"685",
```

```
                "J&G":"701",  "record-date":"10-03-2016"}
{"appid":"3826",  "KScore":"676",  "record-date":"12-19-2016"}
```

Here, the first record would be ignored, because no KScore is reported, and the second would be ignored because the KScore has an invalid value. The third and fourth records might cause the KScore for application number 0000003826 to be updated. If that application's active date (application date for unbooked loans, loan date for booked ones) was earlier than October 3, 2015, no update is performed; if the application's date is between October 3 and December 19, 2016, the KScore for that application would be updated to 685; if the application's date was later than December 19, 2016, the KScore for that application would be updated to 676.

8.8   Loans to Be Excluded

The lender has specified that a small number of loans be excluded entirely from the modeling effort. The loans to be excluded are among those for which XML files are found in the `Excluders` directory. Each XML file corresponds to one loan, identified by that loan's application number in the <APPID> field. Any XML file that contains a field called <EXCLUDE>, for which the value of the <EXCLUDE> field is "Yes" or "Contingent," should be excluded. The <EXCLUDE> field, if it exists, will be found inside an element named DATA. Applications that do not appear in XML files, or whose XML files do not have an <EXCLUDE> field, or whose values of <EXCLUDE> are other than Yes or Contingent, should not be excluded on the basis of their XML data.

8.8.1   Sample Exclusion File

Here, we present a sample file of the sort in the exclusion directory. This file would lead to the exclusion of application number 0134292005, since the value of the EXCLUDE field is Yes. Other fields in the XML files can be ignored.

```
<?xml version="1.0"?>
<rpt><CLASS2 type="a">Supp</CLASS2><APPID>0134292005</APPID>
<DATA><PRELIM>Yes</PRELIM><CR2>25167</CR2>
<EXCLUDE>Yes</EXCLUDE><CATCODE>36H</CATCODE></DATA>
</rpt>
```

8.9   Response Variable

In this section, we describe how to construct the response variable for our modeling effort. This is the measurement that describes the outcome of the loan. In other applications this might be a number, but in this case it will be one of the levels "Good," "Bad," or "Indeterminate." We will construct these values from the payment matrix contained in the `Payments.txt` file. For each loan (identified by a payment identifier found in the portfolio files), this fixed-width file contains information about the last 48 months. For each month, the file records four items: the amount paid, the amount delinquent (which can accumulate from month to month), the billing date, and the number of months since the account was last fully paid. Each payment record also carries a 10-digit application identifier.

The file will carry zeros in all four fields for any month earlier than the loan origination date. For example, a loan that was 10 months old will have 10 sets of payment information (from 1 month ago, 2 months ago, etc.) preceded by 38 sets of zeros. The layout of this file comes to us in the following COBOL code, which we provide because on some occasions our documentation has come to us in the form of COBOL specifications like this one:

```
001000 01  PAY-LAYOUT.
001100     05  APPID                     PIC X(10).
001200     05  FILLER                    PIC X(01).
001300     05  PAYMENT-REC OCCURS 48 TIMES.
001400         10  AMT-PD                PIC S9(9)V99.
001500         10  AMT-DELQ              PIC S9(9)V99.
001600         10  BILL-DATE             PIC 9(8).
001700         10  MONTHS-SINCE-PAID PIC 999.
```

Even without knowing COBOL, you can probably deduce that this record starts with a 10-character payer identifier called APPID. The PIC X(10) tells us to expect 10 alphanumeric characters. The 11th character, indicated by FILLER, can be ignored. Then there follow 48 instances of four fields each. PIC 9 clauses indicate numeric values, so the S9(9)V99 tells us that, for each of the first two fields, we can expect a sign (positive or negative, or a space which also indicates a positive value) and a numeric value of 11 digits, with an "implied" decimal point before the last 2 digits. That is, no actual space is set aside for the decimal point; dollar amounts are represented in pennies, but the layout tells the program where the decimal point is supposed to be. (This sort of storage was very common in COBOL, a language that is no longer widely used.) The third element in each set is an eight-digit date, in YYYYMMDD format, and the fourth is a three-digit number giving the number of months that the account was past due. The months are in order in every set, with the least recent month being associated with the first set of four values and the most recent being the 48th. Examples of this data might look, in part, like the line in the following example. These lines are very long; for display purposes, we have wrapped lines around the page so that two lines in the display correspond to one line of the file.

```
0034344639 00000000000 000000000000000000000000
           00000000000 000000000000000000000000...
```

```
0048268540 00000860623 000000000020101214000
           00000000000 00000860623201101114001...
```

In this example, the first account did not have a loan 48 months ago, so the values for that month are all zeros. The second customer paid $8606.23 (AMT-PD with a space for the sign and the implicit decimal point) in the first month. She was not delinquent, so the AMT-DELQ field carries a space for the sign and then 11 zeros. The billing date for that payment was 2010-12-14, and the customer was up to date, so the "months since paid" field carries the value 000. In the second month, with billing date 2011-01-14, the customer paid nothing and was delinquent by $8606.23; during that month, the "months since paid" field had the value 001. Each row will have a total of 48 of these 33-character sets of payment records.

We are now ready to define our response variable. Of course, this will normally be defined by the client (in this case, Hardy Business Loans) rather than the data cleaner. For this example we will implement these rules, which are handled in priority order, so that, for example, a customer who meets the criterion of rule 1 is not considered by a later rule.

1) Any customer whose loan is six or fewer months old is considered Indeterminate.
2) A customer who is ever 3 months delinquent, or who is 2 months delinquent on two different occasions, is Bad.
3) A customer who is ever more than $50,000 delinquent is Bad.
4) Customers who meet none of these criteria are Good.

Since the payment file has a fixed format, it is natural to read it into R with read.fwf() (Section 6.1.7), although if the file were huge it might be more efficient to read it line by line and decode it ourselves.

8.10 Assembling the Final Data Sets

The final product from this exercise should be two data sets, one with booked loans whose outcome is not "Indeterminate," and one with all other applications – or, if you prefer, one combined data set containing both booked and unbooked applications.

8.10.1 Final Data Layout

At the conclusion of the exercise, each data set should consist of these pieces:

- Identifying information for each entry: application number; application portfolio (Beachside or Wilson); loan number (if any); loan and application dates, or a single column giving the active date.

- The value of the response variable ("Good" or "Bad") for loans. For the unbooked applications we can omit this column, or we might create an empty column so that the two data sets have exactly the same set of columns.
- The remaining columns from Table 8.1.
- Four columns of agency scores, with a suitable indicator to denote missing scores, and with KScores updated as appropriate. It might be of value to keep the corresponding score dates for documentation purposes.
- Four columns of agency scores for co-borrowers, again with a suitable indicator of missingness, and possibly including corresponding dates for these scores as well. For observations without co-borrowers, of course, all of these co-borrower scores will be missing.

It is also important to keep track of your code and your assumptions. You will also want to construct a table giving, for each application number found in any source, its ultimate disposition – whether it appears in the final data set or was deleted, and, if so, why. You may also want to construct a flowchart like the one in Figure 7.1.

8.10.2 Concluding Remarks

The exercise in this chapter is intended to bring together a number of the skills and techniques described throughout the book. If you can complete the exercise in a satisfactory way, we think we are well on your way to mastering the important skills of data cleaning.

Having said that, let us assure you that there are many ways to do data cleaning in general, and this exercise in particular. After the authors devised the data for this book, we set out to do the exercise separately. We took quite different paths: one of us started with Beachside, then moved on to Wilson, and then combined the two data sets into one to create the first big data set of the exercise. The other went column by column through Table 8.1, extracting the Beachside and Wilson versions and cleaning and combining them. One of us turned dates into `Date` objects to ensure that they were sorted correctly; the other used `YYYYMMDD`-style text objects, turning them into `POSIXt`-type dates as needed. One of us turned "unknown" values for the New/Used column into "Used," and the other left them as "unknown." Of course, in real life we would have tried to refer the question of what action to take to the data provider, and possibly to whomever will be doing to modeling as well. Despite our different approaches, our final products agreed almost exactly – "almost" because of the judgments made in handling the small numbers of unexpected values. For the purposes of evaluating our exercise, we worked separately. In real data cleaning work, though, you will probably find it helpful to work in a small group, or at least to show your work to a colleague who can understand and comment on the steps.

When we originally wrote this exercise, it had more steps. The additional ones, inspired though they were by real data we analyze, were tedious and repetitive, so we took them out. But just because they are not in the exercise doesn't mean your data cleaning tasks won't be filled with tedious, detail-oriented actions. For example, you might look at the BUS_TYPE and ASSET_TYPE columns in the Beachside portfolio, which match up, more or less, to the Customer Type and Equipment Class columns in the Wilson one. In order to include those columns in the final output you need to examine the set of labels in the two portfolios and decide how to match them up. For any one column from two sources this task is easy enough, but given dozens of these the workload can be intimidating.

We said at the beginning of the book that data cleaning might take up 80% of the time we devote to a project. It is not always fun or glamorous, but it always needs to be done properly. In order to be good at data cleaning in R, you will need to understand what data is available, and how it is represented. You will need to be familiar with the different formats in which data arrives, and how to combine data from different sources. Perhaps most importantly you will need to know at least a little about how the data is collected and how it is intended to be used. One of the great things about being a data scientist is that you get to learn at least a little bit about a lot of fields, and a lot of that learning comes from practicing with real data.

A

Hints and Pseudocode

Chapter 8 described a data handling task involving acquiring data from spreadsheets, a database, JSON, XML, and fixed-width text files. The formats and layouts of the data are documented in that chapter. In this appendix, we give some extra hints about how to proceed. We recommend trying the exercise first, without referring to this appendix until you need to.

Some of these hints come in the form of "pseudocode." This is the programmer's term for instructions that describe an algorithm in ordinary English, rather than in the strict form of code in R or another computer language. The actual R code we used can be found in the `cleaningBook` package.

A.1 Loan Portfolios

Reading, cleaning, and combining the loan portfolios (Section 8.4) is the first task in the exercise, and perhaps the most time-consuming. However, none of the tasks needed to complete this task is particularly challenging from a technical standpoint.

If you have a spreadsheet program such as Excel that can open the file, the very first step in this process might be to use that program to view the file. Look at the values. Are there headers? Can you see any missing value codes? Are some columns empty? Do any rows appear to be missing a lot of values? Are values unexpectedly duplicated across rows? Are there dates, currency amounts, or other values that might require special handling?

Then, it is time to read the two data sets into R and produce data frames, using one of the `read.table()` functions. We normally start with `quote = ""` or `quote = "\""` and `comment.char = ""`. You might select `stringsAsFactors = FALSE`, in which case numeric fields in the data will appear as numeric columns in the data frame. This sets empty entries in those columns of the spreadsheet to `NA` and also has the effect of stripping leading zeros in fields that look numeric, like the application number. As one

A Data Scientist's Guide to Acquiring, Cleaning, and Managing Data in R, First Edition.
Samuel E. Buttrey and Lyn R. Whitaker.
© 2018 John Wiley & Sons Ltd. Published 2018 by John Wiley & Sons Ltd.
Companion website: www.wiley.com/go/buttrey/datascientistsguide

alternative, you might set `colClasses = "character"`, in which case all of the columns of the data frame are defined to be of type `character`. In this case, empty fields appear as the empty string `" "`. Eventually, columns that are intended to be numeric will have to be converted. On the other hand, leading zeros in application numbers are preserved. From the standpoint of column classes, perhaps the best way to read the data in is to pass `colClasses` as a vector to specify the classes of individual columns – but this requires extra exploration up front to determine those classes.

Pseudocode for the step of reading, cleaning, and combining the portfolio data files might look like this. In this description, we treat the files separately. You might equally well treat them simultaneously, creating the joint data set as you go.

```
for each of {Beachside, Wilson}
    read in file
    examine keys and missing values
    discard unneeded columns
    convert formatted columns (currencies, dates) to R types
    ensure categorical variables have the correct levels
    construct derived variables

ensure categorical variables levels match between data sets
ensure column names match between data sets
ensure keys are unique across data sets
add an identifying column to each data set
join data sets row-wise (vertically)
```

A.1.1 Things to Check

As you will see, the portfolio data sets are messy, just as real-life data is messy. As you move forward, you will need to keep one eye on the data itself, one eye on the data dictionary, and one eye on the list of columns to construct. (We never said this would be easy.) Consider performing the sorts of checks listed here, as well as any others you can think of. Remember to specify `exclude = NULL` or `useNA = "ifany"` in calls to `table()` to help identify missing values.

- What do the application numbers look like? Do they all have the expected 10 digits? Are any missing? Are there duplicate rows or duplicate application numbers? If so, can rows be safely deleted?
- What do missing value counts look like by column? Are some columns missing a large proportion of entries? Are some rows missing most entries, and, if so, should they be deleted?
- Do the values of categorical variables match the values in the data dictionary? If not, are the differences large or small? Can some levels be converted into others? If two categorical variables measure similar things, cross-tabulate

them to ensure that they are associated. At this stage, it might be worthwhile to consider the data from the modeling standpoint. For example, if a large number of categorical values are missing, it might be worthwhile to create a new level called Missing. If there are a number of values that apply to only a few records each, it might be wise to combine them into an Other category.

- Are there columns with special formatting, like, for example, currency values that look like $1,234.56? Convert them to numeric.
- Across the set of numeric columns, what sorts of ranges and averages do you see? Are they plausible? For columns that look like counts, what are the most common values? Are there some values that look as if they might be special indicators (999 for a person's age, 99 or −1 for number of mortgages)? Consider computing the correlation matrix of numeric predictors to see if columns that should carry similar information are in fact correlated.
- What format are the date columns in? If you plan to do arithmetic on dates, like, for example, computing the number of days between two dates, you will need to ensure that dates use one of the Date or POSIXt classes. If all you need to do is to sort dates, you can also use a text format like YYYYMMDD, since these text values will sort alphabetically just as the underlying date values would. Keeping dates as characters can save you a lot of grief when you might inadvertently turn a Date or POSIXt object into numeric form. The date formats are easier to summarize and to use in plots, however. Examine the dates. Are there missing values? What do the ranges look like? Consider plotting dates by month or quarter to see if there are patterns.
- Computing derived variables often involves a table lookup. For example, in the exercise, you can determine each state's region from a lookup into a table that contains state code and region code. The cleaning issue is then a matter of identifying codes not in the table and determining what to do with them.

Once the two loan portfolios have been combined, we can start in on the remaining data sets. In the sections that follow, we will refer to the combined portfolio data set as big. When we completed this step, our big data frame had 19,196 rows and 17 columns; yours may be slightly different, depending on the choices you made in this section.

A.2 Scores Database

The agency scores (Section 8.5) are stored in an SQLite database. The first order of business is to connect to the database and look at a few of its records. Do the extracted records match the descriptions in the data dictionary in Chapter 8? Count the numbers of records. If these are manageable, we might just as well read the entire tables into R, but if there are many millions or tens of millions of records we might be better off reading them bit by bit.

In this case, the tables are not particularly large. Pseudocode for the next steps might look as follows:

```
read Cscore table into an R data frame called cscore
read CusApp table into an R data frame called cusapp
add application number from cusapp to cscore
add active date from big to cscore
discard records for which ScoreMonth > active date
discard records with invalid scores
order cscore by customer number and then by date, descending
for each customer i, for each agency j
      find the first non-missing score and date
```

We did not find a particularly efficient way to perform this last step.

A.2.1 Things to Check

As with almost all data sets, the agency scores have some data quality issues. Items to consider include the following:

- What do the application numbers and customer numbers from cusapp look like? Do they have the expected numbers of digits? Are any duplicated or missing? What proportion of application numbers from cusapp appears in big, and what proportion of application numbers from big appears in cusapp? Are there customer numbers in cscore that do not appear in cusapp or vice versa?
- Summarize the values in the agency score columns. What do missing values look like in each column? What proportion of scores is missing? Are any values outside the permitted range 200–899?
- The ScoreMonth column in the cscore table is in YYYYMM format, without the day of the month. However, the active date field from big has days of the month (and, depending on your strategy, might be in Date or POSIXt format). How should we compare these two types of date?

In the final step, we merge the data set of scores with the big data set created by combining the two loan portfolios. Recall that duplicate keys are particularly troublesome in R's merge () function – so it might be worthwhile to double-check for duplicates in the key, which in this case is the application number, in the two data frames being merged. Does the merged version of big have the same number of rows as the original? If the original has, say, 17 columns and the new version 26, you might ensure that the first 17 columns of the new version match the original data, with a command like all.equal(orig, new[,1:17]).

A.3   Co-borrower Scores

The co-borrower scores (Section 8.6) make up one of the trickiest of the data sets, because of their custom transactional format (Section 7.4). We start by noting that there are 73,477 records in the data set, so it can easily be handled entirely inside R. If there had been, say, a billion records, we would have needed to devise a different approach. We start off with a pseudocode as follows:

```
read data into R using scan() with sep = "\n"
discard records with codes other than ERS or J01
discard ERS records with invalid scores
```

At this point, we are left with the J01 records, which name the application number, and the ERS records, which give the scores. It will now be convenient to construct a data frame with one row for each score. This will serve as an intermediate result, a step toward the final output, which will be a data frame with one row for each application number. This intermediate data frame will, of course, contain an application number field. (This is just one approach, and other equally good ones are possible.) We take the following steps:

```
extract the application numbers from the J01 records
use the rle() function on the part of the string
      that is always either J01 or ERS
```

Recall that each application is represented by a J01 record followed by a series of ERS records. If the data dictionary is correct, the result of the rle() function will be a run of length 1 of J01, followed by a run of ERS, followed by another run of length 1 of J01, followed by another run of ERS, and so on. So, values 2, 4, 6, and so on of the length component of the output of rle() will give the number of ERS records for each account. Call that subset of length values lens. Then, we operate as follows:

```
construct a data frame with a column called Appl,
      produced by replicating the application numbers
      from the J01 records lens times each
add the score identifier (RAY, KSC) etc.
add the numeric score value
add the score date
insert the active date from big
delete records for which the score date > active date
```

At this stage, we have a data set with the information we want, except that some application numbers might still have multiple records for the same agency. A quick way to get rid of the older, unneeded rows is to construct a key consisting of a combination of application number and agency (like, e.g., 3004923564.KSC). Now sort the data set by key, and by date within key, in descending order. We need to keep only the first record for every key – that is, we can delete records for which `duplicated()`, acting on that newly created key field, returns TRUE.

Following the deletion of older scores, we have a data set (call it `co.df`) with all the co-borrower scores, arrayed one per score. (When we did this, we had 4928 scores corresponding to 1567 application numbers.) Now we can use a matrix subscript (Section 3.2.5) to assemble these into a matrix that has one row per application number. We start by creating a data frame with the five desired columns: places for the JNG, KSC, NTH, and RAY scores and the application number. It is convenient to put the application number last. Call this new data frame `co.scores`. Then, we continue as follows:

```
construct the vector of row indices by matching the
    application number from co.df to the application number
    from co.scores. This produces a vector of length 4,928
    whose values range from 1 to 1,567
construct the vector of column indices by matching the score
    id from co.df to the vector c("JNG", "KSC", "NTH",
    "RAY"). This produces a vector of length 4,928
    whose values range from 1 to 4
combine those two vectors into a two-column matrix
use the matrix to insert scores from co.df into co.scores
```

A.3.1 Things to Check

As with the other data sets, the most important issues with the co-borrower data are key matching, missing values, and illegal values. You might examine points like the following:

- What do the application numbers look like? Do they have 10 digits? What proportion of application numbers appears in `big`? In our experience the proportion of loans with co-borrowers has often been on the order of 20%. Are there application numbers that do not appear in `big`? If there are a lot of these we might wonder if the application numbers had been corrupted somehow.
- After reading the data in, check that the fields extracted are what you expect. Do the score identifiers all match JNG, and so on? Are the score values mostly in the 200–899 range? Do the dates look valid?
- We expect some scores to be 999 or out of range. What proportions of those values do we see? Are some months associated with large numbers or proportions of illegal score values? Are these any non-numeric values, which might indicate that we extracted the wrong portion of the record?

When the co-borrowers data set is complete, we can merge it to `big`. Since `big` already has columns names JNG, KSC, NE, and RAY, it might be useful to rename the columns of our `co.score` before the merge to `Co.JNG` and so on. (At this point, you have probably noticed that the NorthEast score is identified by `NE` in the scores database but by `NTH` in the co-borrower scores. It might be worthwhile making these names consistent.)

A final task in this step is to add a co-borrower indicator, which is `TRUE` when an application number from `big` is found in our `co.scores` and `FALSE` otherwise. Actually, this approach has the drawback that it will report `FALSE` for applications with co-borrowers for which every score was invalid or more recent than the active date (if there are any). If this is an issue, you will need to go back and modify the script by creating the indicator before any `ERS` records are deleted. This is a good example of why documenting your scripts as you go is necessary.

A.4 Updated KScores

The updated KScores (Section 8.7) are given in a series of JSON messages. For each message, we need to extract fields named `appid` and `record-date`, if they exist. We start with pseudocode as follows:

```
read the JSON into R with scan() and sep = "\n"
remove messages in which the string "KScore" does not appear
write a function to handle one JSON message: return appid,
    KScore, record-date if found, and (say) "none" if not
apply that function to each message
```

Using `sapply()` in that last command produces a two-row matrix that should be transposed. Using `lapply()` produces a list of character vectors of length 2 that should be combined row-wise, perhaps via `do.call()`. In either case, it will be convenient to produce a data frame with three columns. We continue to work on that data frame with operations as follows:

```
remove rows with invalid scores
add active date from big
remove rows for which KScore date is > active date
keep the most recent row for each application id
```

This final data set contains the KScores that are eligible to update the ones in `big`. Presumably, it only makes sense to update scores for which the one is `big` is either missing, or carries an earlier date than the one in our updated KScore data. When we did this, we found 1098 applications in the updated KScore data set, and they all corresponded to scores that were missing in `big`. So, all 1098 of these KScore entries in `big` should be updated. In a real example, you would have to be prepared to update non-missing KScores as well.

A.4.1 Things to Check

As with the other data sets, the important checks are for keys, missing, duplicated, and illegal values. In this case, we might consider some of the following points:

- Are a lot of records missing application numbers? Examine a few to make sure that it is the data, not the code, at fault. Are any application numbers duplicated? What proportion of application numbers appears in `big`?
- Are many records missing KScores? That might be odd given the specific purpose of this data set. What do the KScores that are present look like? Are many missing or illegal?
- What proportion of update records carries dates more recent than the active date? If this proportion is very large, it can suggest an error on the part of the data supplier.

A.5 Excluder Files

The Excluder files (Section 8.8) are in XML format. We need to read each XML file and determine whether it has (i) a field called `APPID` and (ii) a field called `EXCLUDE`, found under one called `DATA`. In pseudocode form, the task for the excluder data might look as follows:

```
acquire a vector of XML file names from the Excluders dir.
use sapply to loop over the vector of names of XML files:
    read next XML file in, convert to R list with xmlParse()
    if there is a field named "APPID", save it as appid
        otherwise set appid to None
    if there is a field named "EXCLUDE" save it as exclude
        otherwise set exclude to None
    return a vector of appid and exclude
```

The result of this call to `sapply()` will be a matrix with two rows. It will be convenient to transpose it, then convert it into a data frame and rename the columns, perhaps to `Appl` and `ExcCode`. Call this data frame `excluder`.

A.5.1 Things to Check

- Are there duplicate rows or application numbers? This is primarily just a check on data quality. Presumably, if an application number appears twice in the `excluders` data set, that record will be deleted, just as if it had appeared once.
- Do the columns have missing values?
- Are the values in the `ExcCode` column what we expect ("Yes," "No," "Contingent")? We can now drop records for which `ExcCode` is anything other than Yes or Contingent.

- Do the application numbers in `excluder` match the ones in the `big` (combined) data set? Do they have 10 digits? If there are records with no application number, or whose application numbers do not appear elsewhere, they can be dropped from the `excluder` data set.

When we are satisfied with the `excluder` data set, we can remove the matching rows from `big`. When we did this, our data set ended up with 19,034 rows and between 30 and 40 columns, depending on exactly which columns we chose to save.

A.6 Payment Matrix

Recall from Section 8.9 that every row of the payment matrix contains a fixed-layout record consisting of a 10-digit application number, then a space, and then 48 repetitions of numeric fields of lengths 12, 12, 8, and 3 characters. Those values will go into a vector that will define the field widths. We might also set up a vector of column names, by combining names like `Appl` and `Filler` with 48 repetitions of four names like `Pay`, `Delq`, `Date`, and `Mo`. We pasted those 48 replications together with the numbers `48:1` to create unique and easily tractable names. We also know that the first two columns should be categorical; among the repeaters, we might specify that all should be numeric, or perhaps that the two amounts should be numeric and the date and number of months, character.

With that preparation, we are ready to read in the file, using `read.fwf()` and the widths, names, and column classes just created. We called that data frame `pay`.

Our column naming convention makes it easy to extract the names of the date columns with a command like `grep("Date", names(pay))`. For example, recall that we will declare as "Indeterminate" any record with six or fewer non-zero dates. We can use `apply()` across the rows of our `pay` data frame, operating just on the subset of date columns, and run a function that determines whether the number of zero entries is ≤6. (Normally, we are hesitant to use `apply()` on the rows of a data frame. In this case, we are assured that the relevant columns are all of identical types and lengths.)

Now, we create a column of status values, and wherever the result of this `apply()` is `TRUE`, we insert `Indet` into the corresponding spots in that vector. Our code might look something like the following:

```
set up pay$Good as a character vector in the pay data frame
apply to the rows of pay[,grep ("Date", names (pay))]
    a function that counts the number of entries that are
    0 or "00000000"
set pay$Good to Indet when that count is <= 6
```

Our column naming convention also makes it easy to check our work. For example, we might pick out some number haphazardly – say, 45 – and look at the entries in pay for the 45th Indet entry. (This feels wiser than using the very first one, since the first part of the file might be different from the middle part.) In this example, our code might look as follows:

```
pick some number, like, say, 45
extract the row of pay corresponding to the 45th Indet
   -- call that rr
pay[rr, grep ("Date", names (pay))]   shows that row
```

Now we perform similar actions for the other possible outcomes. At this stage, it makes sense to keep the different sorts of bad outcomes separate, combining them only at the end. One bad outcome is when an account is 3 months delinquent. We apply() a function that determines whether the maximum value in any of the month fields is ≥3. For those rows that produce TRUE, we insert a value like bad3 into the pay$Good unless it is already occupied with an Indet value. Again, it makes sense to examine a couple of these records to ensure that our logic is correct.

Another bad outcome occurs when there are at least two instances of month values equal to 2, and a third is when the delinquency value passes $50,000. In each of these cases, we update the pay$Good vector, ensuring that we only update entries that have not already been set. It is a good idea to check a few of the records for each indicator as we did earlier.

Records that do not get assigned Indet nor one of the bad values are assigned Good. Once we have tabulated the bad values separately, we can combine them into a single Bad value. This way, we can compare the frequencies of the different outcomes to see if what we see matches what we expect.

A.6.1 Things to Check

There are lots of ways that these payment records can be inconsistent. The extent of your exploration here might depend on the time available. But we give, as examples, some of the questions you might ask of this data.

- What do the application numbers look like? Do they have 10 digits? Are any missing? Does every booked record have payment information, and does every record with payment information appear in big? What is the right action to take for booked records with no payment information – set their response to Indet?
- What are the proportions of the different outcomes? Do they look reasonable? For example, if 90% of records are marked Indet we might be concerned.
- What do the amounts look like? Are they ever negative, missing, or absurd?
- Are the dates valid? We expect every entry to be a plausible value in the form YYYYMMDD or else a zero or set of zeros. Are they? Are adjacent dates 1

month apart, as we expect? Are there zeros in the interior of a set of non-zero dates?

- Are adjacent entries consistent? For example, if month 8 shows a delinquency of 4 months, and month 10 shows a delinquency of 6 months, then we expect month 9 to show a delinquency of 5 months. Are these expected patterns followed?

Once the response variable has been constructed, we can merge big with pay. Actually, since we only want the Good column from pay, we merge big with the two-column data set consisting of Appl and Good extracted from pay. In this way, we add the Good column into big.

A.7   Starting the Modeling Process

Our data set is now nearly ready for modeling, although we could normally expect to convert character columns to factor first. Moreover, we often find errors in our cleaning processes or anomalous data when the modeling begins – requiring us to modify our scripts. In the current example, let us see if the Good column constructed above is correlated with the average of the four scores. This R code shows one way we might examine that hypothesis using the techniques in the book.

```
> big$AvgScore <- apply (big[,c("RAY", "JNG", "KSC", "NE")],
                         1, mean, na.rm = T)
> gb <- is.element (big$Good, c("Good", "Bad")) &
        !is.na (big$AvgScore)
```

The gb vector is TRUE for those rows of big for which the Good column has one of the values Good or Bad, and AvgScore is present, meaning that at least one agency score was present.

We can now divide the records into groups, based on average agency score. Here we show one way to create five groups; we then tabulate the numbers of Good and Bad responses by group.

```
> qq <- quantile (big$AvgScore, seq (0, 1, len=6),
                  na.rm = TRUE)
> (tbl <- table (big$Good[gb], cut (big$AvgScore[gb], qq,
                include.lowest = TRUE), useNA = "ifany"))
        [420,598] (598,649] (649,696] (696,748] (748,879]
    Bad       641       620       514       449       384
    Good      607       721       811       926      1067
> round (100 * prop.table (tbl, 2), 1)
        [420,598] (598,649] (649,696] (696,748] (748,879]
    Bad      51.4      46.2      38.8      32.7      26.5
    Good     48.6      53.8      61.2      67.3      73.5
```

We can see a relationship between agency scores and outcome from the tables. The first shows the counts, and the second uses `prop.table()` to compute percentages within each column. In the group with the lowest average score (left column), there are about as many Bad entries as Good ones. As we move to the right, the proportion of Good entries increases; in the group with the highest average scores, almost 75% of entries are Good ones. This is consistent with what we expect, since higher scores are supposed to be an indication of higher probability of good response.

Bibliography

Adler, D., Gläser, C., Nenadic, O., Oehlschlägel, J., and Zucchini, W. (2014) *ff: Memory-Efficient Storage of Large Data on Disk and Fast Access Functions*. R Package Version 2.2-13.

Bache, S.M. and Wickham, H. (2014) *magrittr: A Forward-Pipe Operator for R*. R Package Version 1.5.

Bates, D. and Maechler, M. (2016) *Matrix: Sparse and Dense Matrix Classes and Methods*. R Package Version 1.2-6.

Couture-Beil, A. (2014) *rjson: JSON for R*. R Package Version 0.2.15.

Dasu, T. and Johnson, T. (2003) *Exploratory Data Mining and Data Cleaning*, John Wiley & Sons, Inc., Hoboken, NJ.

Dowle, M., Srinivasan, A., Short, T., with contributions from Saporta, R., Lianoglou, S., and Antonyan, E. (2015) *data.table: Extension of Data.frame*. R Package Version 1.9.6.

Dragulescu, A.A. (2014) *xlsx: Read, Write, Format Excel 2007 and Excel 97/2000/XP/2003 files*. R Package Version 0.5.7.

Eddelbuettel, D. and François, R. (2011) Rcpp: seamless R and C++ integration. *Journal of Statistical Software*, **40** (1), 1–18.

Feinerer, I., Hornik, K., and Meyer, D. (2008) Text mining infrastructure in R. *Journal of Statistical Software*, **25** (5), 1–54.

Free Software Foundation (2016) *GNU Bash*, https://www.gnu.org/software/bash/bash.html (accessed 19 November 2016).

Kane, M.J., Emerson, J., and Weston, S. (2013) Scalable strategies for computing with massive data. *Journal of Statistical Software*, **55** (14), 1–19.

Loecher, M. and Ropkins, K. (2015) RgoogleMaps and loa: unleashing R graphics power on map tiles. *Journal of Statistical Software*, **63** (4), 1–18.

Lucas, C. and Tingley, D. (2014) *translateR: Bindings for the Google and Microsoft Translation APIs*. R Package Version 1.0.

Luis (2011) *Reading HTML Pages in R for Text Processing*, http://www.quantumforest.com/2011/10/reading-html-pages-in-r-for-text-processing/ (accessed 13 October 2016).

Matloff, N. (2011) *The Art of R Programming*, No Starch Press, San Francisco, CA.

A Data Scientist's Guide to Acquiring, Cleaning, and Managing Data in R, First Edition.
Samuel E. Buttrey and Lyn R. Whitaker.
© 2018 John Wiley & Sons Ltd. Published 2018 by John Wiley & Sons Ltd.
Companion website: www.wiley.com/go/buttrey/datascientistsguide

Ooms, J. (2014) *The Jsonlite Package: A Practical and Consistent Mapping Between JSON Data and R Objects*, arXiv:1403.2805 [stat.CO].

R Core Team (2013) *R: A Language and Environment for Statistical Computing*, R Foundation for Statistical Computing, Vienna, Austria.

R Core Team (2015) *foreign: Read Data Stored by Minitab, S, SAS, SPSS, Stata, Systat, Weka, dBase,...* R package version 0.8-66.

Ripley, B. and Lapsley, M. (2015) *RODBC: ODBC Database Access.* R Package Version 1.3-12.

RStudio Team (2015) *RStudio: Integrated Development Environment for R.* RStudio, Inc., Boston, MA.

Temple Lang, D. (2014) *RJSONIO: Serialize R objects to JSON, JavaScript Object Notation.* R Package Version 1.3-0.

Temple Lang, D. (2015a) *RCurl: General Network (HTTP/FTP/...) Client Interface for R.* R Package Version 1.95-4.7.

Temple Lang, D. (2015b) *XML: Tools for Parsing and Generating XML Within R and S-Plus.* R Package Version 3.98-1.3.

Warnes, G.R., Bolker, B., Gorjanc, G., Grothendieck, G., Korosec, A., Lumley, T., MacQueen, D., Magnusson, A., Rogers, J. et al. (2015) *gdata: Various R Programming Tools for Data Manipulation.* R Package Version 2.17.0.

Wickham, H. (2011) The split-apply-combine strategy for data analysis. *Journal of Statistical Software*, **40** (1), 1–29.

Wickham, H. (2014) Tidy data. *Journal of Statistical Software*, **59** (10), 1–23, doi: 10.18637/jss.v059.i10.

Wickham, H. (2015) *httr: Tools for Working with URLs and HTTP.* R Package Version 1.0.0.

Wickham, H. and Francois, R. (2015) *dplyr: A Grammar of Data Manipulation.* R package version 0.4.3.

Wickham, H. and Grolemond, G. (2016) *R for Data Science*, O'Reilly, Sebastopol, CA.

Wickham, H., James, D.A., and Falcon, S. (2014) *RSQLite: SQLite Interface for R.* R Package Version 1.0.0.

Index

A Data Scientist's Guide to Acquiring, Cleaning, and Managing Data in R, First Edition.
Samuel E. Buttrey and Lyn R. Whitaker.
© 2018 John Wiley & Sons Ltd. Published 2018 by John Wiley & Sons Ltd.
Companion website: www.wiley.com/go/buttrey/datascientistsguide